John Quincy Adams

THE AMISTAD ARGUMENT & STATE OF THE UNION ADDRESSES

THE AMISTAD ARGUMENT
&
THE STATE OF THE UNION ADDRESSES

John Quincy Adams

Reprinted by Frederick Ellis
8000 E. Girard, Suite 507
Denver CO 80231
ISBN 978-0-9793363-6-8

THE AMISTAD ARGUMENT

Amistad Argument

John Quincy Adams

Argument of John Quincy Adams Before the Supreme Court of the United States in the case of the United States, Appellants, vs. Cinque, and others, Africans, captured in the schooner Amistad, by Lieut. Gedney, Delivered on the 24th of February and 1st of March 1841.

Originally published in 1841 by S.W. Benedict

MAY IT PLEASE YOUR HONORS—

In rising to address this Court as one of its attorneys and counselors, regularly admitted at a great distance of time, I feel that an apology might well be expected where I shall perhaps be more likely to exhibit at once the infinities of age and the inexperience of youth, than to render those services to the individuals whose lives and liberties aren't the disposal of this Court which I would most earnestly desire to render. But as I am unwilling to employ one moment of the time of the Court in anything that regards my own personal situation, I shall reserve what few observations I may think necessary to offer as an apology till the close of my argument on the merits of the question.

I therefore proceed immediately to say that, in a consideration of this case, I derive, in the distress I feel both for myself and my clients, consolation from two sources—first, that the rights of my clients to their lives and liberties have already been defended by my learned friend and colleague in so able and complete a manner as leaves me scarcely anything to say, and I feel that such full justice has been done to their interests, that any fault or imperfection of mine will merely be attributed to its true cause; and secondly, I derive consolation from the thought that this Court is a Court of JUSTICE. And in saying so very trivial a thing I should not on any other occasion, perhaps, be warranted in asking

1

the Court to consider what justice is. Justice, as defined in the Institutes of Justinian, nearly 2000 years ago, and as it felt and understood by all who understand human relations and human rights, is—

"Constans et perpetua voluntas, jus suum cuique tribuendi."

"The constant and perpetual will to secure to every one HIS OWN right."

And in a Court of Justice, where there are two parties present, justice demands that the rights of each party should be allowed to himself, as well as that each party has a right, to be secured and protected by the Court. This observation is important, because I appear here on the behalf of thirty–six individuals, the life and liberty of every one of whom depend on the decision of this Court. The Court, therefore, I trust, in deciding this case, will form no lumping judgment on these thirty–six individuals, but will act on the consideration that the life and the liberty of every one of them must be determined by its decision for himself alone.

They are here, individually, under very different circumstances, and in very different characters. Some are in one predicament, some in another. In some of the proceedings by which they have been brought into the custody and under the protection of this Court, thirty–two or three of them have been charged with the crime of murder. Three or four of them are female children, in. capable, in the judgment of our laws, of the crime of murder or piracy or, perhaps, of any other crime. Yet, from the day when the vessel was taken possession of by one of our naval officers, they have all been held as close prisoners, now for the period of eighteen long months, under custody and by authority of the Courts of the United States. I trust, therefore, that before the ultimate decision of this Court is established, its honorable members will pay due attention to the circumstances and condition of every individual concerned.

When I say I derive consolation from the consideration that I stand before a Court of Justice, I am obliged to take this ground, because, as I shall –show, another Department of the Government of the United States has taken, with reference to this case, the ground of utter injustice, and these individuals for whom I appear, stand before this Court, awaiting their fate from its decision, under the array of the whole Executive power of this nation against them, in addition to that of a foreign nation. And here arises a consideration, the most painful of all others; in considering the duty I have to discharge,

2

in which, in supporting the action to dismiss the appeal, I shall be obliged not only to investigate and submit to the censure of this Court, the form and manner of the proceedings of the Executive in this case, but the validity, and the motive of the reasons assigned for its interference in this unusual manner in a suit between parties for their individual rights.

At an early period of my life it was my fortune to witness the representation upon the stage of one of the tragic masterpieces of the great Dramatist of England, or I may rather say of the great Dramatist of the world, and in that scene which exhibits in action the sudden, the instantaneous fall from unbounded power into irretrievable disgrace of Cardinal Wolsey, by the abrupt declaration of displeasure and dismission from the service of his King, made by that monarch in the presence of Lord Surry and of the Lord Chamberlain; at the moment of Wolsey's humiliation and distress, Surry given vent to his long suppressed resentments for the insolence and injuries which he had endured from the fallen favorite while in power, and breaks out into insulting and bitter reproaches, till checked by the Chamberlain, who says:

"Oh! my Lords;

Press not a falling man too far: 'tis Virtue."

The repetition of that single line, in the relative position of the parties, struck me as a moral principle, and made upon my mind an impression which I have carried with me through all the changes of my life, and which I trust I shall carry with me to my grave.

It is, therefore, peculiarly painful to me, under present circumstances, to be under the necessity of arraigning before this Court and before the civilized world, the course of the existing Administration in this case. But I must do it. That Government is still in power, and thus, subject to the control of the Court, the lives and liberties of all my clients are in its hands. And if I should pass over the course it has pursued, those who have not kind an opportunity to examine the case and perhaps the Court itself, might decide that nothing improper had been done, and that the parties I represent had not been wronged by the course pursued by the Executive. In making this charge, or arraignment, as defensive of the rights of my clients I now proceed to an examination of the correspondence of the Secretary of State with the ambassador of her Catholic Majesty, as officially communicated to Congress, and published among the national documents.

Amistad Argument

The charge I make against the present Executive administration is that in all their proceedings relating to these unfortunate men, instead of that Justice, which they were bound not less than this honorable Court itself to observe, they have substituted Sympathy!—sympathy with one of the parties in this conflict of justice, and antipathy to the other. Sympathy with the white, antipathy to the black—and in proof of this charge I adduce the admission and avowal of the Secretary of State himself. In the letter of Mr. Forsyth to the Spanish Minister d'Argaiz, of 13th of December, 1839, [Document H. R. N. S. 185,] defending the course of the administration against the reproaches utterly ground. less, but not the less bitter of the Spanish Envoy, he says:

"The undersigned cannot conclude this communication without calling the attention of the Chevalier d'Argaiz to the fact, that with the single exception of the vexatious detention to which Messrs. Montes and Ruiz have been subjected in consequence of the civil suit instituted against them, all the proceedings in the matter, on the part both the Executive and Judicial branches of the government have had their foundation in the ASSUMPTION that these persons ALONE were the parties aggrieved; and that their claims to the surrender of the property was founded in fact and in justice." (PP 29, 30.]

At the date of this letter, this statement of Mr. Forsyth was strictly true. All the proceedings of the government, Executive and Judicial, in this case had been founded on the assumption that the two Spanish slave-dealers were the only parties aggrieved— that all the right was on their side and all the wrong on the side of their surviving. self-emancipated victims. I ask your honors, was this JUSTICE, No. It was not so considered by Mr. Forsyth himself. It was sympathy, had he so calls it, for in the preceding page of the same letter referring to the proceedings of this Government from the very first intervention of Lieut. Gedney, he says:

"Messrs. Ruiz and Montes were first found near the coast of the United States, deprived of their property and of their freedom, suffering from lawless violence in their persons, and in imminent and constant danger of being deprived of their lives also.

They were found in this distressing and perilous situation by officers of the United States, who, moved towards them by sympathetic feeling which subsequently became as it were national, immediately rescued them from personal danger, restored them to freedom, secured their oppressor, that they might abide the consequences of the acts of violence perpetrated upon them, and placed under the safeguard of the laws all the property which they claimed as their own, to remain in safety until the competent authority could examine their title to it, and pronounce upon the question of ownership agreeably to the provisions of the 9th article of the treaty of 1795."

This sympathy with Spanish slave–traders is declared by the Secretary to have been first felt by Lieutenant Gedney. I hope this is not correctly represented. It is imputed to him and declared to have become in a manner national. The national sympathy with the slave– traders of the baracoons is officially declared to have been the prime motive of action of the government: And this fact is given as an answer to all the claims, demands and reproaches of the Spanish minister! I cannot urge the same objection to this that was brought against the assertion in the libel— that it said the thing which is not—too unfortunately it was so, as he said. The sympathy of the Executive government, and as it were of the nation, in favor of the slave–traders, and against these poor, unfortunate, helpless, tongueless, defenseless Africans, was the cause and foundation and motive of all these ,proceedings, and has brought this case up for trial before your honors.

I do not wish to blame the first sympathies of Lieut. Gedney, nor the first action of the District and Circuit Courts. The seizure of the vessel, with the arrest and examination of their Africans' was intended for inquiry, and to lead to an investigation of the rights of all parties. This investigation has ultimated in the decision of the District Court, confirmed by the Circuit Court, which it is now the demand of the Executive should be reversed by this Court. The District Court has exercised its jurisdiction over the parties in interest, and has found that the right was with the other party, that the decisions of JUSTICE were not in accordance with the impulses of sympathy, and that consequently the sympathy was wrong before. And consequently it now appears that everything which has flowed from this mistaken or misapplied sympathy, was wrong from the beginning.

For I inquire by what right, all this sympathy, from Lieut. Gedney to the Secretary of State, and from the Secretary of State, as it were, to the nation, was extended to the two Spaniards from Cuba exclusively, and utterly denied to the fifty–two victims of their lawless violence. By what right was it denied to the men who had restored themselves to freedom, and secured their oppressors to abide the consequences of the acts of violence perpetrated by them, and why was it extended to the perpetrators of those acts of violence themselves' When the Amistad first came within the territorial jurisdiction of the United States, acts of violence had passed between the two parties, the Spaniards and Africans on board of her, but on which side these acts were lawless, on which side were the oppressors, was a question of right and wrong, for the settlement of which, if the government and people of the United States interfered at all, they were bound in duty to extend their sympathy to them all; and if they interrened at all between them, the duty incumbent upon this intervention was not of favor, but of impartiality—not of sympathy, but of JUSTICE, dispensing to every individual his own right.

Thus the Secretary of State himself declares that the motive for all the proceedings of the government of the United States, until that time, had been governed by sympathetic feeling towards one of the parties, and by the assumption that all the right was on one side and all the wrong on the other. It was the motive of Lieut. Gedney: the same influence had prevailed even in the judicial proceedings until then: the very language of the Secretary of State in this fetter breathes the same spirit as animating the executive administration, and has continued to govern all its proceedings on this subject to the present day. It is but too true that the same spirit of sympathy and antipathy has nearly pervaded the whole nation, and it is against them that I am in duty bound to call upon this Court to restrain itself in the sacred name of JUSTICE.

One of the Judges who presided in some of the preceding trials, is said to have called this an anomalous case. It is indeed anomalous, and I know of no law, but one which I am not at liberty to argue before this Court, no law, statute or constitution, no code, no treaty, applicable to the proceedings of the Executive or the Judiciary, except that law, (pointing to the copy of the Declaration of Independence, hanging against one of the pillars of the courtroom,) that law, two copies of which are ever before the eyes of your Honors. I know of no other law that reaches the case of my clients, but the law of nature and of Nature's God on which our fathers placed our own national existence. The circumstances are so peculiar, that no code or treaty has provided for such a case. That law, in its application to my clients, I trust will be the law on which the case will be decided by this Court.

In the sequel to the diplomatic correspondence between the Secretary of State and the Spanish minister Argaiz, relating to the case of the Amistad, recently communicated by the President of the United States to the Senate, [Doe. 179. 12 Feb. 1841,] the minister refers with great apparent satisfaction to certain resolutions of the Senate, adopted at the instance of Mr. Calhoun, on the 15th of April, 1840, as follows:

Amistad Argument

1. " Resolved—That a ship or vessel on the high seas, in time of peace, engaged in a lawful voyage, is according to the laws of nations under the exclusive jurisdiction of the state to which her flag belongs as much as if constituting a part of its own domain."

2. " Resolved— That if such ship or vessel should be forced, by stress of weather, or other unavoidable cause into the port, and under the jurisdiction of a friendly power, she and her cargo, and persons on board, with their property, and all the rights belonging to their personal relations, as established by the laws of the state to which they belong, would be placed under the protection which the laws of nations extend to the unfortunate under such circumstances."

Without entering into any discussion as to the correctness of these principles, let as admit them to be true to their fullest extent, and what is their application to the case of the Amistad? If the first of the resolutions declares a sound principle of national law, neither Lieut. Gedney, nor Lieut. Meade, nor any officer of the brig Washington had the shadow of a right even to set foot on board of the Amistad. According to the second resolution, the Africans in possession of the vessel were entitled to all the kindness and good offices due from a humane and Christian nation to the unfortunate; and if the Spaniards were entitled to the same, it was by the territorial right and jurisdiction of the State of New York and of the Union, only to the extent of liberating their persons from imprisonment. Chevalier d'Argaiz, therefore, totally misapprehends the application of the principles asserted in these resolutions of the Senate, as indeed Mr. Forsyth appears by his answer to this letter of the Chevalier to be fully aware. From the decisiveness with which on this solitary occasion he meets the pretensions of the Spanish Envoy, a fair inference may be drawn that the Secretary himself perceived that the Senatorial resolutions, instead of favoring the course of Montes and Ruiz, have a bearing point blank against them.

The Africans were in possession, and had the presumptive right of ownership; they were in peace with the United States; the Courts have decided, and truly, that they were not pirates; they were on a voyage to their native homes—their dulces Argos; they kind acquired the right and so far as their knowledge extended they had the power of prosecuting the voyage; the ship was theirs, and being in immediate communication with the shore, was in the territory of the State of New York; or, if not, at least half the number were actually on the soil of New York, and entitled to all the provisions of the law of nations, and the protection and comfort which the laws of that State secure to every human being within its limits.

Amistad Argument

In this situation Lieut. Gedney, without any charge or authority from his government, without warrant of law, by force of fire arms, seizes and disarms them, then being in the peace of that Commonwealth and of the United States, drives them on board the vessel, seizes the vessel and transfers it against the will of its possessors to another State. I ask in the name of justice, by what law was this done 1 Even admitting that it had been a case of actual piracy, which your courts have properly found it was not, there are questions arising here of the deepest interest to the liberties of the people of this Union, and especially of the State of New York. Have the officers of the U. S. Navy a right to seize men by force, on the territory of New York, to fire at them, to overpower them, to disarm them, to put them on board of a vessel and carry them by force and against their will to another State, without warrant or form of law 1 I am not arraigning Lieut. Gedney, but I ask this Court, in the name of justice, to settle it in their minds, by what law it was done, and how far the principle it embraces is to be carried.

The whole of my argument to show that the appeal should be dismissed, is founded on an averment that the proceedings on the part of the United States are all wrongful from the beginning. The first act, of seizing the vessel, and these men, by an officer of the navy, was a wrong. The forcible arrest of these men, or a part of them, on the soil of New York, was a wrong. After the vessel was brought into the jurisdiction of the District Court of Connecticut, the men were first seized and imprisoned under a criminal process for murder and piracy on the high seas. Then they were libelled by Lieut. Gedney, as property, and salvage claimed on them, and under that process were taken into the Custody of the marshal as property. Then they were claimed by Ruiz and Montes and again taken into custody by the court. The District Attorney of Connecticut wrote to the Secretary of State, September 5th, giving him an account of the matter, stating that " the blacks are indicted for the murder of the captain and mate," and " are now in jail at New Haven ;" that " the next term of our Circuit Court sits on the 17th instant, at which time I suppose," —that is in italics in the printed document—" I suppose it will be my duty to bring them to trial, unless they are in some other way disposed of." This is the first intimation of the District Attorney; it is easy to understand in what "other way" he wished them disposed of. And he closes by saying—"should you hare any instructions to give on the subject, I should line to receive them as soon as may be."

On the 9th of September, he writes again that he has examined the law, which has brought him fully to the conclusion that the Courts of the United States cannot take cognizance of any offense these people may hare committed, as it was done on board a

8

vessel belonging to a foreign state. And then he says,

"I would respectfully inquire, sir, whether there are no treaty stipulations with the Government of Spain that would authorize our Government to deliver them up to the Spanish authorities; and if so, whether it could be done before our court sits".

This is the second intimation from the District Attorney. We shall find others. Now it appears that the Africans were fully in the custody of the Court, first on the criminal charge, and then on the claim to them as property. The Court was to sit in eight days, the District Attorney is satisfied they cannot be tried, and be is anxious to know whether they cannot be disposed of in some way by the Executive, so that the Courts of the United States may have no chance to decide upon the case. May it please your Honors, I am simply pursuing the chain of evidence in this case, to show the effects of the sympathy in favor of one of the parties and against the other, which the Secretary of State says had become in a manner " national." The next document is a letter of the Secretary of State to the District Attorney, Sept. 11, 1839:

"SIR: Since the receipt of your letter of the 5th instant, relative to the case of the Spanish schooner 'Amistad,' brought into the port o, New London on the 26th ultimo, by Lieutenant Gedney, of the surveying brig Washington, a communication has been ad. dressed to this department by the minister of Her Catholic Majesty, claiming the vessel, cargo and blacks," [vessel, cargo and blacks, the Court will observe,] " on board, as Spanish property, and demanding its immediate release. Mr. Calderon's application will be immediately transmitted to the President for his decision upon it, with which you will be made acquainted without unnecessary delay. In the mean time you will take care that no proceeding of your Circuit Court, or of any other judicial tribunal, places the vessel, cargo, or slaves beyond the control of the Federal Executive.

" I am, sir, your obedient servant,

"JOHN FORSYTH."

I know not how, in decent language, to speak of this assertion of the Secretary, that the minister of Her Catholic Majesty had claimed the Africans " as Spanish property." In Gulliver's travels, he is represented as traveling among a nation of beings, who were very rational in many things' although they were not exactly human, and they had a very cool way of using language in reference to deeds that are not laudable. When they wished to characterize a declaration as absolutely contrary to truth, they say the man has " said tee thing that is not." It is not possible for me to express the truth respecting this averment of the Secretary of State, but by declaring that he " has said the thing that is not." This I shall endeavor to prove by allowing what the demand of the Spanish minister was, and that it was a totally different thing from that which was represented.

But I wish first to beg your Honors' special attention to some thing else in this remarkable letter of the Secretary of State. He says, " In the mean time, you will take care that no proceeding of your Circuit Court, or of any other judicial tribunal, places

the vessel, cargo, or slaves beyond the control of the Federal Executive." Here is a ministerial officer of the Executive Government, instructing the District Attorney, before the Judiciary has acted upon the case, to take care that no proceeding of any court places these men beyond reach of the Federal Executive. How was he to do it? In what manner was an Executive officer to proceed, so that neither the Circuit Court of the United States, nor any state Court, could dispose of the vessel or the men in any manner, beyond the control of the Federal Executive. A farther examination of the correspondence in the conclusion, will show how it was intended to be done. But I now come to inquire what was the real demand of the Spanish minister, and to show what was the duty of the Secretary of State on receiving such a de mend.

Here we have the first letter of Mr. Calderon to Mr. Forsyth.

The name of this gentleman is illustrious in the annals of Spain, and for himself personally, during his residence in this country, I have entertained the most friendly and respectful sentiments. I have enjoyed frequent interviews with him, and have found him intelligent, amiable, learned, and courteous. I wish therefore to say nothing respecting him that is personally disrespectful or unkind. But it is my duty to comment with the utmost plainness, and what perhaps your Honors will think severity, on his official letter to the American Secretary of State. His letter begins:—

"NEW YORK, Sept. 6, 1839.

" The undersigned, envoy extraordinary and minister plenipotentiary of her Catholic Majesty the Queen of Spain, has the honor of calling the attention of the honorable John

Amistad Argument

Forsyth, Secretary of State of the United States, to a recent and very public occurrence of which, no doubt, Mr. Forsyth is already informed, and in consequence of which it is the imperious duty of the undersigned to claim an observance of the law of nations' and of the treaties existing between the United States and Spain. The occurrence alluded to is the capture of the Spanish schooner ' Amistad.'

" This vessel sailed from Havana on the 28th of June, bound to Guanaja, in the vicinity of Porto Principe, under the command of her owner, Don Ramon Ferrer, laden with sundry merchandise. and with fifty–three negro slaves on board; and, previous to her departure, she obtained her clearance (alijo) from the custom house, the necessary permit from the authorities for the transportation of the negroes, a passport, and all the other documents required by the laws of Spain for navigating a vessel and for proving ownership of property; a circumstance particularly important in the opinion of the undersigned."

Here your Honors will observe the same distinction of " merchandise and Negroes," which was made by the District Attorney, showing the universal sense of the difference between merchandise and persons. He goes on:

"During the night of the 30th of said month, or about daybreak on the following day, the slaves rose upon the crew, and killed the captain, a slave of his, and two sailors—sparing only two persons, after ill–treating and wounding them, namely, Don Jose Ruiz and Don Pedro Montes: of whom the former was owner of forty–nine of the slaves, and the latter of the other four. These they retained, that they might navigate the vessel and take her to the coast of Africa. Montes, availing himself of his knowledge of nautical affairs, and under favor of Divine Providence— 'the favor of Divine Providence!"—succeeded in directing the vessel to these shores. He was spoken by various vessels, from the captains of which the Negroes bought provisions, but to whom, it seems, he was unable to make known his distress, being closely watched. At length, by good fortune, he reached Long Island, where the 'Amistad' was detained by the American brig–of war 'Washington,' Captain Gedney, who, on learning the circumstances of the case, secured the Negroes, and took them with the vessel to New London, in the state of Connecticut.

"The conduct of that commander and his subalterns toward the unfortunate Spaniards has been that which was to be expected from gentlemen. and from officers in the service of an enlightened nation friendly to Spain. That conduct will be appreciated as it deserves by my august sovereign, and by the Spanish government, and will be reciprocated on similar occasions by the Spaniards— a people ever grateful for benefits received." [We shall see some proofs of Spanish gratitude, as we proceed in the case.]

" The act of humanity thus performed would have been complete, had the vessel at the same time been set at liberty, and the Negroes sent to be tried by the proper tribunal, and by the violated laws of the country of which they are subjects. The under signed is willing to believe that such would have been the case, had the general government been able to interpose its authority in the first instance, as it has probably done during the short interval between the occurrence of this affair and the period when the undersigned received an authentic statement of the facts."

This is what the Spanish minister demanded, that the vessel should be set at liberty, and the Negroes sent to Cuba to be tried. And he is so confident in the disposition the United States in favor of this demand, that he even presumes the President of the United States had already immediately dispatched an order to the Court in Connecticut, to stay its proceedings and deliver up the Negroes, to the Government of Spain.

What combination of ideas led to that conclusion, in the mind of Mr. Calderon, I am not competent to say. He evidently supposes the President of the United States to possess what we understand by arbitrary power—the power to decide cases and to dispose of persons and of property, mero motu, at his own discretion, and without the intervention of any court. What led him to this imagination I am unable to say. He goes on to say that the officers of the Washington, in the service of the United States, have presented to that incompetent Court,—the U. S. District Court in Connecticut—a petition, claiming salvage: " a claim which, in view of existing treaties, the undersigned conceives can. not be allowed in the sense in which it is made." This is that most grateful nation! The deliverers of these two Spaniards, the representative of a most grateful nation insists, are not deserving of any recompense whatever!

Now, I beg your Honors to see if there is, among all these specifications, any one demand that corresponds with that which the Secretary of State appears to have been made. He demands,

1st. That the vessel be immediately delivered up to her owner, together with every article found on board at the time of her capture by the Washington, without any payment being exacted on the score of salvage, or any charges made, other than those specified in the

Amistad Argument

treaty of 1795, article 1st.

Yet he had already said the captain, and owner, Ferrer, was killed.

" 2d. That it be declared that no tribunal in the United States has the right to institute proceedings against, or to impose penalties upon, the subjects of Spain, for crimes committed on board a Spanish vessel, and in the waters of the Spanish territory."

Declared, by whom? By the President of the United States. Of course, he does not demand that the " incompetent tribunal" in Connecticut, before which the suit was brought, should declare this, but that the President of the United States should issue a proclamation, declaring that no court in this country could hold cognizance of the case. Is there in this a demand that the net "roes should be delivered up as Spanish property? It is a direct protest against any judicial tribunal taking cognizance of the case, and that the President should issue a proclamation to prevent any such proceedings whatever.

"3d. That the Negroes be conveyed to Havana, or be placed at the disposal of the proper authorities in that part of Her Majesty's dominions, in order to their being tried by the Spanish laws which the, have violated; and that, in the mean time, they be kept in safe custody, in order to prevent their evasion."

In what capacity does he demand that the President of the United States should place himself? Is it a demand to deliver up these people as property? No. Is it that they should deliver them to the minister himself, as the representative of the Spanish government, to be disposed of according to the laws of Spain ? No. It demands of the Chief Magistrate of this nation that he should first turn himself into a jailer, to keep these people safely, and then into a tipstaff to take them away for trial among the slave–traders of the baracoons. Was ever such a demand made upon any government? He must seize these people and keep them safely, and carry them, at the expense of the United States, to another country to be tried for their fires! Where in the law of nations there a warrant for such a demand?

May it please your Honors—If the President of the United States had arbitrary and unqualified power, he could not satisfy these demands. He must keep them as a jailer; he must then send them beyond seas to be tried for their lives. I will not recur to the Declaration of Independence—your Honors have it implanted in your hearts—but one of the grievous charges brought against George III. was, that he had made laws for sending men beyond areas for trial. That was one of the most odious of those acts of tyranny which occasioned the American revolution. The whole of the reasoning is not applicable to this case, but I submit to your Honors that, if the President has the power to do it in the case of Africans. and vend them beyond seas for trial, he could do it by the same authority in the case of American citizens. By a simple order to the marshal of the district, he could just as well seize forty citizens of the United States, on the demand of a foreign minister, and send them beyond seas for trial before a foreign court. The Spanish minister farther demands—

"4th. That if, in consequence of the intervention of the authorities of Connecticut, there should be any delay in the desired delivery of the vessel and the slaves, the owners both of the former be indemnified for the injury that may accrue to them."

Now, how are all these demands to be put together? First, he demands that the United States shall keep them safely, and send them to Cuba, all in a lump, the children as well as Cinque and Grabbo. Next, he denies the power of our courts to take any cognizance of the case. And finally, that the owners of the slaves shall be indemnified for any injury they may sustain in their property. We see in the whole of this transaction, a confusion of ideas and a contradiction of positions from confounding together the two capacities in which these people are attempted to be held. One moment they are viewed as merchandise, and the next as persons. The Spanish minister, the Secretary of State, and every one who has had anything to do with the case, all have run into these absurdities. These demands are utterly inconsistent. First, they are demanded as persons, as the subjects of Spain, to be delivered up as criminals, to be tried for their lives, and liable to be executed on the gibbet. Then they are demanded as chattels, the same as so many bags of coffee, or bales of cotton, belonging to owners, who have a right to be indemnified for any injury to their property.

I now ask if there is, in any one or in all those specifications, that demand which the Secretary of State avers the Spanish Minister had made, and which is the basis of the whole proceeding in this case on the part of the Executive.

The letter of the Secretary, which is the foundation of the whole proceeding of the District Attorney, in making the United States a party, on the ground of a demand by the Spanish Minister for the delivery of these people as property, " says the thing that is not." The letter proceeds.

Amistad Argument

"In support of these claims, the undersigned invokes the law of nations, the stipulations of existing treaties, and those good feelings"—[good feelings, indeed, he might well say' where all the feelings were in favor of his demand]—" so necessary to the maintenance of the friendly relations that subsist between the two countries, and are so interesting to both.

" The undersigned would be apprehensive of offending Mr. Forsyth by supposing it in t;.e least degree necessary to bring to his recollection his own well−known Construction (`disposiciones) of the law of nations, in a case analogous to the one under consideration."

This is what the logicians call argumentum ad hominem—an appeal, first to the feelings of the individual, not to his sense of justice. He then brings up to Mr. Forsyth his own construction of the law of nations, as given in another case, which he deems analogous. Perhaps I may be justified in conjecturing to what case he alludes, and I will say that, if he alludes to any case of public notoriety, I shall be able to show, before I close, that there is no analogy to this case.

M. Calderon de la Barca then refers to several treaty stipulations in support of his demand, and particularly the 8th, 9th, and 10th articles of the treaty of 1795, continued in force by the treaty of 1819.

"ART. 8. In case the subjects and inhabitants of either party, with their shipping, whether public and of war, or private and of merchants, be forced, through stress of weather, pursuit of pirates or enemies, or any other urgent necessity, for seeking of shelter and harbor, to retreat and enter into any of the rivers, bays, roads, or ports, belonging to the other party, they shall be received and treated with all humanity, and enjoy all favor, protection, and help; and they shall be permitted to refresh and provide themselves, at reasonable rates, with victuals and all things needful for the subsistence of their persons, or reparation of their ships, and prosecution of their voyage; and they shall no ways be hindered from returning out of the said ports or roads, but may remove and depart when and whither they please, without any let or hindrance."

This is a provision for vessels with their owners, driven into port by distress. Who was the Spanish owner here with his ship? There was none. I say the Africans were here with their ship. If you say the original owner is referred to, in whose name the ship's register was given, he was dead, he was not on board, and would not claim the benefit of this article. The vessel either belonged to the Africans, in whose possession it was found, and who certainly kind what is everywhere the first evidence of property, or there was no person to whom this article could apply, and it was not casus foederis. The truth is, this article was not intended to apply to such a case as this, but to the common case, in regard to which it has doubtless been carried into execution hundreds of times, in meeting the common disasters of maritime life.

The Africans, who certainly had the prima facie title to the property, did not bring the vessel into our waters themselves, but were brought here against their will, by the two Spaniards, by stratagem and deception. Now, if this court should consider, as the courts below have done, that the original voyage from Lomboko, in Africa, was continued by the Spaniards in the Amistad, and that pursuing that voyage was a violation of the laws of the United States, then the Spaniards are responsible for that offense. The deed begun in Africa was not consummated according to its original intention, until the Negroes were landed at their port of final destination in Porto Principe. The clandestine landing in Havana, the unlawful sale in the barracoons, the shipment on board the Amistad, were all parts of the original transaction. And it was in pursuit of that original unlawful intent that the Spaniards brought the vessel by stratagem into a port of the United States. Does the treaty apply to such voyages ? Suppose the owner had been on board, and his voyage lawful, what does the treaty secure to him? Why, that he might repair his ship, and purchase refreshments, and continue his voyage. Ruiz and Montes could not continue the voyage. But, suppose the article applicable, and what were the United States to do ? They must place those on board the ship in the situation they were in when taken, that is, the Africans in possession, with the two Spaniards as their prisoners, or their slaves, as the case might be; the Negroes as masters of the ship, to continue their voyage, which on their part was certainly lawful.

If any part of the article was applicable to the case it was in favor of the Africans. They were in distress, and were brought into our waters by their enemies' by those who sought, and who are still' seeking, to reduce them from freedom to slavery, as a reward for having spared their lives in the fight. If the good offices of the government are to be rendered to the proprietors of shipping in distress, they are due to the Africans only, and the United States are now bound to restore the ship to the Africans, and replace the Spaniards on board as prisoners. But the article is not applicable at all. It is not a casus federis. The parties to the treaty never could have had any such case in view.. The transaction on board of the vessel after leaving Havana entirely changed the circumstances of the parties, and conferred rights on my most unfortunate clients, which cannot but be regarded by this honorable court.

Next we have article 9:

ART. 9. All ships and merchandise, of what nature so ever, which shall be rescued out of the hands of any pirates or robbers on the high seas, shall be brought into some port of either state, and shall be delivered to the custody of the officers of that port, in order to be taken care of, and restored entire to the true proprietor, as soon as due and sufficient proof shall be made concerning the property thereof."

Was this ship rescued out of the hands of pirates and robbers? Is this Court competent to declare it ? The Courts below have decided that they have no authority to try, criminally, what happened on board the vessel. They have then no right to regard those who forcibly took possession of the vessel as pirates and robbers. If the sympathies of Lieutenant Gedney, which the Secretary of State says had become national, had been felt for all the parties, in due proportion to their sufferings and their deserts, who were the pirates and robbers, Were they the Africans? When they were brought from Lomboko? in the Tecora, against the laws of Spain, against the laws of the United States, and against the law of nations, so far as the United States, and Spain, and Great Britain, are concerned, who were the robbers and pirates? And when the same voyage, in fact, was continued in the Amistad, and the Africans were in a perishing condition in the hands of Ruiz, dropping dead from day to day under his treatment, were they the pirates and robbers ? This honorable Court will observe from the record that there were fifty–four Africans who left the Havana. Ruiz says in his libel that nine had died before they reached our shores. The marshal's return shows that they were dying day after day from the effects of their sufferings. One died before the Court sat at New London. Three more died before the return was made to the Court at Hartford—only seventeen days—and three more between that and November. Sixteen fell victims before November, and from that time not one has died. Think only of the relief and benefit of being restored to the absolute wants of human nature. Although p]aced in a condition which, if applied to forty citizens of the United States, we should call cruel, shut up eighteen months in a prison, and enjoying only the tenderness which our laws provide for the worst of criminals, so great is the improvement of their condition from what it was in the hands of Ruiz, that they have perfectly recovered their health, and not one has died; when, before that time, they were

17

perishing from hour to hour.

At the great day of accounts, may it please the Court, who is to be responsible for those sixteen souls that died I Ruiz claims those sixteen as his property, as merchandise. How many of them, at his last hour, will pass before him and say, " Let me sit heavy on thy soul to–morrow !"

Who, then, are the tyrants and oppressors against whom our laws are invoked? Who are the innocent sufferers, for whom we are called upon to protect this ship against enemies and robbers Certainly not Ruiz and Montes.

But, independently of this consideration, the article cannot apt ply to slaves. It says ships and merchandise. Is that language applicable to human beings? Will this Court so affirm? It says they shall be restored entire. Is it a treaty between cannibal nations, that a stipulation is needed for the restoration of merchandise entire, to prevent parties from cutting off the legs and arms of human beings before they are delivered up? The very word entire in the stipulation is of itself a sufficient exclusion of human beings from the scope of the article. But if it was intended to embrace human beings, the article would have included a provision for their subsistence until they are restored, and an indemnification for their maintenance to the officers who are charged with the execution of the stipulation. And there is perhaps needed a provision with regard to the institutions of the free states, to prevent a difficulty in keeping human beings in the custom house, without having them liable to the operation of the local law, the habeas corpus, and the rights of freedom.

But with regard to article 9, I will speak of my own knowledge, for it happened that on the renewal of the treaty in 1819, the whole of the negotiations with the then minister of Spain passed through my hands, and I am certain that neither of us ever entertained an idea that this word merchandise was to apply to human beings.

Mr. Calderon also quotes article 10.

"ART. 10. When any vessel of either party shall be wrecked, foundered, or otherwise damaged, on the coasts or within the do minion of the other, their respective subjects or citizens shall receive, as well for themselves as for their vessels and effects, the same assistance which would be due to the inhabitants of the country where the damage happens, and shall pay the same charges and dues only as the said inhabitants would be subject to pay in a like case; and if the operations of repair should require that the whole or any part of the cargo be unladen, they shall pay no duties, charges, or fees, on the pelt which they shall relayed and carry away."

This article, again, has nothing to do with the case. The Amistad was neither wrecked nor foundered, nor otherwise damaged. She came into our waters voluntarily, so far as the Spaniards were concerned, but involuntarily, so far as concerned the Africans, who were in possession of the vessel. They were intentionally prosecuting a voyage to Africa, but were brought to our shores by deception, and against their wills. This is not casus federis. The treaty has no application here. But if, by any latitude of construction, it could be applied, its benefits belong to the Africans, for they were pursuing a lawful voyage, and not to the Spaniards, who were on an unlawful voyage, in the prosecution of the slave trade.

But the article says the same assistance shall be afforded that our own citizens would be entitled to receive in like circumstances. Let us apply the rule. Suppose the Amistad had been a vessel of the United States, owned and manned by citizens of the United States, and in like circumstances. Say it was a Baltimore clipper, fitted for the African slave trade, and having performed a voyage, had come back to our shores, directly or indirectly, with fifty—four African victims on board, and was thus brought into port—what would be the assistance guaranteed by our laws to American citizens, in such circumstances? The captain would be seized, tried as a pirate, and hung! And every person concerned, either as owners or on board the ship, would be severely punished. The law makes it a capital offense for the captain, and no appeal to this Court would save him from the gibbet. Is that the assistance which the Spanish minister invokes for Ruiz and Montes ? That is what our laws would secure to our own citizens in like circumstances. And perhaps it would be a reward nearer their merits than the restoration of these poor Negroes to them, or enabling them to complete their voyage.

But my clients are claimed under the treaty as merchandise, rescued from pirates and robbers. Who were the merchandise, and who were the robbers? According to the construction of the Spanish minister, the merchandise were the robbers, and the robbers were the merchandise. The merchandise was rescued out of its own hands, and the robbers were rescued out of the hands of the robbers. Is this the meaning of the treaty ? Will this Court adopt a rule of construction in regard to solemn treaties that will sanction

19

such conclusions, There is a rule in Vattel that no construction shall be allowed to a treaty which makes it absurd. Is any thing more absurd than to say these forty Africans are robbers, out of whose hands they have themselves been rescued? Can a greater absurdity be imagined in construction than this, which applies the double character of robbers and of merchandise to human beings ?

May it please your Honors, there is not one article of the treaty that has the slightest application to this case, and the Spanish minister has no more ground for appealing to the treaty, as a warrant for his demand, than he has for relying on the law of nations.

The next argument that follows is so peculiar that I find it difficult to give a distinct idea of its purpose or application. He says,

"The crime in question is one of those which, if permitted to pass unpunished, would endanger the internal tranquillity and the safety of the island of Cuba, where citizens of the United States not only carry on a considerable trade, but where they possess territorial properties which they cultivate with the labor of African slaves. These, on learning that the crime alluded to had been committed with impunity, (and their friends would not fail to acquaint them with the fact) would lose none of the opportunities for attempting revolt and evasion, which are afforded by the frequent and daily necessity of conveying Negroes by sea from one quarter of the island to another; and to guard against this it would be necessary to use additional precautions at a great expense."

I believe, may it please the Court, that this is not a good argument before this court to determine questions of law and justice by the consideration that there are American citizens who own plantations in the island of Cuba, which they cultivate by the labor of slaves. They own their plantations and slaves there, subject to the laws of Spain, which laws declare the African slave trade to be felony. The Spanish minister has no right to appeal to our courts to pass a particular sentence between parties in a suit, by considerations of their personal interest, or that of other American citizens in the Island óf Cuba. What would become of the liberties of this nation if our courts are to pass sentence between parties, upon considerations of the effect it may have upon the interest of American citizens, scattered as they may be in all parts of the world? If it is a valid consideration when applied to Cuba and the American owners of sugar estates and slaves there, it applies equally to all other countries where American citizens may have property; to China, Hindostan, or the Feejee Islands. It was no proper argument for the

20

Amistad Argument

Spanish minister to urge upon the American Secretary of State. It was undoubtedly calculated and designed to influence his sympathy in the case—that sympathy with one of the parties which he says had become national It was calculated to excite and to influence the Secretary of State not only by the effect to be produced in the island of Cuba, but perhaps also by a reward to certain interests nearer home. But was that JUSTICE? Was that a ground on which courts of justice will decide cases ? I t rust not.

There are a few portions of this letter, which I had rather your Honors would read when you are together in consultation, than to read them myself in this place. I will not trust myself to comment upon them as they deserve. I trust that your Honors, in the pursuit of JUSTICE, will read them, as the document will be in your hands, and you will see why I abstain from doing it. Mr. Calderon proceeds to say,

"If, on the other hand, they should be condemned by the incompetent tribunal that has taken upon itself to try them as pirates and assassins, the infliction of capital punishment in this case would not be attended with the salutary effects had in view by the law when it resorts to this painful and terrible alternative, namely, to prevent the commission of similar offenses. In such case, the indemnification I officially ask for the owners would be n very slender compensation; for, if the property remained unimpaired, as it would remain, the satisfaction due to the public would not be accorded."

And that is a reason why the President of the United States was to issue his lettrede cachet, and send these unfortunate individuals to Cuba. I abstain now from reading the subsequent passages. He concluded by saying,

"In the islands above mentioned the citizens of the United States have always met with a favorable reception and kind treatment. The Spanish Government, for the protection of their property, would immediately accord the extradition of any slaves that might take refuge there from the southern states. Being itself exact in the observance of treaties, it claims the more justly the execution of them, and a reciprocal good correspondence, from a nation, the ally and neighbor of Spain, to whom so many proofs have been afforded of the high degree in which her friendship is esteemed."

They will readily yield fugitive slaves! Was this an argument, I ask the honorable Court, to be addressed to the Secretary of State? Is it upon these principles that cases are to be decided? Is it by these considerations that the action of governments? to be determined?

21

Amistad Argument

Shall these men be given up on the offer of an equivalent ? " If you will deliver these Africans to me, for whose blood all the slave–traders of Cuba thirst, and any slave from the south shall make his escape and came to Cuba, we will readily deliver him up." What is this argument as addressed to the Secretary of State I It may be a very easy thing for the Governor at Havana to seize a fugitive southern slave, or a pretended fugitive, as the case may be, and put him on board a vessel and send him to one of our Southern states. The learned Attorney General, I think, read some authorities to show that this Governor has royal powers, about equal to those of the King, and it may be easy for him to seize any man, black or white, slave or free, who may be claimed as a slave, and send him beyond seas for any purpose. But, has the President of the United States any such powers Can the American Executive do such things? If he is to do them, I should hope, at least, that it might be under treaty stipulations rather more adapted to the object than these. It was going quite far enough, I should think, to require the President of the U. S. to keep these men safely, and send them back at the expense of this nation, without making this—what shall I call it? I will not undertake to qualify it in words—this offer to send back the fugitive slaves of the South as an equivalent, provided the President will consent to deliver up these MEN, by a despotic act, to satiate the vengeance of the slave–traders at Havana.

I have now, may it please the Court, examined at great length, and with tedious detail, the letter of the Spanish minister demanding the interposition of the national Executive to restore these unfortunate Africans to the island of Cuba. And now I may in. quire of your Honors, what, in your opinion, was the duty of the Secretary of State, on receiving such a letter. And in the first place, what did he do ?

His first act was, to misrepresent the demand, and to write to the District Attorney in Connecticut, directing him to pursue a claim for the possession of these people on behalf of the United States, on the ground that the Spanish minister had demanded their delivery to him, as the property of Spanish subjects, and ordering him to take care that no court should place them beyond the control of the Executive. That is what he did. And the consequence is the case now before the court. The Attorney of the United States pursued his orders. He stated, in his claim before the District Court, that the Spanish minister had demanded their restoration as property; and then' as if conscious that this claim might not secure the other purpose, of keeping them at all events within the control of the Executive, he added, of his own head, (for it does not appear that he had any instructions on this point,) a second count, claiming, on behalf of the United States, that if the court should find they were not slaves by the laws of Spain, but that they were brought to our shores in violation of the act of Congress for the suppression of the slave trade, then they should be placed at the disposal of the President, to be sent to Africa, according to the provisions of that act. This count was undoubtedly added in consequence of the order not to let them be placed beyond the control of the Executive. In a subsequent term of the court, he filed a new libel, in which this alternative demand was omitted. Why was that done ? I can conceive no other reason than that he had received such instructions from the Executive.

Those instructions do not appear among the printed documents but it does not follow that none were given, for the communication of the President, in answer to the call of the House of Representatives, was not a full one, as I know of my own knowledge. The demand was for all information not incompatible with the public interest, and under that proviso many things were kept back. But there can be no doubt that it was for the purpose of complying with the first order of the District Attorney inserted in the second count, and that it was by the instructions of the department he afterward withdrew it.

[Mr. Baldwin. The count was not withdrawn. A new libel was entered, having only one count, but the first libel was not withdrawn.] Very well—it amounts to this: that the Executive did not choose to hold itself responsible for that construction of the act of Congress. This appears from the appeal. What have the United States appealed from? Why, from n decree of the court, giving them precisely what they had claimed by the District Attorney. The Attorney knew that the libel grounded on the demand of the Spanish minister, (ostensibly, for I have shown that it was a falsification of the terms of that demand by the Secretary of State,) was not sufficient to place the Africans beyond the control of the Executive, in a certain alternative, and therefore he calls upon the Court to put them in the hands of the President, to be sent to Africa—that is, to complete their own voyage.

Well, the District Court investigated the case, and dissipated entirely the pretension that these Africans could be claimed in any way as merchandise. They went the length of declaring that the only lading on board, the boy Antonio, concerning whom there was the slightest pretext of a claim that he was a slave, should be delivered up to the Spanish consul, on behalf of the representatives of his late owner, Captain Ferrer. The United States do not appeal from that decision, and there has been no appeal, although we might have appealed with propriety. And I confess that, had I been of counsel in that stage of the proceedings, I should have been much disposed to appeal, on the ground that there was no article of the treaty which has any thing to do with the case. I conceive that this part of the decree of the District Court is not warranted by any law or treaty whatever.

But I do not desire to argue that question now, for I perceive that the district judge, in giving his decision, places it partly on the ground that the boy is desirous of returning. And as volenti non fit injuria, I reconcile my mind to that part of the decision, for we could certainly have no possible motive to interfere with the wishes of the boy. If he really has the desire to return to slavery in Cuba, it would be far from my desire to interfere with his wishes, however strange and unnatural I might deem them to be. But I must, at the same time, as an individual, protest against his delivery by any compulsion, or on any ground of obligation in the treaty; for I must maintain, that there is no one of the articles in the treaty cited that has any application whatever to the ease.

And now, may it please your Honors, so strange and singular is every thing that happens, connected with this most singular case, I am informed that, after all, this boy has not been sent to Cuba, notwithstanding his anxiety to go, and the desire of the Spanish consul for his restoration, with a decree of the Court agreeable to his demand. I am informed that he has remained a whole year in prison with the Africans, and is, at this moment, in the custody of the marshal, by what warrant or process I know not, or at whose expense.

The reason for this extended analysis of the demand by the Spanish minister is, that we may be prepared to inquire what answer he ought to have received from the American Secretary. I aver, that it was the duty of the Secretary of State instantly to answer the letter, by showing the Spanish minister that all his de. minds were utterly inadmissible, and that the government of the United States could do nothing of what he required. It could not deliver the ship to the owner, and there was no duty resting on the United States to dispose of the vessel in any such manner. And as to the demand that no salvage should be taken, the Spanish minister should have been told that it was a question depending exclusively on the determination of the courts, before whom the case was pending for trial according to law. And the Secretary aught to have shown Mr. Calderon, that the demand for a proclamation by the President of the United States, against the jurisdiction of the courts, was not only inadmissible but offensive —it was demanding what the Executive could not do, by the constitution. It would be the assumption of a control over the judiciary by the President, which would overthrow the whole fabric of the constitution; it would violate the principles of our government generally and in every particular; it would be against the rights of the Negroes, of the citizens, and of the States.

The Secretary ought to have done this at once, without waiting to consult the President, who was then absent from the city. The claim that the negroes should be delivered was equally inadmissible with the rest; the President has no power to arrest either citizens or foreigners. But even that power is almost insignificant compared with that of sending men beyond seas to deliver them up to a foreign government. The Secretary should have called upon the Spanish ambassador to name an instance where such a demand had been made by any government of another government that was independent. He should have told him, that such a demand was treating the President of the United States, not as the head of a nation, but as a constable, a catch pole—a character that it is not possible to express in gentlemanly language. That i8 what this demand makes of the President of the United States.

The Secretary should also have set the Spanish Minister right with regard to the authorities before whom the question was pending. He should have told him that they were not the authorities of the state of Connecticut but of the United States, the courts of the Union in the state of Connecticut. He should have corrected this mistake of the minister at the beginning. It was a real misapprehension, which has continued through the whole proceeding to the present time, and it ought to have been corrected at first. And what is still more remarkable, the same mistake of calling it the court of Connecticut was made by Mr. Forsyth himself long after.

But what did the Secretary do in fact? He barely replies to Mr. Calderon, that he had sent his letter to the President for his consideration, and that "no time will be needlessly lost, after his decision upon the demand it prefers shall have reached me, in communicating to you his views upon the subject."

And now, from that day to this, the Secretary of State has never answered one of these demands, nor arrested one of these misapprehensions, nor asserted the rights and the honor of the nation against one of these most extraordinary, inadmissible, and insolent demands. He has degraded the country, in the face of the whole civilized world, not only by allowing these demands to remain unanswered, but by proceeding, I am obliged to say, throughout the whole transaction, as if the Executive were earnestly desirous to comply with every one of the demands. In the very misrepresentations of those demands, in his instructions to the District Attorney, under which this case is brought here, why does he take such a course? The Spanish Minister pronounced the Court before which the Secretary brought the question, an incompetent tribunal—and this position has been maintained by the Legation of Spain down to this very month, that a letter of Chevalier d'Argaiz officially protests against the jurisdiction of the courts before which the Secretary professes to be prosecuting the claim of this very minister!

Why does the Spanish Minister persist– in such inadmissible pretensions? It is because they were not met in limine in a proper manner—because he was not told instantly, without the delay of an hour, that this Government could never admit much claims, and would be offended if they were repeated, or any portion of them. Yet all these claims, monstrous, absurd and inadmissible as they are, have been urged and repeated for eighteen months, upon our Government, and an American Secretary of State evades answering any of them—evades it to such an extent that the Spanish Minister reproaches him for not meeting his arguments.

The demand of Mr. Calderon was dated September 6. The order of the Secretary to the District Attorney, in regard to the suit, was dated September 11, in which he says that "a communication has been addressed to this department by the Minister of Her Catholic Majesty, CLAIMING TEE VESSEL, CARGO, AND BLACKS ON BOARD, As SPANISH PROPERTY, and demanding its immediate release." On the 23d of September, the Secretary writes to the Spanish Minister as follows:

SIR: In the examination of the case of the Spanish schooner "Amistad," the only evidence at present within reach of this department is that presented by the ship's paper; and the proceedings of the court of inquiry held by a district judge of Connecticut, on board the schooner, at the time the Negroes in whose possession she was found, were imprisoned for the alleged murder of the captain and mate of the vessel. If you have any other authentic documents relating to the question or evidence of facts which can be useful to a proper understanding of it, I have the honor to request by the direction of the President, that you will communicate them to me with as little delay as practicable.

Here the Secretary reiterates the error of the Spanish minister, instead of correcting it, with regard to the character of the Court before which the case was pending. The Secretary of State calls the United States District for Connecticut "a District Court of Connecticut." The Spanish Minister could not be expected to acquire a correct understanding of the case, unless he was informed, but here he has his error confirmed.

Amistad Argument

The Secretary further requests the ambassador, if he has any farther documents, " that you will communicate them to me." What had he to do with this evidence? The Spanish minister had made a certain demand upon the government of the United States. Whether it was what it appears to be, or whether it was what the Secretary represented it to be in his orders to the District Attorney, it was no part of the business of the American Secretary of State to look after the evidence. Still, if he had requested the minister to communicate the evidence to the Court, it might not have been exactly improper, but only officious. If the Spanish Minister chose to go into our courts in support of the private claims of Spanish subjects, he could do it, and it was his business to bring forward the proper evidence in support of his claim. Why, then, does the Secretary call upon him to furnish these documents to the Executive Department? Your Honors will judge whether this letter is or is not evidence of a determination then existing on the part of the Executive, to decide this case independently of the judiciary, and ex parte.

Mr. Calderon replies that he has no other evidence to furnish. The next document is the letter of his successor, the Chevalier d'Argaiz:

NEW–YORK October 3, 1839.

The undersigned, envoy extraordinary and minister plenipotentiary of Her Catholic Majesty, has the honor of commencing his official correspondence with you, sir, by soliciting an act of justice, which, not being in any way connected with the principal question as yet remaining unsettled by the cabinet, relative to the Negroes, found on board the schooner Amistad on her arrival on these coasts, he does not doubt will be received by you in the manner which he has every reason to expect, from the circumstance that all preceding acts of the department under your charge have been dictated by the principles of rectitude and reciprocity.

Her Majesty's vice–consul at Boston, under date of the 24th of September last, says, among other things:

"As it appears from the papers of the schooner that she, as well as her cargo, are exclusively Spanish property, it seems strange that the Court of New London has not yet ordered the delivery of one or both to the owners, if they are present, or to me, as their agent, born in that part of the Union"—[This is a mis–translation; it means the official agent in that part of the Union]— "agreeably to the articles of the treaty now in force

27

between the two countries. The delay in the delivery would not be of so much consequence to the proprietors if the vessel did not require immediate repairs, in order to preserve her from complete destruction, and if it were not material that a large part of the cargo should be sold on account of its bad condition.

Here we see the same unfortunate misapprehension continued. The new Spanish minister calls upon the Secretary of State to put the "Court of New London" into speedy action, to lessen the danger of loss to the proprietors by delay, and the Secretary of State takes no pains to correct the error.

On the 24th of October, the Secretary of State wrote again to Mr. Argaiz, on another subject, which is not now before this Court,—the arrest of Ruiz and Montes, at the suit of some of the Africans, in the courts of the State of New York. Mr. Argaiz protested against the arrest, and claims "the interposition of the Executive in procuring their liberation, and indemnity for the losses and injury they may have sustained. To that the Secretary replies:

"It appears from the documents accompanying the note of the Chevalier d'Argaiz, that the two Spanish subjects referred to were arrested on process issuing from the Superior Court of the city of New York, at the suit of, and upon affidavits made by certain colored men, natives of Africa, for the purpose of securing their appearance before the proper tribunal, to answer for wrongs alleged to have been inflicted by them upon the persons of the said Africans; and, consequently, that the occurrence constitutes a simple case of resort by individuals against others to the judicial courts of the country, which are equally open to all without distinction, and to which it belongs exclusively to decide, as well upon the right of the complainant to demand the interposition of their authority, as upon the liability of the defendant to give redress for the wrong alleged to have been committed by him. This being the only light in which the subject can be viewed, and the constitution and laws having secured the judicial power against all interference on the part of the Executive authority, the President, to whom the Chevalier d'Argaiz's note has been communicated, has instructed the undersigned to state, that the agency of this government to obtain the release of Messrs. Ruiz and Montes cannot be afforded in the manner requested by him. The laws of the state of New York, of which the constitution and laws of the United States and their treaties with foreign powers form a part, afford to Messrs. Ruiz and Montes all the necessary means to procure their release from imprisonment, and to obtain any indemnity to which they may be justly entitled, and therefore would render

Amistad Argument

unnecessary any agency on the part of this department for those purposes."

There is a complete answer to all these demands of the Spanish legation. "The constitution and laws have secured the judicial power against All interference of the Executive authority." That is very true. The laws of the state of New York, of which the constitution and laws of the United States and their: treaties with foreign powers form a part, afford to Messrs. Ruiz and Montes all the necessary: means for the security of their rights, and therefore "render unnecessary any agency on the part of" the Executive. That is very correct. There is a perfect answer, worthy of an American statesman But is that all? No. The Secretary finds, after all these disclaimers, one Executive power yet in reserve, which may be put forth to take part against poor Africans, and at least afford evidence of the national sympathy. The Secretary says:

"But inasmuch as the imprisonment of those persons connects itself with another occurrence which has been brought under the President's consideration, in consequence of a correspondence between the Spanish legation and this department, instructions (of which a copy is inclosed) have been given to the Attorney of the United States for the District of New York to put himself in communication with those gentlemen, to offer them his advice (and his aid, if necessary) as to any measure which it may be proper for them to adopt to procure their release, and such indemnity as may be due to them. under our laws, for their arrest and detention."

Because the case "connects itself with another occurrence." What is all this? The independence of the judiciary is first firmly and bravely sustained. It is a question of private rights between parties, with which the executive has nothing to do, and the Government of the United States has no power to interpose. And then the President instructs the District Attorney, the law officer of the government, to "put himself in communication" with one of the parties, to throw all the weight and influence of the government on their side, in order to secure a favorable decision for them in the Courts of the state of New York. May it please your Honors, I will not here enter into an inquiry of the effect of this interference of the Executive of the United States with the Courts of a State, or the extent and operation of the principle which would authorize such interference. I really do not know, my imagination cannot present to me the compass of its effects on the rights of the people of the United States. again ask the attention of this honorable court to this subject. The letter begins with a declaration of the independence of the judiciary of the State of New York, the sufficiency of the laws to secure justice and the incompetency of the Executive to interfere; and yet, because the case connects itself" with another case in which the Executive has considered itself entitled to act, the whole influence of the Government is brought to bear upon the judicial authorities of the State of New York.

I said the Secretary of State had never to this hour undertaken to contest any one of the actual demands of Mr. Calderon, as preferred in his letter of 5th September. He had suffered both Mr. Calderon and his successor to remain under the impression that if their demands were not complied with, for the kidnapping of these people by the Executive, it was not for the want of a will to do it, or of a disposition to contest the claims put forth in so extraordinary a manner upon our government. Let us now see how Mr. Argaiz himself regarded the conduct of the Secretary. On the 5th of November, he writes again to Mr. Forsyth, acknowledging the receipt of Mr. Forsyth's letter, inclosing the instructions of the Attorney of the United States for the District of New York, " that he should offer to these persons his advice and assistance, if needed, with regard to the most proper means of obtaining their liberty." He says:

" Although this answer did not entirely satisfy the desire expressed by the undersigned in the note of October 22d to which he was impelled by the sense of his duty, and by the terms of existing treaties, yet he received it with pleasure and with thanks; with pleasure, because he saw that the Secretary of State did not refuse to admit the reasons which the undersigned had the honor to state in that note; and with shanks, because he saw that the sentiments which had urged him to request with warmth a prompt reply, had been kindly interpreted. The undersigned in consequence, went immediately to New York, where he visited on the 29th ultimo, the Attorney of the United States with whom he had a long conversation, which left him delighted with the affability and courtesy of Mr. Butler, although he did not have the happiness to remain satisfied as to the principal matter, as that officer of justice declared that he could find no other means of obtaining the liberty of Ruiz Montes being already free) than by waiting the determination of the court or courts, against the jurisdiction of which the undersigned had already especially protested."

The Spanish ambassador was not satisfied with the letter, and yet he received it with pleasure, " because he saw that the Secretary did not refuse to admit his reasons." How is that? The Secretary of State took no measures to repel the improper demand made, or to correct the erroneous idea cherished by the Spanish legation; and this neglect Mr. Argaiz construes as a virtual admission of his " reasons ' Why should he not so construe it? Here is also a renewal of the protest, which has uniformly been maintained by the legation, against the right of any court in this country to exercise jurisdiction in the case. And yet this suit is carried on by the Executive, as in pursuance of a demand by the Spanish minister. Mr. Argaiz then refers to two personal conferences which he had with the Secretary, and he is well persuaded that what he had said, together with the indications in his note of October 22, would have been sufficient to convince " one so enlightened and discriminating as the Secretary, of the justice of his claim; that this persuasion has gained strength, from the circumstance that the Secretary of State has made no attempt in his answer to oppose those arguments, but has confined himself to endeavoring to explain the course of civil causes in the courts of this country, in order to show that the government of the United States could not interfere in the manner which her Catholic Majesty's representative requested; it becomes necessary to advance farther arguments, at the risk of being importunate."

And a little farther on, after adverting to the various excuses and palliations which seem to have been presented in these confidential conferences, for not seizing these Negroes and sending them to Cuba by the Executive power, in which he says: "it is allowed by the whole world" that "petitions or accusations of slaves against their masters cannot be admitted in a court,', he concludes by asking—

"As the incompetence of the courts of the United States, with regard to this matter, is so clearly demonstrated, is there no power in the Federal Government to declare it so, and to interpose its authority to put down the irregularity of these proceedings, which the court is not competent to perform? It seems impossible that there should be no such power; but unfortunately there is none"

"Her Catholic Majesty's envoy extraordinary and minister plenipotentiary, nevertheless, seeing that his previous protest did not produce the result which he expected, renews it now, declaring this government responsible for the consequences which may grow out of this affair; and he asks the Secretary of State whether or not he possesses sufficient authority and force to carry into fulfillment the treaty of 1795. If he has not, then there cad be no treaty binding on the other party."

He thinks it impossible there should not be a power in the Federal Government to put down these proceedings of the courts, but he admits that unfortunately there is no such power, and then asks the Secretary of State if he cannot find a power, somewhere, to take the matter out of the hands of the judiciary altogether. And if not, he shall hold this Government responsible for the consequences, for if it has not power to fulfill the treaty, no treaty is binding on either party.

On the 26th of November, the trial of the case having been postponed by the District Court from November to January, he writes again, that he is under the necessity of renewing his former complaints.

"To the first complaint, made by his predecessor, on the 6th September last, nothing more than an acknowledgment of its receipt was thought necessary, which was made on the 16th of the same month. In the answers which the Secretary has pleased to give to the notes of the undersigned, of the 22d of October, and the 5th of November last, that gentleman did not think proper to combat the argument advanced. Whose which the undersigned now proposes to present will be no less powerful, and he hopes will be such that the Secretary will not be able .o deny their Justice.

"The undersigned has the honor to ask in what law, act, or statute, does the said court base its right to take cognizance of the present case? There can be no doubt as to the reply: on no law, act, or statute."

Here he denies again that the Court, before which the Secretary of State had made a demand with the averment that it came from the Spanish minister, has any power to take cognizance of the case. He says there is no law, act, or statute for it, and then he goes on:—

" For, if any such existed, it is, or should be, anterior or posterior to the treaty of 1795. If anterior, it clearly became annulled, because a treaty is one of the superior laws of the State, or the treaty should never have been signed, or ratified, or sanctioned by the legislative bodies. If posterior to the treaty, the legislative bodies, in drawing it up, discussing it, and voting on it, must have seen that it was at variance with a subsisting treaty, which was already a law of the Union. All which serves to show that, in the existing state of the laws, this affair cannot and should not be decided by the common law, but by the international law."

Amistad Argument

That is to say, the treaty stipulation has taken away the power of the courts of the United States to exercise jurisdiction between parties. Is that a doctrine to be heard by the Secretary of State of the United States from a foreign ambassador without answering it' The ambassador proceeds to urge that "if the General Government of the Union had decided this matter of itself, gubernativamente"—here is a word, used several times in this correspondence, that no American translator has been able to translate into our language. It means, by the simple will or absolute fiat of the Executive, as in the case of the lettres de cachet—or a warrant for the BASTILE—that is what the Spaniard means by gubernativamente, when he asks the Executive of the United States, by his own fiat, to seize these MEN, wrest them from the power and protection of the courts, and send them beyond seas! Is there any such law at Constantinople ? Does the Celestial Empire allow a proceeding like this? Is the Khan of Tartary possessed of a power competent to meet demands like these? I know not where on the globe we should look for any such authority, unless it be with the Governor General of Cuba with respect to Negroes.

" If the General Government had proceeded gubernativamente" —it is not necessary now to consider what would have followed. " But," says the Chevalier d'Argaiz, "very different, however, have been the results; for, in the first place the treaty of 1795 has not been executed, as the legation of her Catholic Majesty has solicited; and the public vengeance has not been satisfied."

" The public vengeance! "What public vengeance ? The vengeance of African slave traders, despoiled of their prey and thirsting for blood! The vengeance of the barracoons! This " public vengeance" is not satisfied. Surely, this is very lamentable. Surely, this is a complaint to be made to the Secretary of State of this government. " For," says he, "be it recollected that the legation of Spain does not demand the delivery of slaves, but of assassins."

How is it possible to reconcile this declaration of the Spanish minister with the libel of the District Attorney, entered by order of the Secretary of State, setting forth what was said to be the demand of the Spanish minister? It is an explicit contradiction.

The Constitution of the United States recognizes the slaves, held within some of the States of the Union, only in their capacity of persons— persons held to labor or service in a State under the laws thereof—persons constituting elements of representation in the popular branch of the National Legislature—persons, the migration or importation of whom should not be prohibited by Congress prior to the year 1808. The Constitution no where recognizes them as property. The words slave and slavery are studiously excluded from the Constitution. Circumlocutions are the fig–leaves under which these parts of the body politic are decently concealed. Slaves, therefore, in the Constitution of the United States are recognized only as persons, enjoying rights and held to the performance of duties.

But, in all countries where men are held as slaves, when they are charged with the commission of crimes, the right of their owners to their persons is, and must necessarily be, suspended; and when they are convicted of capital crimes, the right of the owner is extinguished. Throughout the whole correspondence between the Spanish ministers and our Department of State, concerning the surrender of these most unfortunate persons, this broad distinction appears to have been entirely and astonishingly overlooked, not only by the Spanish ministers, but by the Secretary of State and by the Attorney General.

Mr. Calderon demands that the President should keep these persons all—all—adult males and children of both sexes included— in close custody, and convey them to Cuba to be tried for their lives. Is it not palpable that if this demand had been complied with, they could not have been restored to their pretended owners, Ruiz and Montes, as merchandise of what nature soever? With what face, then, could the 9th article of the treaty with Spain be alledged to support a demand for the safekeeping and delivery of the captives, not as slaves, but as assassins—not as merchandise, but as men— as infant females, with flesh, and blood, and nerves, and sinews, to be tortured, and with lives to be forfeited and consumed by fire, to appease the public vengeance of the lawless slave–traders in Cuba.

Mr. Forsyth, by a most unaccountable oversight of this distinction between persons and things, misrepresents this demand of Mr. Calderon.

He instructs the District Attorney, Mr. Holabird, (11th Sept., 1839, Doc. p. 39, 40,) that the Spanish minister had addressed a communication to the Department of State, claiming the vessel, cargo, AND BLOCKS on board, as Spanish property, and demanding its immediate release.

The District Attorney, on the 19th of September, files, accordingly, his libels, (Record, p. 13,) stating the demand of the Spanish minister, not as it had really been made, but according to the statement of it in his instructions from the Department of State; and he prays the Court that, if the claim of the Spanish minister is well founded and conformable to treaty, the Court should make such order for the disposal of the said vessel, cargo, AND SLAVES, as may best enable the United States, in all respects, to comply with their treaty stipulations, and preserve the public faith inviolate.

But if it should be made to appear that the persons aforesaid, described as slaves are Negroes and persons of color, who have been transported from Africa in violation of the laws of the United States, and brought into these United States contrary to the same laws, he claims that, in such case, the Court shall make such further order as may enable the United States, if deemed expedient, to remove such persons to the coast of Africa, to be delivered there to such agent or agents as may be authorized to receive and provide for them, pursuant to the laws of the United States; or to make such other order as to the court should seem fit, right, and proper in the premises.

Here were three alternatives prayed for—1st. That the vessel, cargo, and blacks, assumed to be slaves, should be so disposed of as to enable the United States to comply with their treaty stipulations, and preserve the public faith inviolate. It was stated that this demand was made at the instance of the Spanish minister, but that was true only of the vessel and cargo, but not of the persons. Of them, he had demanded, by necessary implication, that they should not be restored to their pretended owners, but kept in close custody, and, in defiance of all judicial authority, conveyed to the Havana Govermnentally, that is, by the arbitrary mandate of the President of the United States, to satisfy public vengeance. The Court could not have complied with this alternative of restoring the Negroes, as property, to their owners, but by denying and defying the real demand of the Spanish minister, that they should be sent to Cuba as criminals.

The second alternative was, that the Court should enable the United States to send the Negroes home to Africa, if deemed expedient; and to this the decree of the Court said, soit fait comme il est desire— it as the District Attorney desires. Let the said Africans, in the custody of the Marshal, be delivered to the President of tile United States by the Marshal of the District of Connecticut, to be by him transported to Africa, in pursuance of the law of Congress passed March 3, 1829, entitled " An act in addition to the acts prohibiting the slave–trade."

Yet, from this sentence, claimed by the District Attorney, the representative of the Executive Administration before the Court, it is he himself that appeals. Should the Court sustain that apt peal, what judgment could they possibly render? Should they reverse the decision of the District and Circuit Courts, they would indeed determine that these forty persons should not be delivered to the President of the United States, to be sent home to Africa —but what shall the Court decree to be done with them ? Not surely, that they should be delivered up to their pretended owners, for against that the Spanish minister solemnly protests ! He demands not even that they should be delivered up to himself! He demands that it should be declared, that no tribunal in the United States has the right even to institute proceedings against them. Be declared— by whom? He demands of the Executive Administration—(will the Court please to consider what the purport of this demand is?)—that the President of the United States should issue n proclamation, that no tribunal of the United States has the right to institute proceedings against the subjects of Spain for crimes committed on board a Spanish vessel, and in the waters of the Spanish territory.

When this demand was made, the Africans of the Amistad were in the custody of a judicial tribunal of the United States, upon proceedings instituted against them as criminals charged with piracy and murder. They were also claimed by two Spaniards as merchandise, their property; and the faith of a treaty was solemnly invoked to sustain the claim that this merchandise, rescued out of the hands of pirates or robbers, (that is to say, out of the hands of itself,) should be taken care of by the officers of the port into which they had been brought, and restored entire to them—Ruiz and Montes—as soon as due and sufficient proof should be made concerning the property thereof.

Now, if no tribunal in the United States had the right to institute proceedings against the subjects of Spain for crimes committed on board a Spanish vessel and in the waters of the Spanish territory, how could the Court know that these same Spanish subjects were, at the same time, the merchandise rescued out of the hands of pirates and robbers and the pirates or robbers out of whose hands the merchandise was rescued? How could the Court know that they were subjects of Spain—that they were pirates or robbers—or that they were merchandise—if the Court had no right to institute proceedings against them ?

The very phraseology of the 9th article of the treaty with Spain proves, that it was not and could not be intended to include persons under the denomination of merchandise, of what nature soever, for it provides that the merchandise shall be delivered to the custody of the officers of the port, in order to be taken care of and restored entire to the true proprietor. Now, this provision, that the merchandise shall be restored entire, is absurd if applied to human beings, and the use of the word conclusively proves that the thought and intention of the parties could not be construed to extend to human beings. A stipulation to restore human beings entire might suit two nations of cannibals, but would be absurd, and worse than absurd, between civilized and Christian nations. Again, the article provides that the rescued merchandise shall be delivered to the custody of the officers of the port into which it is brought, in order to be taken care of; but, by what Constitution or law of the United States, or of Connecticut, could the officers of the port of hew London receive into their custody, and take care of, the Africans of the Amistad?

The demand of the Spanish minister, Calderon, was, that the President of the United States should first turn man–robber; rescue from the custody of the Court, to which they had been committed, those forty odd Africans, males and females, adults and children; next turn jailer, and keep them in his close custody, to prevent their evasion; and lastly, turn catchpoll and convey them to the Havana, to appease the public vengeance of the African slave–traders of the barracoons.

Is it possible to speak of this demand in language of decency and moderation? Is there a law of Habeas Corpus in the land? Has the expunging process of black lines passed upon these two Declarations of Independence in their gilded frames? Has the 4th of July, '76, become a day of ignominy and reproach? Is there a member of this Honorable Court of age to remember the indignation raised against a former President of the United States for causing to be delivered up, according to express treaty stipulation, by regular judicial process, a British sailor, for murder on board of a British frigate on the high seas? At least, all your Honors remember the case of the Bambers? You all remember your own recent decision in the case of Dr. Holmes ? And is it for this Court to sanction such monstrous usurpation and Executive tyranny as this at the demand of a Spanish minister? And can you hear, with judicial calmness and composure, this demand of despotism, countenanced and supported by all the Executive authorities of the United States, though not yet daring to carry it into execution?

The third alternative prayed for in the name and behalf of the United States in the libel of the 19th of September, 1839, is, that the court should make such other order in the premises as it should think fit, right, and proper.

To this expedient it was necessary for the court to resort. The court did not know—it could not know that the demand of the Spanish Minister, Calderon, was not only widely different from that which the libel of the District Attorney represented it to be, but absolutely incompatible with it. The court took it for granted that the statement in the libels, at least so far as concerned the demand of the Spanish Minister, was true—and so far as respected the only Ladino on board the Amistad, the boy Antonio, did accede to the supposed demand of the Minister—did actually admit the treaty stipulation as applicable to him—and did decree that he should be restored to the legal representatives of his deceased master. The judge of the District Court relieved Antonio from his right of appeal— from that decision by stating that Antonio himself desired to be restored to his widowed mistress. But as the whole decree was the result of a deception practiced upon the court, and as in that part of it relating to Antonio, are involved principles of the deepest interest to human freedom, and to the liberties of my country, I will only express my most earnest hope, with profound respect for the court, that that portion of its decision will never tee adduced as authority for the surrender of any other individual situated as Antonio was on that trial.

And here I must avail myself of the occasion to state my objections to the admission of the case of the Antelope as an authoritative precedent in this or any other court of the United States— I had almost said for any thing, certainly for the right of the court itself to deliver up to slavery any human individual at the demand of any diplomatic or consular agent of any foreign power. And that I may be enabled to set forth at large, my reasons for resisting the application of that case as precedent or authority for the settlement of any principle now under the consideration of the Court, I must ask the permission of the Court to review the case of the Antelope itself, as it appears on the face of the Reports.

[See the review of the case of the Antelope, at the close of the argument.]

And this declaration of the Spanish minister not only contradicts it, but shows that it was impossible any such demand should have been made. "For, let it be remembered," he says, "that the Spanish legation demands not slaves but assassins." No despotism could comply with both demands, had they been made, but the Spanish Minister explicitly declares that only one demand was made by the legation, and that not the one affirmed by the Secretary of State—not property but assassins—not for the benefit of individuals, but to satisfy "public vengeance." There is something follows in the letter about " fanaticism," which I will not read to the Court, for reasons that will be obvious. Indeed, I do not know as I understand it, and it is possible that I have indulged, or may indulge in what, in certain dialects, may be called "fanaticism," myself. The Chevalier proceeds to reason:

"Thus it appears that a court of one of the States of the confederacy has assumed the direction of an affair over which it has no jurisdiction; that there can be no law, either anterior or posterior to the treaty, upon which a legal sentence can be based; that this court, by the repeated delays which it orders, contributes to delay the satisfaction demanded by public justice; and that, in consequence, the affair should only be determined by reference to international right, and, therefore, by the exercise of the power of the government, (gubernativamente ;) that, for its determination, the treaty exists to which Spain appeals; that, from the delay on this determination have proceeded injuries requiring indemnification, to demand which the undersigned reserves his right for a future occasion. The undersigned may, without indiscretion, declare that this must be the opinion of the cabinet, which, possessing already the necessary and even indispensable powers, may immediately act (gubernativamente) in this matter, in virtue of the actual state of the law, and without awaiting the decision of any court. Not to do so may give rise to very complicated explanations with regard to reciprocity in the execution and fulfillment of treaties."

Here it is. " Gubernativamente," again; that is the idea which was in the mind of the Spanish minister all the while, gubernativamente. That is what he was insisting on, that was the demand which the Secretary of State never repelled as he ought, by telling Mr. Argaiz that it was not only inadmissible under our form of government, but would be offensive if repeated. But where will your Honors find any thing like a demand for property' under the treaty, and by the decision of a court of the United States? He says, if the Executive does not at once act gubernativamente, and take the case out of the judiciary, and send these people to Cuba. it "may give rise to complicated explanations with regard to reciprocity in the execution and fulfillment of treaties.)" Is that language for a foreign minister to use to the American Secretary of State, and not to be answered. He then says:

"The undersigned flatters himself with the hope that his Excellency the President will take into his high consideration this communication, to which the undersigned hopes for a speedy answer, as a new proof of the scrupulousness and respect with which this nation fulfills the treaties existing with other nations. If, contrary to this hope, the decision should not be such as the undersigned asks, he can only declare the General Government of the Union responsible for all and every consequence which the delay may produce."

Amistad Argument

There is the language used by the representative of her Catholic Majesty to the Secretary of State of the United States, and to which the Secretary never thought it necessary to make a suitable reply. There is another correspondence published among the documents of the present session of Congress, connected too with this very case, which shows that the Secretary knows how to be very sensitive with regard to any thing that looks like foreign interference with the action of our courts and government. It is in his answer to Mr. Fox the British ambassador, who addressed a letter to Mr. Forsyth, January 20th, 1841, saying he had been instructed to represent to the President that the attention of his government " has been seriously directed to the case" of these Africans, and in consequence of the treaty between Great Britain and Spain, in which the former paid a valuable consideration for the abandonment of the trade, it is "moved to take a special and peculiar interest in the fate of these unfortunate Africans." And he says:

"Now the unfortunate Africans, whose case is the subject of the present representation, have been thrown by accidental circumstances into the hands of the authorities of the United States; and it may probably depend upon the action of the United States Government, whether these persons shall recover the freedom to which they are entitled, or whether they shall be reduced to slavery, in violation of the known laws and contracts publicly passed, prohibiting the continuance of the African slave trade by Spanish subjects.

"It is under these circumstances that Her Majesty's Government anxiously hope that the President of the United States will find himself empowered to take such measures in behalf of the aforesaid Africans as shall secure to them the possession of their liberty, to which, without doubt, they are by law entitled."

The Secretary of State, in his reply, consents to receive the communication, " as an evidence of the benevolence of her Majesty's Government, under which aspect alone," he says, " it could be entertained by the Government of the United States." What a different tone is here! Mr. Fux merely referred to the relations of his own government with that of Spain, and to the 10th article of the treaty of Ghent, between Great Britain and the United States, in which both nations bound themselves " to use their best endeavors for the entire abolition of the African slave trade." His letter was courteously worded throughout. It casts no imputations upon any branch of our government, it pronounces no part of it incompetent to its functions, it asks no unconstitutional and despotic interference of the Executive with the judiciary gubernativamente, but simply, announces the interest his

40

government feels in the case, and its "anxious hope that the President of the United States will find himself empowered to take such measures in behalf of the aforesaid Africans as shall secure to them their liberty, to which," he says, "without doubt, they are by law entitled." To this the Secretary of State replies:

" Viewing this communication as an evidence of the benevolence of her Majesty's Government—under which aspect alone it could be entertained by the Government of the United States— I proceed, by direction of the President, to make, in reply, a few observations– suggested by the topics of your letter. The narrative presented therein, of the circumstances which brought these Negroes to our shores, is satisfactory evidence that her Majesty's Government is aware that their introduction did not proceed from the wishes or direction of the Government of the United States. A formal demand having been made by the Spanish minister for the delivery of the vessel and property, including the Negroes on board, the grounds upon which it is based have become the subject of investigation before the judicial tribunals of the country, which have not yet pronounced their final decision thereupon You must be aware, sir, that the Executive has neither the power nor the disposition to control the proceedings of the local tribunals when acting within their own appropriate jurisdiction."

How sensitive the Secretary is now! How quick to perceive an impropriety! How slave to the honor of the country—much more so, indeed, than the case required. How different his course from that pursued toward the Spanish minister, who had been from the beginning to the end pressing upon our government demands the most inadmissible, the most unexampled, the most offensive, and yet received from the Secretary no answer, but either a prompt compliance with his requirements, or a plain demonstration of regret that compliance was impracticable. Not one attempt do we find by the Secretary to vindicate the honor of the country, or to press the Spanish minister to bring forward his warrant for such unexampled, such humiliating demands. Neither does he intimate in the case of the Spanish claim, that it i8 received on the ground of "benevolence." Indeed he could not very well offer that as an apology. Benevolence ! The burning of these forty Africans at the stake, as the result of a compliance by our Executive with the Spanish demand, would hardly tend to exhibit or inspire " benevolence."—No, it was for vengeance that they were demanded, admitted to be so in this very letter.

In the same letter the Secretary of State does not undertake to controvert the principles set forth by Mr. Calderon, nor the arguments urged by Mr. Argaiz; but repeats that they had

41

been submitted to the President for consideration. And that is all the answer ever given to the Spanish legation. He then refers to various personal conversations with the minister of Spain.

It was hoped that, in the various conversations which have since taken place with the Chevalier d'Argaiz at this department, on the same subject, he would have discovered additional evidence of the desire of the United States Government to do justice to the demand and representation addressed to it in the name of that of Spain, as fully and as promptly as the peculiar character of the claim admitted. From the repeated communications of the Chevalier d'Argaiz, pressing for the disposal of the question; from his reiterated over of suggestions as to the course by which he deems it incumbent upon this Government to arrive at a final decision; and from the arguments in support of those suggestions, which the undersigned does not perceive the utility of combating at the present stage of the transaction.

The Secretary makes no pretension to contest the claims of Spain—not even a suggestion of the idea that these claims are inadmissible, or that, if pressed, they would be offensive. In these conversations, many things may hare been said which perhaps it would not have been deemed compatible with the public interest to make public. I shall justify this intimation before I am through with this remarkable correspondence. But it is evident there was no resistance of the claims in question as to their justice, no examination of their principles. The Secretary says he does not perceive the utility of combating any of these demands or allegations, and he refers to these private conversations as evidence that the Government is perfectly disposed to do all that is demanded. He continues by saying—

" The Government of the United States cannot but perceive with regret that the Chevalier d'Argaiz has not formed an accurate conception of the true character of the question, nor of the rules by which, under the constitutional institutions of the country, the examination of it must be conducted; nor a correct appreciation of the friendly disposition toward Her Catholic Majesty's Government, with which that examination was so promptly entered upon. In connection with one of the points in the Chevalier d'Argaiz's last note, the undersigned will assure him, that whatever be, in the end, the disposal of the question, it will be in consequence of a decision emanating from no other source than the Government of the United States; and that, if the agency of the judicial authority shall have been employed in conducting the investigation of the case, it is because the judiciary is, by the organic law of the land, a portion, though an independent one, of that Government."

That is to say, so it is, and we can't help it, the judiciary is independent, it must have its course, and we cannot help it. He proceeds:

" As to the delay which has already attended, and still may attend, a final decision, and which the Chevalier d'Argaiz considers as a legitimate subject of complaint, it arises from causes which the undersigned believes that it would serve no useful purpose to discuss at this time, farther than to say that they are beyond the control of this department, and that it is not apprehended that they will affect the course which the Government of the United States may think it fit ultimately to adopt."

The Spanish minister is here given to understand, in his ear, that care had been taken to prevent the Africans from being placed beyond the control of the Executive, and therefore he need be under no apprehension that the decision of the courts, whatever it may be, " will affect the course which the Government of the United States may think it fit ultimately to adopt." What other construction can possibly he given to this paragraph? If any other is possible from the words there are facts in the case which prove that this was what was intended. The Secretary proceeds with his explanations and apologies.

" The undersigned indulges the hope that, upon a review of the circumstances of the case, and the questions it involves, the Chevalier d'Argaiz will agree with him in thinking that the delay which has already occurred is not more than commensurate with the importance of those questions; that such delay is not uncommon in the proceedings and deliberations of governments desirous of taking equal justice as the guide of their actions; and that the caution which it has been found necessary to observe in the instance under consideration, is yet far from having occasioned such procrastination as it has been the lot of the United States frequently to encounter in their intercourse with the Government of Spain."

"With regard to the imprisonment of Don Jose Ruiz, it is again the misfortune of this Government to have been entirely misapprehended by the Chevalier d'Argaiz, in the agency it has had in this, an entirely private concern of a Spanish subject. It was no more the intention of this department, in what has already been done, to draw the Chevalier d'Argaiz into a polemical discussion with the Attorney of the United States for the district of New York, than to supply Don Jose Ruiz, gratis, with counsel in the suit in which he had been made a party. The offer made to that person of the advice and assistance of the District Attorney, was a favor— an entirely gratuitous one—since it was not the province of the United States to interfere in a private litigation between subjects of a foreign state, for which Mr. Ruiz is indebted to the desire of this government to treat with due respect the application made in his behalf in the name of her Catholic Majesty, and not to any right he ever had to be protected against alleged demands of individuals against him or his property."

Here, then, it is avowed that the Executive government of this nation had interposed in a suit between two parties, by extending a favor entirely gratuitous to one of the parties, who, it is at the same time admitted, had no claim whatever to this gratuitous aid. And then comes the exhibition which I have already read, of the national sympathy, in which all the authorities of the country are alleged to have participated, and the assumption, under which all the proceedings have been carried on, that there was but one party aggrieved in the case, and that party was the Spanish slave traders.

On the 25th of December the Chevalier d'Argaiz addressed a long letter to the Secretary of State, in which he acknowledges the receipt of the last letter, to which " it would be superfluous" —the word is ocioso, idle—to reply, inasmuch as the Secretary of State does not seem to have considered it requisite in the present situation of the affair, to combat the arguments adduced by the undersigned. The delicacy of the undersigned does not, however, allow him to pass over (desoir) certain insinuations (remarks) contained in the said note; and it will, perhaps, be difficult for him to avoid adducing some new argument in support of his demands."

The Secretary had never met these claims and arguments, as it was his duty to do, nod the Spanish minister is continually reminding him that he does not answer his arguments. He then refers him to his own course, and says, "The undersigned would not have troubled the Government of the Union with his urgent demand, if the two Spaniards (who, as the Secretary of State, in his note of the 12th, says, 'were found in this distressing and perilous situation by officers of the United States, who, moved by sympathetic feelings, which subsequently became national,') had not been the victims of an intrigue, as accurately shown by Mr. Forsyth, in the conference which he had with the undersigned on the 21st of October last."

Amistad Argument

He here refers to a private conference in which the Secretary of State had accurately shown that the two Spaniards in New York were the "victims of an intrigue." The Secretary of State of the United States, then, had confidentially and officially informed the Spanish minister that the two Spaniards, in being arrested at the suit of some of these Africans, were the victims of an intrigue." What the Secretary meant by " victims of an intrigue, "is not for me to say. These Spaniards had been sued in the courts of the state of New York by some of my clients, for alleged wrongs done to them on the high seas—for cruelty, in fact, so dreadful, that many of their number had actually perished under the treatment 'These suite were commenced by lawyers of New York—men of character in their profession. Possibly they advised with a few other individuals—fanatics, perhaps, I must call them, according to the general application of language, but if I were to speak my own language in my own estimate of their character, so far as concerns this case, and confining my remarks exclusively to this present case, I should pronounce them the FRIENDS OF HUMAN NATURE—men who were unable to see these, their fellow men, in the condition of these unfortunate Africans, seized, imprisoned, helpless, friendless, without language to complain, without knowledge to understand their situation or the means of deliverance—I say they could not see human beings in this condition and not undertake to save them from slavery and death, if it was in their power—not by a violation of the laws, but by securing the execution of the laws in their favor. These are the men whom the American Secretary of State arraigns in a confidential conversation with the minister of Spain, as the instigators of "an intrigue" of which he holds these disappointed slave–holders to be the unfortunate victims. The Chevalier goes on:

"The Secretary of State, however, says that 'he cannot but perceive with regret that the Chevalier d'Argaiz has not formed an accurate conception of the true character of the question, nor of the rules by which, under the constitutional institutions of this country, the examination of it must be conducted.' Possibly the undersigned may not have formed such an accurate conception, of this affair, since it has been carried within the circle of legal subtleties, as he has not pursued the profession of the law; but he is well persuaded that, if the crew of the Amistad had been composed of white men, the court, or the corporation to which the Government of the Union might have submitted the examination of the question, would have observed the rules by which it should be conducted under the constitutional institutions of the country, and would have limited itself to the ascertainment of the facts of the murders committed on the 30th of June; and the undersigned does not comprehend the privilege enjoyed by Negroes, in favor of whom an interminable suit is commenced, in which everything is deposed by every person who pleases; and, for that object, an English doctor, who accuses the Spanish government of not complying with its treaties, and calumniates the Captain General of the island of Cuba, by charging him with bribery."

Here it is made the subject of complaint from a foreign ambassador to the Executive Government of the United States, that in a court of the United States, in a trial for the life and liberty of forty human beings, the testimony, of "an English doctor" was received. And this complaint also was received without a reply. The "English doctor," thus spoken of, was Doctor Madden, a man of letters, and in the official employ of the British Government, in a post of much importance and responsibility, as the superintendent of liberated Africans at Havana. His testimony was highly important in the case and was admitted in the court below, and now forms a part of the record now before your Honors. He does not use the word bribery in reference to the Governor General of Cuba.

DEATH OF JUDGE BARBOUR—THE PROCEEDINGs OF THE COURT SUSPENDED.

Washington, Feb. 25, 1841.

The proceedings of the Court in this solemn case have been interrupted by the solemn voice of death. One of the learned and honorable judges of the Court, who sat yesterday in his place, listening with profound and patient attention to the argument of a counselor many years older than himself, reasoning eloquently in behalf of justice on earth, has been summoned to his own dread account, at the bar of Eternal Justice above. Judge Barbour, of Virginia, the seventh in rank on the bench, died last night in his bed—in his sleep, it is probable, without a groan or a struggle. The servant at his lodgings went at the usual hour this morning to the rooms of the different Judges, to call them to breakfast. 4s the Chief Justice was passing the door of Judge Barbour's room, the man said to him, "Chief Justice, will you please to come here, sir—I think Judge Barbour is dead." Judge Taney went to the bed, and there saw his associate lying on his side, as if in a gentle sleep, but dead and cold, with the exception of a slight remaining warmth at the chest. Not a muscle was distorted, nor were the bed-clothes in the slightest degree disturbed, so that it is probable his heart ceased to beat in an instant, while he was asleep!

At the usual hour for opening the Court this morning, none of the Judges were seen in the court-room, which was already filled with persons come to hear the continuation of Mr.

Amistad Argument

Adams' speech.

At length the Judges came in together, and their countenances looked pale, distressed, and sorrowful. As soon as they had taken their seats, the Crier opened the Court in the usual form, and the Chief Justice addressed the gentlemen of the bar—"Gentlemen a painful event has occurred—Judge Barbour died suddenly last night—and the Court is therefore adjourned until Monday."

The Crier then made proclamation to that effect, the Judges all rose, and retired again to their private apartment, and the assembly withdrew.

I did not expect an announcement of so overwhelming a Providence in a manner so severely simple and subdued, but it struck me as eminently appropriate for the Supreme Court of this nation. It was in keeping with the strictest propriety and suitableness. It was sublime.

RESUMPTION OF THE TRIAL.

Washington March 1, 1841.

On the re–opening of the Court, the Attorney General of the United States, H. D. Gilpin, Esq. presented a series of appropriate resolutions in reference to the decease of Judge Barbour, which had been adopted on Friday, at a meeting of the Bar of officers of the court, and which he moved to have entered on the records of the court. The Chief Justice responded in a short address, and concluded with ordering the resolutions to be entered on the records. Mr. Adams then resumed his argument, as follows:—

May it please your Honors,

The melancholy event which has occurred since the argument of this case was begun, and which has suspended for a time the operations of the Court itself, and which I ask permission to say that I give my cordial, and painful concurrence in the sentiments of the Bar of this Court—has imposed on me the necessity of re– stating the basis and aim of the argument which I am submitting to the Court, in behalf of the large number of individuals, who are my unfortunate clients.

47

Amistad Argument

I said that my confidence in a favorable result to this trial rested mainly on the ground that I was now speaking before a Court of JUSTICE. And in moving the dismissal of the appeal taken on behalf of the United States, it became my duty, and was my object to show, by an investigation of all the correspondence of the Executive in regard to the case that JUSTICE had not been the motive of its proceedings, but that they had been prompted by sympathy with one of the two patties and against the other. In support of this, I must scrutinize, with the utmost severity every part of the proceedings of the Executive Government. And in doing it, I think it proper for me to repeat, that in speaking of the impulse of sympathies, under which the government acted, I do not wish to be understood to speak of that sympathy as being blamable in itself, or as inducing me to feel unfriendly sentiments towards the Head of the Government, or the Secretary of State, or any of the Cabinet. I feel no unkind sentiments towards any of these gentlemen. With all of them, I am, in the private relations of life, on terms of intercourse, of the most friendly character. As to our political differences, let them pass for what they are worth, here they are nothing. At the moment of the expiration of this administration, I feel extreme reluctance at the duty of bringing its conduct before the court in this manner, as affecting the claims of my clients to JUSTICE. My learned friend, the Attorney General, knows that I am not voluntary in this work. I here descended to personal solicitation with the Executive, that by the withdrawal of the appeal, I might be spared the necessity of appearing in this cause. I have been of the opinion that the case of my clients was so clear, so just, so righteous, that the Executive would do well to cease its prosecution, and leave the matter as it was decided by the District Court, and allow the appeal to be dismissed. But I did not succeed, and now I cannot do justice to my clients, whose lives and liberties depend on the decision of this Court—however painful it may be, to myself or others.

In my examination of the first proceedings of the Executive in this case, I did scrutinize and analyze most minutely and particularly, the four demands first made upon our government by the late Spanish minister, Mr. Calderon, in his letter to the Secretary of State of Sept. 5, 1839. I tested the principles there laid down, both by the laws of nations and by the treaties between the two Nations to which he had appealed. And I showed that every one of these demands was inadmissible, and that every principle of law and every article of the treaty, he had referred to, was utterly inapplicable. At the close of my argument the other day, I was commenting upon the complaint of the present minister, the Chevelier d'Argaiz, addressed to the Secretary of State on the 25th of December, 1839, in relation to the injustice he alledges to have been done to the two Spanish subjects, Ruiz and Montes, by their arrest and imprisonment in New York, at the suit of some of the Africans. He says he "does not comprehend the privilege enjoyed by Negroes, in favor of whom an interminable suit is commenced, in which everything is deposed by every person who pleases; and, for that object, an English doctor who accuses the Spanish Government of not complying with its treaties, and calumniates the Captain General of the island of Cuba, by charging him with bribery."

This English Doctor is Dr. Madden, whose testimony is given in the record. He certainly does not charge the Captain General with bribery, although he says that both he and the other authorities of Cuba are in the habit of winking or conniving at the slave trade. That this is the actual state of affairs, I submit to the Court, is a matter of history. And I call the attention of the Court to this fact, as one of the most important points of this case. It is universally known that the trade is actually carried on, contrary to the laws of. Spain, but by the general connivance of the Governor General and all the authorities and the people of the island. The case of this very vessel, the visit of Ruiz and Montes to the barracoon in which these people were confined, the vessel in which they were brought from Africa, are all matters of history. I have a document which was communicated by the British government to the Parliament, which narrates the whole transaction. Mr. A. here read from the Parliamentary documents, a letter from Mr. Jerningham, the British Minister at Madrid, to the Spanish Secretary of State, dated January 5th, 1840, describing the voyage of the Tecora from Africa, the purchase of these Africans who were brought in her, with the subsequent occurrences, and urging the Spanish Government to take measures both for their liberation, and to enforce the laws of Spain against Ruiz and Montes.

He says " I have consequently been instructed by my government to call upon the government of her Catholic Majesty to issue, with as little delay as possible, strict orders to the authorities of Cuba, that, if the request of the Spanish minister at Washington be complied with, these Negroes may be put in possession of the liberty of which they were deprived, and to the recovery of which they have an undeniable title.

"I am further directed to express the just expectations of Her Majesty's government that the Government of her Catholic Majesty will cause the laws against the slave–trade to be enforced against Messrs. Jose Ruiz and Pedro Montes, who purchased these newly imported negroes, and against all such other Spanish subjects as have been concerned in this nefarious transaction."

Amistad Argument

These facts, said Mr. A., must be well known to the Spanish minister. If he complains of injustice in the charge of general connivance made by Dr. Madden why has he not undertaken to prove that it is a calumny? Not the slightest attempt has been made to bring forward any evidence on this point, for the very plain reason that there could be none. The fact of the slave trade is too notorious to be questioned. I will read, said he, from another high authority, a book filled with valuable and authentic information on the subject of the slave trade' written by one of the most distinguished philanthropists of Great Britain, Sir Thomas Fowell Buxton. Mr. A. then read as follows:—

"It is scarcely practicable to ascertain the number of slaves imported into Cuba: it can only be a calculation on, at best, doubtful data. We are continually told by the Commissioners, that difficulties are thrown in the way of obtaining correct information in regard to the slave trade in that island. Everything that artifice, violence, intimidation, popular countenance, and official connivance can do, is done, to conceal the extent of the traffic. Our ambassador, Mr. Villiers, April, 1837, says, 'That a privilege (that of entering the harbor after dark) denied to all other vessels, is granted to the slave–trader; and, in short, that with the servants of the Government, the misconduct of the persons concerned in this trade finds favor and protection. The crews of captured vessels are permitted to purchase their liberation; and it would seem that the persons concerned in this trade have resolved upon setting the government of the mother country at defiance.' Almost the only specific fact which I can collect from the reports of the Commissioners, is the statement 'that 1835 presents a number of slave vessels (arriving at the Havana) by which there must have been landed, at the very least, 15,000 Negroes.' But in an official letter, date 28th May, 1836, there is the following remarkable passage: 'I wish I could add, that this list contains even one fourth of the number of those which have entered after having landed cargoes, or sailed after having refitted in this harbor.' This would give an amount of 69,000 for the Havana alone; but is Havana the only port in Cuba in which Negroes are landed? The reverse is notoriously true. The Commissioner says, 'I have every reason to believe that several of the other ports of Cuba, more particularly the distant city of St. Jago de Cuba, carry on the traffic to a considerable extent.' Indeed, it is stated by Mr. Hardy, the consul at St. Jago, in a letter to Lord Palmerston, of the 18th February, 1837, 'That the Portuguese brig Boca Negra, landed on the 6th inst. at Juragua, a little to windward of this port, (St. Jago,) 400 Africans of all ages, and subsequently entered this port.' But in order that we may be assuredly within the mark, no claim shall be made on account of these distant ports. Confining ourselves to the Havana, it would seem probable, if it be not demonstrated, that the number for that port, a fortiori, for the whole island, may fairly be estimated at 60,000."

This evidence is important to show what is the real value of this certificate of the Governor General. There is one other proof which I will read to the court, and leave it to your Honors to judge of its bearing, and of the conclusion to which it arrives It is the statement of the Spanish vice consul, Mr. Vega.

"The following statement was made to me by A. G. Vega, Esq., Spanish consul, as near as I can now recollect, and according to my best knowledge and belief, 10th January, 1840.

W. S. HOLABIRD.

"That he is a Spanish subject; that he resided in the Island of Cuba several years; that he knows the laws of that island on the subject of slavery; that there was no law that was considered in force in the Island of Cuba, that prohibited the bringing in African slaves; that the court of mixed commissioners had no jurisdiction except in case of capture on the sea; that newly imported African Negroes were constantly brought to the island, and after landing were bona fide transferred from one owner to another, without any interference by the focal authorities or the mixed commission? and were held by the owners and recognized as lawful property; that slavery was recognized in Cuba by all the laws that were considered in force there; that the native language of the slaves was kept up on some plantations for years. That the barracoons are public markets, where all descriptions of slaves are sold and bought; that the papers of the Amistad are genuine, and are in the usual form; that it was riot necessary to practice any fraud to obtain such papers from the proper officers of the government; that none of the papers of the Amistad are signed by Martinez, spoken of by R. R. Madden, in his deposition; that he (Martinez) did not hold the office from whence that paper issued."

This is the statement given to the District Attorney by Mr. Yega, and by him made a part of this case. This Spanish functionary declares positively, that he knows there is no law in force in Cuba against the African slave trade, and that recent Africans are held and sold bona fide as slaves. It is conclusive to prove this fact, that the illegal importation and purchase of Africans is openly practiced in Cuba, although it is contrary to the laws of Spain, but those laws are not considered in force, that is, the violation of them is constantly connived at by the authorities.

Amistad Argument

It may not be universally known, but is doubtless known to members of this court, that there is a volume of correspondence

this subject, by our consul at Havana, which will be communicated to Congress for publication in a few days, and I can state from my personal knowledge that it confirms every word of Mr. Madden's statements on this point, and will show how much reliance is to be placed on this certificate of the Governor–General.

But I will return to the letter of the Chevalier d'Argaiz. I have not the honor of knowing this gentleman personally, as I knew his predecessor, but I certainly entertain no feeling of unkindness towards him. And in examining his correspondence, al. though it is my duty to show that his demands are utterly inadmissible and unprecedented, yet it must be admitted that his sympathy and partiality for his own countrymen are at least natural; and if his zeal and earnestness are somewhat excessive, they are at least pardonable. There is in this letter, I must say, a simplicity, what the French call bonhommie, which gives me a favorable impression of his character, and I certainly feel the farthest possible from a disposition to pass any censure on him. I repeat that, so far as this sympathy is concerned, if it is not entirely excusable, it is much more reasonable than it is in some others who have not the same interests to defend. He goes on to express his pleasure at the assurance received from, the Secretary, that " whatever may be the final settlement of the question, it will be in consequence of a decision emanating from the government, and not from any other source ;" and he adds, that " he doubts not such decision will be conformable with the opinion which was confidentially communicated to him at the Department of State on the 19th of November, as founded on that of a learned lawyer, and which he was assured had been adopted by the cabinet."

I take it for granted that the opinion referred to is the opinion of the Attorney–General of that time, Mr. Grundy, contained in the Congressional document.. It will be necessary for me to examine that document before I close, as well as the other papers, and I wish to say that the decease of that gentleman, under the circumstances in which it occurred, has made such an impression on my mind, as could not have but disarmed me of any disposition to censure him, if I had before entertained it. It will be a painful duty to me to examine, as I must, with the utmost severity, that document. And I shall show that it is such, that neither the courts nor the cabinet ought ever to have acted on it.

Amistad Argument

In another part of his letter, M. d'Argaiz says of Ruiz and Montes, that they were not exempted from the persecutions of an atrocious intrigue, and the undersigned Is not the first who has so styled this persecution.' This is a pretty plain intimation that the American Secretary of State was the first who called the suit of my clients for legal redress " an atrocious intrigue," in his " confidential conversation" with the Spanish minister. This is followed by an idea so novel and ingenious that it is necessary to repeat the whole of it. After complaining that Negroes should be allowed to be complainants, he goes on to argue that they ought to be considered, "morally and legally, as not being in the United States," and of course, if they should be delivered up physically, I suppose it was to be inferred that the Executive would not incur any responsibility.

"They are morally and legally not in the United States, because the court of Connecticut has not declared whether or not it is competent to try them. If it should declare itself incompetent, it declares that they are under the cover of the Spanish flag; and, in that case, they are physically under the protection of a friendly government, but morally and legally out of the territory and jurisdiction of the United States; and, so long as a doubt remains on this subject, no judge can admit the complaint. If this argument be of any value to the Secretary of State of the Government of the Union, the undersigned entreats him to prevail on the President to cause a protest, founded on this argument, to be officially addressed to the court of New York."

His predecessor, M. Calderon, called upon the President for a proclamation forbidding the courts to take up the case, and the present minister of Spain insists that he shall send forth his protest to take it out of the hands of the courts—and this on the ground, that my clients, although personally imprisoned for eighteen months by the U.S. Marshal, under order of the U. S. Court, yet are "not morally and legally in the United States." There is another argument of the same gentleman, very much of the same character. The court will find it in his first letter after the arrest of Ruiz and Montes at New York. He says:

"It would be easy to demonstrate the illegality of these arrests, the orders for which have possibly been obtained from the attorney by surprise: as it would also be easy to show the ignorance of the declarant, Tappan, in declaring that Ruiz is known by the name of Pipi, whereas he would have been known and distinguished throughout Spain, as all other Joses are, by the diminutive of Pepe, and thus it appears that a Pepe has been imprisoned instead of a Pipi, which I believe the law does not permit."

Amistad Argument

The argument is certainly ingenious, and if it is sound at all, it is worth more in favor of the Africans than of the Spaniards, as I may hereafter have occasion to show, when I come to consider the case of nine–and forty persons with Spanish names, who have been arrested and brought into court by African names.

The Chevalier d'Argaiz, in the close of this letter, exhibits his loyalty towards the then acting sovereign of his nation.

" At the moment when the heart of the august Queen Governess is filled with delight on account of the termination of a civil war, and the assurance of the throne of her august daughter, her minister in the United States has to perform the painful duty of diminishing her happiness by communicating to her, as he did by letter on the 19th instant, the disagreeable event which forms the subject of this communication, The desire of calming the disquiet which this news may occasion in the mind of her Majesty, together with that of alleviating the lot of the two prisoners, urge the undersigned to entreat you, Mr. Secretary of State, to take into consideration what he has here set forth, and to afford him the means, in a prompt reply, of satisfying those just desires, which will be completely done if he is able to transmit such a reply to his Government by the packet sailing for Havre on the 1st of November next."

It must doubtless, said Mr. A., be some consolation to this loyal minister, to reflect that before the august Queen Governess could have received the painful intelligence of the imprisonment of two such meritorious subjects as Ruiz and Montes to diminish her happiness her heart had been gratified in a much better manner. In the pursuit of that happiness for which she longed, it seems that she retired altogether from the cares of state, into the comforts of domestic life, with a husband that, I hope has calmed her disquiet, and if it should ultimately turn out that the lives of these poor Africans are saved, there will be no further occasion to diminish the happiness of the august Queen–Governess.

On the 30th of December, five days after the date of the letter I have been commenting upon, the Chevalier d'Argaiz wrote again to the Secretary of State.

(WASHINGTON, December 30, 1839.)

Amistad Argument

"SIR—In the conversation which I had with you on the morning of the day before yesterday, you mentioned the possibility that the Court of Connecticut might, at its meeting on the 7th of January next, declare itself incompetent, or order the restitution of the schooner Amistad, with her cargo, and the Negroes found on board of her; and you then showed me that it would be necessary for the legation of her Catholic Majesty to take charge of them as soon as the Court should have pronounced its sentence or resolution; and, although I had the honor to state to you that this legation could not possibly transfer the said Negroes to Havana, still it appears proper for me now to declare that—

" Considering that the schooner Amistad cannot make a voyage, on account of the bad condition in which she is, of her being entirely without a crew:

"Considering that it would be difficult to find u vessel of the United States willing to take charge of these Negroes, and to transport them to Havana; and, also, that these Negroes have declared before the Court of Connecticut that they are not slaves; and that the best means of testing the truth of their allegation is to bring them before the Courts of Havana:

" Being at the same time desirous to free the Government of the United States from the trouble of keeping the said Negroes in prison, I venture to request you to prevail upon the President to allow to the Government of her Catholic Majesty the assistance which it asks under the present circumstances from that of the United States, by placing the Negroes found on board of the said schooner, and claimed by this legation, at the disposition of the Captain General of the Island of Cuba, transporting them thither in a ship belonging to the United States. Her Catholic Majesty's Government, I venture to assert, will receive this act of generosity as a most particular favor, which would serve to strengthen the bonds of good and reciprocal friendship now happily reigning between the two nations."

Here is no longer a demand for the delivery of slaves to their owners, nor for the surrender of the Africans to the Spanish minister as assassins, but an application to the President of the United States to transport forty individuals beyond the seas, to be tried for their lives. Is there a member of this Honorable Court that ever heard of such a demand made by a foreign minister on any government? Is there in the whole history of Europe an instance of such a demand made upon an independent government? I have never in the whole course of my life, in modern or ancient history, met with such a demand by one government on another. Or, if such a demand was ever made, it was when the nation on which it was made was not in the condition of an independent power.

What was this demand? It was that the Executive of the United States, on his own authority, without evidence, without warrant of law, should seize, put on board a national armed ship, and send beyond seas, forty men, to be tried for their lives. I ask the learned Attorney General in his argument on this point of the case, to show what is to be the bearing of this proceeding on the liberties of the people. I ask him to tell us what authority there is for such an exercise of power by the Executive. I ask him if there is any authority for such a proceeding in the case of these unfortunate Africans, which would not be equally available, if any President thought proper to exercise it, to seize and send off forty citizens of the United States. Will he vindicate such an authority? Will this Court give it a judicial sanction ?

But, may it please your Honors, what was the occasion, the cause, the motive, which induced the Secretary of State to hold this personal communication with the Spanish minister on the 28th of December ? What had occurred, to induce the Secretary of State to send for the Chevalier d'Argaiz, and tell him that the court of Connecticut was about to pass a decree that these Africans should be delivered up, and that our government would be ready to deliver them to him! What induced the Secretary of State to come to the conclusion that there was any sort of probability that the Court of Connecticut would so adjudge? The documents do not inform us at whose suggestion or by what information the Secretary of State acted in this remarkable manner. We are left to infer, that his course was founded, probably, on the opinion of the late Attorney General, with a suggestion from the District Attorney' of Connecticut. I refer to a letter of the Secretary of – State to Mr. Holabird, January 6, 1840, in connection with this letter of the Spanish minister, of December 30. The Secretary says—" Your letter of the 20th ultimo," that is, the 20th of December, " was duly received." Now, said Mr. Adams, it is a remarkable fact, that this letter of the District Attorney, of December 20 1839, was not communicated with the rest of the documents. Why it was not communicated is not for me to say. The call of the House of Representatives was in the usual form, for information "not incompatible with the public interest ;" which, of course, gives the President the right to withhold any documents that he thinks proper. That letter, therefore, is not communicated, and I cannot reason from it, any farther than its contents may be presumed, from the intimations in the letter of the Spanish minister, in connection with the subsequent proceedings. The Secretary says—

Amistad Argument

(WASHINGTON, January 6, 1840)

" Sir—Your letter of the 20th ultimo was duly received, and has been laid before the President. The Spanish minister having applied to this department for the use of n vessel of the United States in the event of the decision of the circuit court in the case of the Amistad being favorable to his former application, to convey the Negroes to Cuba, for the purpose of being delivered over to the authorities of that island, the President has, agreeably to your suggestion taken in connection with the request of the Spanish minister, ordered a vessel to be in readiness to receive the Negroes from the custody of the marshal as soon as their delivery shall have been ordered by the court "

Now, what could that suggestion have been? It will be remembered that the Secretary of State had before directed the District Attorney, Sept. 11, "In the mean time you will take care that no proceeding of your circuit court' or of any other judicial tribunal places the vessel, cargo, or slaves, beyond the control of the Federal Executive." The District Attorney had repeatedly inquired of the Secretary if they could not be disposed of by an Executive act, or before the court met. Until this time he had received no orders from the Department. From the intimation now given, it is evident that the purport of that suppressed letter was an intimation that the district court would undoubtedly deliver them up, and the difficulty then was, how to get them out of the way. There might be a Habeas Corpus from the State courts at the moment of their delivery to the Spaniards, and some new difficulties would intervene. There must have been some such suggestion to warrant or account for the subsequent proceedings. The Secretary goes on to say—

"As the request of the Spanish minister for the delivery of the Negroes to the authorities of Cuba has, for one of its objects, that those people should have an opportunity of proving, before the tribunals of the island, the truth of the allegations made in their behalf in the course of the proceedings before the circuit court, that they are not slaves, the President, desirous of affording the Spanish courts every facility that may be derived from this country towards a fair and full investigation of all the circumstances, and particularly of the allegations referred to with regard to the real condition of the Negroes, has directed that Lieutenants Gedney and Meade be directed to proceed to Cuba, for the purpose of giving their testimony in any proceedings that may be instituted in the premises; and that complete records of all those which have been had before the circuit court of your district, including the evidence taken in the cause, be, with the same view, furnished to the Spanish colonial authorities. In obedience to this last mentioned order, you will cause to be prepared an authentic copy of the records of the court in the case, and of all the documents and evidence connected with it, so as to have it ready to be handed over to the commander of the vessel which is to take out the Negroes, who will be instructed as to the disposition he is to make of them."

In every thing I have said of the arguments, and the zeal of the Spanish minister, I have admitted that the principles which may be supposed to govern him might go far to justify the sympathy he has shown for one party exclusively. But I cannot give the same credit for the sympathy shown by our own government. In this letter we meet, for the first time, something that might appear like sympathy for the poor wretches whose liberties and lives were in peril. Here is a desire intimated that they might go to Cuba, for the purpose of having an opportunity to prove in the courts of Spain their right to be free by the laws of Spain. And the President, in the abundance of his kindness, orders Lieutenants Gedney and Meade to be sent along with them, as witnesses in the case, " particularly," the Secretary says, "with regard to the real condition of the Negroes, "that is, whether they were free or slaves. But what did Lieutenants Gedney and Meade know about that? They could testify to nothing but the circumstances of the capture. And as to the other idea, that these people should have an opportunity to prove their freedom in Cuba, how could that be credited as a motive, when it is apparent that, by sending them back in the capacity of slaves, they would be deprived of all power to give evidence at all in regard to their freedom! I cannot, therefore, give the Executive credit for this sympathy towards the Africans. It was a mere presence, to blind the public mind with the idea that the Africans were merely sent to Cuba to prove they were not slaves. So far from giving any credit for this sympathy, the letter itself furnishes incontestable evidence of n very different disposition, which I will not qualify in words.

Pursuing the case chronologically, according to the course of the proceedings, I now call the attention of the Court to the opinion of the late Attorney General of the United States, which the Secretary of the State told Mr. Argaiz had been adopted by the Cabinet, and which has been the foundation, to this day, of all the proceedings of the Executive in the case. Before considering this, however, I will advert to the letter of Messrs. Staples and Sedgwick; to the President These gentlemen were counsel for those unfortunate men. There had been reports in circulation, which is by no means surprising, considering the course of the public sympathy, that the President intended to remove these people to Cuba, by force, gubernativamente, by virtue of his Executive authority—that inherent power which I suppose has been discovered, by which the President. at his discretion?

can seize men, and imprison them, and send them beyond seas for trial or punishment by a foreign power.

Hear Messrs. Staples and Sedgwick to the President of the United States.

NEW YORK, September 13, 1839.

"Sir—We have been engaged as counsel of the Africans brought in by the Spanish vessel, the Amistad; and, in that capacity, take the liberty of addressing you this letter.

" These Africans are now under indictment in the circuit court of the second circuit, on a charge of piracy, and their defense to this accusation must be established before that tribunal. But we are given to understand, from authority not to be doubted, that a demand has already been made upon the Federal Government, by the Spanish minister, that these Negroes be surrendered to the authorities of his country; and it is on this account that we now address you.

" We are also informed, that these slaves are claimed under the 9th article of the treaty of 1795, between this country and Spain by which all ships and merchandise rescued out of the hands of pirates and robbers on the high seas are to be restored to the true proprietor, upon due and sufficient proof.

" We now apply to you, sir, for the purpose of requesting that no order may be made by the Executive until the facts necessary to authorize its interposition are established by the judicial authority in the ordinary course of justice. We submit that this is the true construction of the treaty; that it is not a mere matter of Executive discretion; but that, before the Government enforces the demand of the Spanish claimant, that demand must be substantiated in a court of justice.

" It appears to us manifest that the treaty could never have meant to have submitted conflicting rights of property to mere official discretion; but that it was intended to subject them to the same tribunals which, in all other cases, guard and maintain our civil rights. Reference to the 7th article, in our opinion, will confirm this position.

" It will he recollected that, that if we adopt this as the true construction of the treaty, should any occasion ever arise when our citizens shall claim the benefit of this section,

Amistad Argument

Spain would be at liberty to give it the same interpretation; and that the rights of our citizens will be subjected to the control of subordinate ministerial

agents, without any of those safeguards which courts of justice present for the establishment of truth and the maintenance of rights. We submit, further, that it never could be intended that the Executive of the Union should be harassed by the investigation of claims of this nature, and yet, assuredly, if the construction contended for be correct, such must be the results for, if he is to issue the order upon due and sufficient proof, the proof must be sufficient to his mind.

"We further submit, that, in regard to the Executive, there are no rules of evidence nor course of proceeding established; and that, in all such cases, unless the claimant be directed to the courts of justice, the conduct of the affair must, of necessity, be uncertain. vague, and not such as is calculated to inspire confidence in the public or the parties. We can find nothing in the treaty to warrant the delivery of these individuals as offenders; and the Executive of the Union has never thought itself obliged, under the laws of nations, to accede to demands of this nature.

" Those suggestions are of great force in this case, because we, with great confidence, assert, that neither according to the law of this, nor that of their own country, can the pretended owners of these Africans establish any legal title to them as slaves.

" These Negroes were, it is admitted, carried into Cuba contrary to the provisions of the treaty between Spain and Great Britain of 1817, and of the orders made in conformity therewith; orderes which have been repented, at different times, to as late a date as the 4th November, 1838, by which the trade is expressly prohibited; and if they had been taken on board the slaver, they would have been unquestionably emancipated.

" They were bought by the present claimants, Messrs. Ruiz and Montes, either directly from the slaver, or under circumstances which must beyond doubt, have apprised them that they were illegally introduced into the Havana; and on this state of facts we, with great respect, insist that the purchasers of Africans illegally introduced into the dependencies of a country which has prohibited the slave trade, and who make the purchase with knowledge of this fact, can acquire no right. We put the matter on the Spanish law and we affirm, that Messrs. Ruiz and Montes hare no title, under that law, to these Africans.

Amistad Argument

"If this be so, then these Negroes have only obeyed the dictates of self–defense. They have liberated themselves from illegal restraint; and it is superfluous to say, that Messrs. Ruiz and Montes have no claim whatever under the treaty.

" It is this question, sir, fraught with the deepest interest, that we pray you to submit for adjudication to the tribunals of the land. It is this question that we pray may not be decided in the recesses of the cabinet, where these unfriended men can have no counsel and can produce no proof, but in the halls of Justice, with the safeguards that she throws around the unfriended and oppressed.

" And, sir, if you should not be satisfied with the considerations here presented, we then submit that we are contending for a right upon a construction of a treaty: that this point, at least, should be presented to the courts of justice; and, should you decide to grant an order surrendering these Africans, we beg that you will direct such notice of it to be given, as may enable us to test the question as we shall be advised, by habeas corpus or otherwise.

"We have only, sir, to add, that we have perfect confidence that you will decide in this matter with a single regard to the interests of justice and the honor of the country, and that we are, with the greatest respect, your most obedient servants,

' SETH P. STAPLES,

"THEODORE SEDGWICK, JR. "

MARTIN VAN BUREN, ESQ.

" President of the United States."

I read the whole of this letter, said Mr. A., to show that this extraordinary course of proceeding was not entered upon by the Executive without warning and counsel. The President of the United States was informed, on the receipt of that letter, in the month of September, 1839, of the deep principles, involving the very foundation of the liberties of this country, that were concerned in the disposal which the Executive might make of these men. That letter was with the late Attorney General when he examined the case, and when he made up his opinion. His opinion, addressed to the Secretary of State,

Amistad Argument

begins thus:

"Sir,—I have the honor to acknowledge the receipt of yours of the 24th of September, in which, by direction of the President, you refer to this office the letter of the Spanish minister of the 6th of September, addressed to you; also the letter of Seth P. Staples and Theodore Sedgwick, Jr. Esqrs., who have been engaged as counsel for the Negroes. taken on board the schooner Amistad, addressed to the President of the United States; and asking my opinion upon the different legal questions presented by these papers.

" I have given to the subject all the consideration which its importance demands, and now present to you, and through you to the President, the result of my reflections upon the whole subject.

" The following is the statement of facts contained in your communication: 'Fine Amistad is a Spanish vessel; was regularly cleared from Havana, a Spanish port in Cuba, to Guanaja, in the neighborhood of Puerto Principe, another Spanish port; that her papers were regular; that the cargo consisted of merchandise and slaves, and was duly manifested as belonging to Don Jose Ruiz and Don Pedro Montes; that the Negroes after being at sea a few days, rose upon the white persons on board; that the captain, his slave and two seamen, were killed, and the vessel taken possession of by the Negroes, that two white Spaniards, after being wounded, were compelled to assist in navigating the vessel, the Negroes intending to carry her to the coast of Africa; that the Spaniards contrived, by altering the courts of steering at night, to keep her on the coast of the United States; that on seeing land off New−York, they come to the coast, and some of the Negroes landed to procure water and provisions; that being on the point of leaving the coast, the Amistad was visited by a boat from Captain Gedney's vessel, and that one of the Spaniards, claiming protection from the officer commanding the boat, the vessel and cargo, and all the persons on board, were sent into New London for examination, and such proceedings as the laws of nations and of the United States warranted and required."

Here the Court will see he assumes, through the whole argument that these Negroes were slaves. This corresponds with the assumption of the Executive, which Mr. Forsyth, in his letter to the Spanish minister afterwards declared the Government had carried out, that the Negroes were slaves, and that the only parties injured were Montes and Ruiz. The late Attorney General says it appears that the "cargo consisted of merchandise and slaves," that the papers were " all regular," that after the capture of the vessel by the Negroes, the two white Spaniards " were compelled to assist in navigating the vessel, the Negroes intending to carry her to the coast of Africa, "but" the Spaniards contrived, by altering the course of steering at night, to bring her to the United States." This last is an admission of some importance, as the Court will easily see, in deciding upon the character of the voyage which the vessel was pursuing when taken by Lieutenant Gedney. He proceeds to say:

In the intercourse and transactions between nations, it has been found indispensable that due faith and credit should be given by each to the official acts of the public functionaries of others. Hence the sentences of prize courts under the laws of nations, or admiralty, and exchequer or other revenue courts, under the municipal law, are considered as conclusive as to the proprietary interest in, and title to, the things in question; nor can the same be examined into in the judicial tribunals of another country. Nor is this confined to judicial proceedings! The acts of other officers of a foreign nation, in the discharge of their ordinary duties, are entitled to the like respect. And the principle seems to be universally admitted, that, whenever power or jurisdiction is delegated to any public officer or tribunal, and its exercise is confided to his or their discretion, the acts done in the exercise of that discretion, and within the authority conferred, are binding as to the subject matter; and this is true, whether the officer or tribunal be legislative, executive, judicial, or special.—Weaton's Elements of International Law, page 121; 6th Peter's, page 729."

There is the basis of his opinion; that the comity of nations requires, that such a paper, signed by the Governor General of Cuba, is conclusive to all the world as a title to property. If the life and liberty of men depends on any question arising out of these papers, neither the courts of this country nor of any other can examine the subject, or go behind this paper. In point of fact, the voyage of the Amistad, for which these papers were given, was but the continuation of the voyage of the slave trader, and marked with the horrible features of the middle passage. That is the fact in the case, but this government and the courts of this country cannot notice that fact, because they must not go behind that document. The Executive may send the men to Cuba, to be sold as slaves, to be put to death, to be burnt at the stake, but they must not go behind this document, to inquire into any facts of the case. That is the essence of the whole argument of the late Attorney–General. At a subsequent part of my argument I shall examine this document, and I undertake to show that it is' not even valid for what it purports to be, and that as a passport it bears on its face the insignia of imposture. But at present I will only observe that it is n most unheard–of thing, that in a question of property, a passport should be supposed to give a valid title. Papers of foreign courts and functionaries are to be credited for that which they intend to do. A passport, if it is regular, is to be credited as a passport. But when was it ever supposed that a passport stating what a person carries with him is evidence of his property in that which is described ? All the decisions of this court agree that foreign papers are good only for that which they propose and purport, but not as evidence of property. And yet the opinion of the late Attorney—General rests on that ground. In a case involving the lives and liberties of a large number of men, he has not a word to say of the principles of justice or humanity concerned, but goes entirely on the force of this document, on the ground that we cannot go behind the certificate of the Spanish Captain General. He says:

"Were this otherwise, all confidence and comity would cease to exist among nations; and that code of international law, which now contributes so much to the peace, prosperity and harmony of the world, would no longer regulate and control the conduct of nations."

This principle of national comity, I have no desire to contest, so far as it is applicable to this case. The Attorney says:—

" In the case of the Antelope, (10 Wheaton, page 66,) this subject was fully examined, and the opinion of the Supreme Court of the United States establishes the following points:—

"1. That, however unjust and unnatural the slave trade— may be, it is not contrary to the law of nations.

" 2. That, having been sanctioned by the usage and consent of almost all civilized nations, it could not be pronounced illegal, except so far as each nation may have made it so by its own acts or laws; and these could only operate upon itself, its own subjects or citizens; and, of course, the trade would remain lawful to those whose Government had not forbidden it.

"3. That the right of bringing in and adjudicating upon the case of a vessel charged with being engaged in the slave trade, even where the vessel belongs to a nation which has prohibited the trade, cannot exist. The courts of no country execute the penal laws of another, and the court of the American Government on the subject of visitation and search would decide any case in which that right had been exercised by an American cruiser, on the vessel of a foreign nation not violating our municipal laws, against the captors.

" It follows, that a foreign vessel engaged in the African slave trade, captured on the high seas in time of peace, by an American cruiser, and brought in for adjudication, would be restored.

" The opinions here expressed go far beyond the present case; they embrace cases where the Negroes never have been within the territorial limits of the nation of which the claimant is a citizen."

Here reference is made to the case of the Antelope, in 10 Wheaton, to which I shall hereafter solicit the particular attention of the Court, as I purpose to examine it in great detail, as to all the principles that have been supposed to be decided by that case, and especially on the point here alluded to, concerning which Chief Justice Marshall says that the Court was divided, therefore , no principle is decided. That was the most solemn and awful decision that ever was given by any Court. The Judges did not deliver their opinions for publication, or the reasons, because the court was divided. This case is laid at the foundation of the argument or opinion of the Attorney–General on which this whole proceeding is based, and it is appealed to in all the discussions as authority against the rights of these unfortunate people. I shall, therefore, feel it to be my duty to examine it to the bottom.

The second principle drawn by the late Attorney General, if he had reasoned on the subject as men ought to reason, is in favor of the claims of the Africans. The Antelope was engaged in the slave trade south of the Line, where it was not then prohibited by the laws of Spain. The decision of the Supreme Court, such as it was, was in affirmance of the decree of the court below. Judge Davies, in the District Court of Georgia, and Judge Johnson, of the Circuit Court, said that, if the slave trade had at that time been abolished by Spain, their decision would have been otherwise. That trade is now abolished by Spain.

The late Attorney General says ii the courts of no country execute the penal laws of another." I may ask, does any nation execute the slave laws of another country ? Is not the slave system, the Code Noir, as peculiar as the revenue system or the criminal code? These men were found free, and they cannot now be decreed to be slaves, but by making them slaves. By what authority will this court undertake to do this ? What right has Ruiz to claim these men as his property, when they were free, and so far from being in his possession when taken, he was in theirs. If there is no right of visitation and search by the cruisers of one nation over those of another, by what right has this ship been taken from the men who had it in their possession? The captors in this case, are Gedney and Meade, the owners are the Africans. The Attorney says,

" This vessel was not engaged in the slave trade; she was employed lawfully in removing these Negroes, as slaves, from one part of the Spanish dominions to another, precisely in the same way that slaves are removed, by sea, from one slave State to another in our own country. I consider the facts as stated, so far as this government is concerned, as establishing a right of ownership to the Negroes in question, in the persons in whose behalf the minister of Spain has made a demand upon the government of the U. States."

Now, here I take issue The vessel was engaged in the slave trade. The voyage in the Amistad was a mere continuation of the original voyage in the Tecora. The voyage in its original intention was not accomplished until the slaves had reached their final destination on the plantation. This is the principle universally applicable to coasting vessels. I say further, that the object of Ruiz and Montes was illegal, it was a part of the voyage from Lomboko, and when they fell into the hands of Lieutenant Gedney, they were steering in pursuance of that original voyage. Their object was to get to Porto Principe, and of course the voyage was to them an unlawful one. The object of the Africans was to get to a port in Africa, and their voyage was lawful. And the whole character of the affair was changed by the transactions that fool; place on board of the ship. The late Attorney, however, comes to the conclusion that the courts of the United States cannot proceed criminally against these people, that the provisions of the Acts of Congress against the slave trade are not applicable to Ruiz and Montes, and so he recurs to the 9th Article of the Treaty of 1795. I have nothing to add to what I have before said respecting the treaty. It can have no possible application in this case.

The late Attorney General now comes to a conclusion as to what is to be done—a conclusion which it is not in my power to read to the Court without astonishment, that such an opinion should ever have been maintained by an Attorney General of the United States.

Amistad Argument

" My opinion further is, that the proper mode of executing this article of treaty, in the present case, would be for the President of the United States to issue his order, directed to the Marshal in whose custody the vessel and cargo are, to deliver the same to such persons as may be designated by the Spanish minister to receive them. The reasons which operate in favor of a delivery to the order of the Spanish minister are—

" 1. The owners of the vessel and cargo are not all in this country and, of course, a delivery cannot be made to them.

"2. This has become a subject of discussion between the two Governments, and, in such a case, the restoration should be made to that agent of the Government who is authorized to make, and through whom the demand is made.

" 3. These Negroes are charged with an infraction of the Spanish laws; therefore, it is proper that they should be surrendered to the public functionaries of that Government, that if the laws of Spain have been violated, they may not escape punishment.

" 4. These Negroes deny that they are slaves; if they should be delivered to the claimants, no opportunity may be afforded for the assertion of their right to freedom. For these reasons, it seems to me that a delivery to the Spanish minister is the only safe course for this Government to pursue."

That is the opinion, which the Secretary of State told the Spanish minister the American Cabinet had adopted! That these MEN, being at that time in judicial custody of the Court of the United States, should be taken out of that custody, under an order of the President, and sent beyond seas by his sole authority! The Cabinet adopted that opinion; why, then, did they not act upon it? Why did not the President send his order to the Marshal to seize these men, and ship them to Cuba, or deliver them to the order of the Spanish Minister? I am ashamed ! I am ashamed that such an opinion should ever have been delivered by any public officer of this country, executive or judicial. I am ashamed to stand up before the nations of the earth, with such an opinion recorded as official, and what is worse, as having been adopted by the government:—an opinion sanctioning a particular course of proceeding, unprecedented among civilized countries, which was thus officially sanctioned, and yet the government did not dare to do it. Why did they not do it? If this opinion had been carried into effect, it would have settled the matter at once, so far as it related to these unfortunate men. They would have been wrested from that protection, which above all things was their due after they had been taken into custody by order of the Court, and would have been put into the power of " public vengeance" at Havana. Yet there was not enough. There seems to have been an impression that to serve an order like that would require the aid of a body of troope.— The people of Connecticut never would, never ought to have suffered it to be executed on their soil, but by main force. So the Spanish minister says his government has no ship to receive these people, and the President must therefore go further, and as he is responsible for the safekeeping and delivery of the men, he must not only deliver them up, but ship them off in a national vessel, so that there may be no Habeas Corpus from the State Courts coming to the rescue as soon as they are out of the control of the judiciary. The suggestion, which first came from the District Attorney, that the Court would undoubtedly place the Africans at the mercy of the Executive, is carried out by an announcement from the Secretary of State, of an agreement with Mr. Argaiz to send them to Cuba in a public ship. Here is the memorandum of the Secretary of State to the Secretary of the Navy.

" DEPARTMENT OF STATE, January 2, 1840.

" The vessel destined to convey the Negroes of the Amistad to Cuba, to be ordered to anchor off the port of New Haven, Connecticut, as early as the 10th of January next, and be in readiness to receive said Negroes from the marshal of the United States, and proceed with them to Havana, under instructions to be hereafter transmitted.

" Lieutenant Gedney and Meade to be ordered to hold themselves in readiness to proceed in the same vessel, for the purpose of affording their testimony in any proceedings that may be ordered by the authorities of Cuba in the matter.

" These orders should be given with special instructions that they are not to be communicated to any one."

Well, the order was given by the Secretary of the Navy, that the schooner Grampus should execute this honorable service.

The Secretary of the Navy to the Secretary of State.

" NAVY DEPARTMENT, Jan. 2, 1840.

Amistad Argument

" SIR,—I have the honor to state that, in pursuance of the memorandum sent by you to this department, the United States schooner Grampus, Lieutenant Commanding John S. Paine, has been ordered to proceed to the bay of New Haven, to receive the Negroes captured in the Amistad. The Grampus will probably be at the point designated a day or two before the 10th inst., and will there await her final instructions in regard to the Negroes."

A celebrated state prisoner, when going to the scaffold, was led by the statue of Liberty, and exclaimed, " O, Liberty! how many crimes are committed in thy name!" So we may say of our gallant navy, "What crimes is it ordered to commit! To what uses is it ordered to be degraded!"

On the 7th of January, the Secretary of State writes to the Secretary of the Navy, acknowledging the receipt of his letter of the 3d, informing him that the schooner Grampus would receive the Negroes of the Amistad, " for the purpose of conveying them to Cuba, in the event of their delivery being adjudged by the circuit court, before whom the case is pending." This singular blunder, in naming the court, shows in what manner and with how little care the Department of State allowed itself to conduct an affair, involving no less than the liberties and lives of every one of my clients. This letter inclosed the order of the President to the Marshal of Connecticut for the delivery of the Negroes to Lieut. Paine. Although disposing of the lives of forty human beings, it has not the form or solemnity of a warrant, and is not even signed by the President in his official capacity. It is a mere order.

"The Marshal of the United States for the district of Connecticut will deliver over to Lieut. John S. Paine, of the United States Navy, and aid in conveying on board the schooner Grampus, under his command, all the Negroes, late of the Spanish schooner Amistad, in his custody, under process now pending before the Circuit court of the United States for the district of Connecticut. For so doing, this order will be his warrant.

" Given under my hand, at the city of Washington, this 7th day of January, A. D. 1840.

" M. VAN BUREN.

"By the President:

Amistad Argument

"JOHN FORSYTH, Sec. of State."

That order is good for nothing at all. It did not even describe the court correctly, under whose protection these unfortunate people were. And on the 11th of January, the District Attorney had to send n special messenger, who came, it appears all the way to Washington in one day, to inform the Secretary that the Negroes were not holden under the order of the Circuit Court but of the District Court. And he says, "Should the pretended friends of the Negroes"—the pretended friends!—" obtain a writ of Habeas Corpus, the Marshal could not justify under that warrant." And he says, " the Marshal wishes me to inquire "—a most amiable and benevolent inquiry—" whether in the event of a decree requiring him to release the Negroes, or in case of an appeal by the adverse party, it is expected the Executive warrant will be executed " that is, whether he is to carry the Negroes on board of the Grampus in the face of a decree of the court. And he requests instructions on the point. What a pretty thing it would have been, if he had received such instructions, in the face of a decree of the court! I should like to ask him which he would have obeyed. At least, it appears, he had such doubts whether he should obey the decree of the court' that he wanted instructions from the President. I will not say what temper it shows in the Marshal and the District Attorney.

On the 12th of January, the very next day after the letter of the District Attorney was written at New Haven, the Secretary of State replies in a dispatch which is marked " confidential."

[CONFIDENTIAL.]

" DEPARTMENT OP STATE, Jan. 12, 1840.

" SIR,—Your letter of the 11th instant has just been received. The order for the delivery of the Negroes of the Amistad is here with returned, corrected agreeably to your suggestion. With reference to the inquiry from the Marshal, to which you allude, I have to state, by direction of the President, that, if the decision of the court is such as is anticipated, the order of the President is to be carried into execution, unless an appeal shall actually have been interposed. You are not to take it for granted that it will be interposed. And if, on the contrary, the decision of the court is different, you are to take out an appeal, and allow things to remain as they are until the appeal shall have been decided.

Amistad Argument

" I am, sir, your obedient servant,

" W. S. HOLABIRD, Esq.,

Attorney U. S. for Dist. of Conn."

"JOHN FOR FORSYTH.

Now, may it please your Honors, this corrected order, the final order of the President of the United States, is not in evidence, it does not appear among the documents communicated to Congress, and I feel some curiosity to know how it was corrected I have heard it intimated that the President of the United States never knew it had been changed, and that the alternative was made, perhaps by a clerk in the State Department, just by drawing his pen through the word circuit, and interlining the word district. I put it to your Honors to say what sort of regard is here exhibited for human life and for the liberties of these people. Did not the President know, when he signed that order for the delivery of MEN to the control of an officer of the navy to be carried beyond seas, he was assuming a power that no President had ever assumed before, It is questionable whether such a power could have been exercised by the most despotic government of Europe. Yet this business was coolly dispatched by a mere informal order, which order was afterwards altered by a clerk.

The Secretary of State further instructs the District Attorney, that " if the decision of the Court shall be such as is anticipated, the order of the President is to be carried into execution, unless an appeal is actually interposed," and he is " NOT TO TAKE IT FOR GRANTED THAT IT WILL BE INTERPOSED." The Government then confidently "anticipated" that the Negroes would be delivered up; and the Attorney was directed not to allow them a moment of time to enter an appeal. They were to be put on board of the Grampus instantly, and deprived, if possible, of the privilege of appealing to the higher Courts. Was this JUSTICE ?

But after all, the order did not avail. The District Judge, contrary to all these anticipations of the Executive, decided that the thirty–six Negroes taken by Lieut. Gedney and brought before the Court on the certificate of the Governor General of Cuba, were FREEMEN; that they had been kidnapped in Africa; that they did not own these Spanish names; that they were not ladinos, and were not correctly described in the passport, but were new

Amistad Argument

Negroes bought by Ruiz in the depot of Havana, and fully entitled to their liberty.

Such was the disposal intended, deliberately intended, by a President of the United States to be made, of the lives and liberty of thirty–six human beings!—The Attorney General of the United States, at once an Executive and a judicial officer of the American people, bound in more than official duty to respect the right of personal liberty and the authority of the Judiciary Department had given a written opinion, that, at the instigation of a foreign minister, the President of the United States should issue his order, directed to the marshal to whose custody these persons had been committed, by order of the judge, as prisoners and witnesses, and commanding that marshal to wrest them from the hands of justice, and deliver them to such persons as should be designated by that same foreign minister to receive them. Will this Court please to consider for one moment, the essential principle of that opinion ? Will this Court inquire, what, if that opinion had been successfully carried into execution, would have been the tenure by which every human being in this Union, man, woman, or child, would have held the blessing of personal freedom? Would it not have been by the tenure of Executive discretion, caprice or tyranny? Had the precedent once been set and submitted to, of a nameless mass of judicial prisoners and witnesses, snatched by Executive grasp from the protective guardianship of the Supreme Judges of the land, (gubernativamente,) at the dictate of a foreign minister, would it not have disabled forever the effective power of the Habeas Corpus? Well was it for the country—well V/OS it for the President of the United States himself that he paused before stepping over this Rubicon !—[hat he said—"We will proceed no further in this business." And yet, he did not discard the purpose, and yet he saw that this executive trampling at once upon the judicial authority and upon personal liberty would not suffice, either to satisfy the Spanish Minister or to satiate the public vengeance of the barracoon slave traders. Had the unfortunate Africans been torn away from the protection of the Court, and delivered up to the order of the Spanish Minister, he possessed not the means of shipping them off to the Island of Cuba. The indignation of the freemen of Connecticut, might not tamely endure the sight, of thirty–six free persons, though Africans, fettered and manacled in their land of freedom, to be transported beyond the seas, to perpetual hereditary servitude or to death, by the servile submission of an American President to the insolent dictation of a foreign minister. There were judges of the State Courts in Connecticut, possessing the power of issuing the Writ of Habeas Corpus, paramount even to the obsequiousness of a federal marshal to an Executive mandate. The opinion of the Attorney General, comprehensive as it was for the annihilation of personal liberty, carried not with it the means of accomplishing its object.

Amistad Argument

What then was to be done? To save the appearance of a violent and shameless outrage upon the authority of the judicial courts, the moment was to be watched when the Judge of the District Court should issue his decree, which it was anticipated would be conformable to the written opinion of the Attorney General. From that decree the Africans would be entitled to an appeal, first to the Circuit and eventually to the Supreme Court of the United States—but with suitable management, by one and the same operations they might be choused out of that right, the Circuit and Supreme Courts ousted of their jurisdiction, and the hapless captives of the Amistad delivered over to slavery and to death.

For this purpose at the suggestion of the District Attorney Holabird, and at the requisition of the dictatorial Spanish Minister, the Grampus, one of the smallest public vessels of the United States, a schooner of burden utterly insufficient to receive and contain under the shelter of her main deck, thirty-six persons additional to the ship's company, was in the dead of winter, ordered to repair from the navy yard at Brooklyn to New Haven where the Africans were upon trial, with this secret order which I have read to the Court, signed " Martin Van Buren," commanding the Marshal of the District of Connecticut to deliver over to Lieut. John S. Paine, commander of the Grampus, and aid in conveying on board that schooner all the Negroes, late of the Spanish schooner Amistad, in his custody, under process [now] pending before the Circuit Court of the United States for the District of Connecticut.

Of this ever memorable order, this Court will please to observe that it is in form and phraseology, perfectly conformable to the written opinion which had been given by the Attorney General. It is not conditional, to be executed only in the event of a decision by the court against the Africans, but positive and unqualified to deliver up all the Africans in his custody, under process now pending. There was nothing in the order itself to prevent Lieut. Paine from delivering it to the marshal, while the trial was pending; it carries out in form the whole idea of the Attorney General's opinion, that the President's order to the marshal is of itself all sufficient to supersede the whole protective authority of the judiciary—and with this pretension on the face of the order, i6 associated another, if possible still more outrageous upon every security to personal liberty, in the direction to the marshal to deliver over to Lieut. Paine all the Negroes, late of the Amistad, under his custody.

Amistad Argument

Is it possible that a President of the United States should be ignorant that the right of personal liberty is individual. That the right to it of every one, is his own—JUS SUMM; and that no greater violation of his official oath to protect and defend the Constitution of the United States, could be committed, than by an order to seize and deliver up at a foreign minister's demand, thirty—six persons, in a mass, under the general denomination of all, the Negroes, late of the Amistad. That he was ignorant, profoundly ignorant of this self—evident truth, inextinguishable till under gilt framed Declarations of Independence shall perish in the general conflagration of the great globe itself. I am constrained to believe—for to that ignorance, the only alternative to account for this order to the Marshal of the District of Connecticut, is willful and corrupt perjury to his official presidential oath.

But ignorant or regardless as the President of the United States might be of the self—evident principles of human rights, he was bound to know that he could not lawfully direct the delivery up to a foreign minister. even of slaves, of acknowledged undisputed slaves, in an undefined, unspecified number. That the number must be defined, and individuals specifically designated, had been expressly decreed by the Supreme Court of the united States in that very case of the Antelope so often, and as I shall demonstrate so erroneously quoted as a precedent for the captives of the Amistad.

"Whatever doubts (said in that case Chief Justice Marshall) may attend the question whether the Spanish claimants are entitled to restitution of all the Africans taken out of their possession with the Antelope we cannot doubt the propriety of demanding ample proof of the extent of that possession. Every legal principle which requires the plaintiff to prove his claim in any case, applies with full force to this point; and no countervailing consideration exists. The onus probandi, as to the number of Africans which were on board, when the vessel was captured, unquestionably lies on the Spanish libellants. Their proof is not satisfactory beyond 93. The individuals who compose this number must be designated to the satisfaction of the Circuit Court." 10 Wheaton 128. And this decision acquires double authority, as a precedent to establish the principles which it affirms, inasmuch as it was given upon appeal, and reversed the decision of the Circuit Court, which had resorted to the drawing of lots; both for the designation of the number' and for the specification of individuals.

Lawless and tyrannical; (may it please the Court—Truth, Justice, and the Rights of humankind forbid me to qualify these epithets) Lawless and Tyrannical, as this order thus

74

was upon its face, the cold blooded cruelty with which it was issued—was altogether congenial to its spirit—I have said that it was issued in the dead of winter—and that the Grampus was of so small a burden as to be utterly unfit for the service upon which she was ordered. I now add that the gallant officer who commanded her remonstrated, with feelings of indignation' controlled only by the respect officially due from him to his superiors against it. That he warned them of the impossibility of stowing this cargo of human flesh and blood beneath the deck of the vessel, and that if they should be shipped in the month of January, on her deck, and the almost certain casualty if a storm should befall them on the passage to Cuba, they must all inevitably perish. He remonstrated in vain! He was answered only by the mockery of an infraction, to treat his prisoners with all possible tenderness and attention.— If the whirlwind had swept them all into the ocean he at least would have been guiltless of their fate.

But although the order of delivery was upon its face absolute and unconditional, it was made conditional, by instructions from the Secretary of State to the District Attorney. It was to be executed only in the event of the decision of the court being favorable to the pretended application of the Spanish minister, and Lieutenant Paine was to receive the Negroes from the custody of the marshal as soon as their delivery should have been ordered by the court.

" Letting I dare not wait upon I would," a direct collision with the authority of the judicial tribunals was cautiously avoided; and a remarkable illustration of the thoughtless and inconsiderate character of the whole Executive action in this case, appears in the fact, that with all the cunning and intricate stratagems to grab and ship off these poor wretches to Cuba, neither the President of the United States who signed, nor the Secretary of State who transmitted the order knew, but both of them mistook the court, before which the trial of the Africans was pending. The supposed it was the Circuit, when in fact it was the District Court.

The Grampus arrived at New Haven three days before the decision of Judge Judson was pronounced. Her appearance there, in January, when the ordinary navigation of Long Island Sound is suspended, coming from the adjoining naval station at Brooklyn, naturally excited surprise, curiosity, suspicion. What could be the motive of the Secretary of the Navy for ordering a public vessel of the United States upon such a service at such a time

Amistad Argument

Why should her commander, her officers and crew be exposed, in the most tempestuous and the coldest month of the year, at once to the snowy hurricanes of the northeast, and the ice−bound shores of the northwest? These were questions necessarily occurring to the minds of every witness to this strange and sudden apparition. Lieut. Paine and his officers were questioned why they were there, and whither they were bound ? They could not tell. The mystery of iniquity sometimes is but a transparent veil and reveals its own secret. The fate of the Amistad captives was about to be decided as far as it could be by the judge of a subordinate tribunal. The surrender of them had been demanded of the Executive by a foreign minister, and earnestly pressed upon the court by the President's officer, the District Attorney. The sudden and unexpected appearance of the Grampus, with a destination unavowed, was a very intelligible signal of the readiness' of the willingness, of the wish of the President to comply with the foreign minister's demand. It was a signal equally intelligible to the political sympathies of a judge presumed to be congenial to those of a northern President with southern principles, and the District Attorney in his letter of 20th December had given soothing hopes to the Secretary of State, which he in turn had communicated in conference, on the 28th of December, to the Spanish minister, that the decree of the judge, dooming the Africans to servitude and death in Cuba, would be as pliant to the vengeful thirst of the barracoon slave−traders, as that of Herod was in olden times to the demand of his dancing daughter for the head of John the Baptist in a charger.

But when Lieut. Paine showed to the District Attorney the Executive warrant to the marshal for the delivery of the Negroes, he immediately perceived its nullity by the statement that they were in custody under a process from the " Circuit Court" and that the same error had been committed in the instructions to the marshal. "In great haste," therefore, he immediately dispatched Lieut. Meade, as a special messenger to Washington, requesting a correction of the error in the warrant and instructions; giving notice that if the pretended friends of the Negroes obtain a writ of habeas corpus, the marshal could not justify under the warrant as it was; and that the decision of the court would undoubtedly be had by the time the bearer of the message would be able to return to New Haven.

This letter was dated the 11th of January, 1840. The trial had already been five days "progressing." The evidence was all in, and the case was to be submitted to the court on that day. Misgivings were already entertained that the decision of the judge might not be so complacent to the longings of the Executive department as had been foretold and almost promised on the 20th of December. Mr. Holabird, therefore, at the desire of the Marshal propounds that decent question, and requests precise instructions," whether in the event of a decree by the court requiring the Marshal to release the Negroes, or in case of an appeal by the adverse party, it was expected the EXECUTIVE warrant [to ship off the prisoners in the Grampus to Cuba,] would be executed?" These inquiries may account perhaps for the fact that the same Marshal, after the District and Circuit Courts had both decided that these Negroes were free, still returned them upon the census of the inhabitants of Connecticut as Slaves.

The Secretary of State was more wary. The messenger, Lieut. Meade, bore his dispatch from New Haven to Washington in one day. On the 12th of January, Mr. Forsyth in a confidential letter to Mr. Holabird informs him that his missive of the day before had been received. That the order for the delivery of the Negroes to Lieut. Paine of the Grampus was returned, corrected agreeably to the District Attorney's suggestion—by whom corrected no uninitiated man can tell. Of the final warrant of Martin Van Buren, President of the United States, to the Marshal of the District of Connecticut, to ship for transportation beyond the seas, an undefined, nameless number of human beings, not a trace remains upon the records or the files of any one of the Executive Departments, and when nearly three months after this transaction the documents relating to it were, upon a call from the House of Representatives, communicated to them by massage from Mr. Van Buren himself, this original, erroneous, uncorrected order of the 7th of January, 1810, was the only one included in the communication.

But in the confidential answer of the Secretary of State of the 12th of January to the inquiries of the Marshal, he says, " I have to state by direction of the President, that if the decision of the Court is such as is anticipated, (that is, that the captives should be delivered up as slaves,) the order of the President is to be carried into execution, unless an appeal shall actually have been interposed, you are not to take it for granted that it will be interposed. And if on the contrary the decision of the Court is different, you are to take out an appeal, and allow things to remain as they are until the appeal shall have been decided." The very phraseology of this instruction is characteristic of its origin, and might have dispensed the Secretary of State from the necessity of stating that it emanated from the President himself. The inquiry of the Marshal was barefaced enough; whether, if the Executive warrant and the judicial decree should come in direct conflict with each other, it was expected that he should obey the President, or the Judge ? No ! says the Secretary of State. If the decree of the Judge should be in our favor, and you can steal a march upon the Negroes by foreclosing their right of appeal, ship them off without mercy and without delay: and if the decree should be in their favor, fail not to enter an instantaneous appeal to the Supreme Court where the chances may be more hostile to self– emancipated slaves.

Was ever such a scene of Liliputian trickery enacted by the rulers of a great, magnanimous, and Christian nation? Contrast it with that act of self emancipation by which the savage, heathen barbarians Cinque and Grabeau liberated themselves and their fellow suffering countrymen from Spanish slave–traders, and which the Secretary of State, by communion of sympathy with Ruiz and Montes, denominates lawless violence. Cinque and Grabeau are uncouth and barbarous names. Call them Harmodius and Aristogiton, and go back for moral principle three thousand years to the fierce and glorious democracy of Athens. They too resorted to lawless violence, and slew the tyrant to redeem the freedom of their country. For this heroic action they paid the forfeit of their lives: but within three years the Athenians expelled their tyrants themselves, and in gratitude to their self–devoted deliverers decreed, that thenceforth no slave should ever bear either of their names. Cinque and Grabeau are not slaves. Let them bear in future history the names of Harmodius and Aristogiton.

This review of all the proceedings of the Executive I have made with the utmost pain, because it was necessary to bring it fully before your Honors, to show that the course of that department had been dictated, throughout, not by justice but by sympathy—and a sympathy the most partial and unjust. And this sympathy prevailed to such a degree, among all the persons concerned in this business, as to have perverted their minds with regard to all the most sacred principles of law and right, on which the liberties of the people of the United States are founded; and a course was pursued, from the beginning to the end, which was not only an outrage upon the persons whose lives and liberties were at stake, but hostile to the power and independence of the judiciary itself.

I am now, may it please your Honors, obliged to call the attention of the Court to a very improper paper, in relation to this case, which was published in the Official Journal of the Executive Administration, on the very day of the meeting of this Court, and introduced with a commendatory notice by the editor, as the production of one of the brightest intellects of the South. I know not who is the author, but it appeared with that almost official sanction, on the day of meeting of this Court. It purports to be a review of the present case. The writer begins by referring to the decision of the District Court and says the case is " one of the deepest importance to the southern states." I ask, may it please your Honors, is that an appeal to JUSTICE ? What have the southern states to do with the case, or what has the case to do with the southern states ? The case, as far as it is known to the courts of this country, or cognizable by them, presents points with which the southern states have nothing to do It is a question of slavery and freedom between foreigners; of the lawfulness or unlawness of the African slave trade; and has not, when properly considered, the remotest connection with the interests of the southern states.

What was the purpose or intent of that article, I am not prepared to say, but it was evidently calculated to excite prejudice, to arouse all the acerbities of feeling between different sections of this country, and to connect them with this case, in such a manner as to induce this Court to decide it is favor of the alledged interests of the southern states, and against the suppression of the African slave trade. It is not my intention to review the piece at this time. It has been done, and ably done, by more than one person. And after infinite difficulty, one of these answers has been inserted in the same official journal in which the piece appeared. I now wish simply, to refer your Honors to the original principle of slavery' as laid down by this champion of the institution. It is given by this writer as a great principle of national law and stands as the foundation of his argument. I wish, if your Honors deem a paper of this kind, published under such circumstances, worthy of consideration in the decision of a case, that your Honors would advert to that principle, and say whether it is a principle recognized by this Court, as the ground on which it will decide cases.

" The truth is, that property in man has existed in all ages of the world, and results from the natural state of man, which is war. When God created the first family and gave them the fields of the earth as an inheritance, one of the number, in obedience to the impulses and passions that had been implanted in the human heart, rose and slew his brother. This universal nature of' man is alone modified by civilization and law. War, conquest, and force, have produced slavery, and it is state necessity and the internal law of self preservation, that will ever perpetuate and defend it."

There is the principle, on which a particular decision is demanded from this Court, by the Official Journal of the Executive, on behalf of the southern states? Is that a principle recognized by this Court? Is it the principle of that DECLARATION? [Here Mr. A. pointed to the Declaration of Independence, two copies of which hang before the eyes of the Judges on the bench.] It is alleged in the Official Journal, that war gives the right to

Amistad Argument

take the life of our enemy, and that this confers a right to make him a slave, on account of having spared his life. Is that the principle on which these United States stand before the world?. That DECLARATION says that every man is "endowed by his Creator with certain inalienable rights," and that among these are life, liberty, and the pursuit of happiness." if these rights are inalienable, they are incompatible with the rights of the victor to take the life of his enemy in war, or to spare his life and make him a slave. If this principle is sound, it reduces to brute force all the rights of man. It places all the sacred relations of life at the power of the strongest. No man has a right to life or liberty, if he has an enemy able to take them from him. There is the principle. There is the whole argument of this paper. Now I do not deny that the only principle upon which a color of right can be attributed to the condition of slavery is by assuming that the natural state of man is war The bright intellect of the South, clearly saw, that without this principle for a corner stone, he had no foundation for his argument. He assumes it therefore without a blush, as Hobbes assumed it to prove that government and despotism are synonymous words. I will not here discuss the right or the rights of slavery, but I say that the doctrine of Hobbes, that War is the natural state of man, has for ages been exploded, as equally disclaimed and rejected by the philosopher and the Christian. That it is utterly incompatible with any theory of human rights, and especially with the rights which the Declaration of Independence proclaims as self-evident truths. The moment you come, to the Declaration of Independence, that every man has a right to life and liberty, an inalienable right, this case is decided. I ask nothing more in behalf of these unfortunate men, than this Declaration. The opposite principle is]aid down, not by an unintelligent or unthinking man, but is given to the public and to this Court, as coming from one of the brightest intellects of the South. Your Honors see what it comes to, when carried out. I will call the attention of the Court to one more paragraph:—

"Instead of having the Negroes placed in a situation to receive punishment for what offenses they may have committed against their masters, those who have been in Cuba in undisputed possession of property under the Spanish flag were instantly deprived of that possession, and their final title to the property peremptorily decided upon by an American court, in defiance of the plainest treaty stipulations. Not only that, but Ruiz and Montes, Spanish citizens, thus forced into our territory under appalling circumstances, where common humanity, independent of all law, demanded that they should be treated with hospitality as unfortunate guests were actually thrown into prison under charges which the Negroes were instigated to make, for offenses committed against the Negroes while they were in Cuba, under the Spanish jurisdiction. This is the justice of an American court, bowed down in disgraceful subserviency before the bigoted mandates of that blind fanaticism which prompted the Judge upon the bench to declare in his decree, in reference to one of these Negroes, that, 'Although he might be stained with crime, yet he should not sigh in vain for Africa ;' and all because his hands were reeking with the blood of murdered white men! ! It is a base outrage (I can use no milder language,) upon all the sympathies of civilized life."

That is the complimentary manner in which the courts of the United States are treated by the brightest intellects of the South, in the Official Journal, and under the immediate supervision of the Executive Administration of the Government.

During the present session, a further correspondence between the Secretary of State and the Spanish minister has been communicated to Congress. The Spanish minister seems to be ever attentive to all that is going on, in all the departments of Government, with relation to this case. In a letter dated the 20th of March, 1840, he observes that the Secretary of State had confidently asked him to furnish a copy of the existing laws of Cuba relative to Negro slavery. What was this for? Was the President of the United States under the impression that before he carried into effect this exercise of despotic power, to seize MEN, by his own warrant, and send them to foreign countries for punishment by his own order—there would be some sort of decency, at least, in having a show of evidence to show that the Spanish law required that they should be delivered up? The Secretary of State asked Mr. Calderon for evidence in the case, but he had none to give He then "confidently" asked Mr. Argaiz for the law of Spain in the case—the law, be it remembered, on which the United States were presenting a suit against individuals, solely, as they alledge, in pursuance of a demand made by the minister of Spain to that effect. What is the reply ? Mr. Argaiz says he cannot communicate the law officially because he cannot recognize the jurisdiction of the Court over the case. Here is another point–blank contradiction of the serial averment of the claim which the United States Government is prosecuting here— that the suit is in pursuance of the demand of Spain now pending against the Government. Mr. Argaiz, therefore, communicates a certain memorandum, "confidentially." This memorandum begins.

"Mr. Forsyth way pleased, some time since, to state to the Chevalier de Argaiz, that it would be expedient to obtain a copy of the laws now in force in the island of Cuba relative to slavery The Chevalier de Arnaiz therefore immediately requested from the Captain General of that island every thing on the subject, which has been determined since the treaty concluded in 1818, between Spain and England."

Now, may it please the Court, may I inquire why this demand was limited to laws subsequent to the treaty of 1818? The decree for abolishing the slave trade was issued in 1817. Why did the Spanish minister limit his request to laws passed after 1818? Why was not the decree of 1817 brought forward? Was it kept back because he thought, with Mr. Vega, that the laws had been broken so much in Cuba, that they were not in force ? Or did he think the authentication of that Decree might have some injurious effect in the trial here ? Whatever was the reason, it is certain that, to Mr. Forsyth's request for " a copy of the laws now in force in the Island of Cuba relative to slavery," only the laws since 1818 were communicated, and the Decree of 1817, making the slave trade unlawful and its victims free, was kept beck. Even the treaty of 1835, which was communicated, " the Chevalier de Argaiz requests maybe returned to him," and consequently it does not appear among these papers.

In another letter, dated April 24th, 1840, the Chevalier de Argaiz refers to certain resolutions of the United States Senate passed the 15th of the same month, commonly called Mr. Calhoun's resolutions. I showed the other day, that if these principles are just, and if they have any application to this case, Lieut. Gedney had no right to seize the vessel at all. The resolution declares that—

" A ship or vessel on the high seas, in time of peace, engaged in a lawful commerce, is, according to the laws of nations, under the exclusive jurisdiction of the State to which her flag belongs; as much so as if constituting a part of its own domain ;" and " if such ship or vessel should be forced, by stress of weather, or other unavoidable cause, into the port and under the jurisdiction of a friendly power, she, and her cargo, and persons on board, with their property, and all the rights belonging to their personal relations as established by the laws of the state to which they belong, would be placed under the penalty which the laws of nations extend to the unfortunate under such circumstances."

Here it is plain that the vessel was in the hands of the Africans, it was not under the Spanish flag, they were at peace with the United States, their voyage is lawful, the personal relations established among the persons Oh board were that the Africans were masters and the Spaniards captives subjects;—perhaps by the laws of Mendi they were slaves. So much for the resolutions, which the Secretary of State says coincide "with principles which the President considers as founded in law and justice," but which does not alter "the determination he found himself obliged to make on the reclamation" made for the Amistad " and the property found on board of her."

I will now make a few observations on the passport, or permit, as it has been called, which is relied on as of authority sufficient to bind this Court and Government to deliver up my clients irrevocably as slaves, on a claim of property by Ruiz and Montes... Here we have what appears to be a blank passport, filled up with forty-nine Spanish names of persons, who are described as ladinos and as being the property of Don Jose Ruiz. Now, this on the face of it is an imposture. It is not a passport, that can be inspected as such by this Court, or by any tribunal. It appears on the face of it to be a passport designed for one person, a man, as there are blanks in the margin, to be filled up with a description of the person, as to his height, age, complexion, hair, forehead, eyebrows, eyes, nose, mouth, beard, and particular marks. This particular description of the person is the very essence of a passport, as it is designed to identify the individual by the conformity of his person to the marks given; and a passport is nothing, and is good for nothing, if it does not accord with the marl;s given. The man who presents it must show by this accordance that he is the person named Every body who has ever had occasion to use passports knows this. We are not in the habit of using passports in this country; you may go through the country from State to State, freely without any passport to show who and what you are and what is your business. But throughout the continent of Europe, passports are everywhere necessary. At every town you show your passport to a public officer, who instantly compares your person with the description' and if it corresponds, you proceed, but if the description varies from the reality, you cannot pass. That is the nature of a passport. It says, let the person who bears these marks pass the custom-house, or the guard, as the case may be. And its validity depends on the accuracy of the description.

I once had occasion, many years ago to see the operation of these things in a very remarkable case. I was a passenger in n merchant vessel, bound to the north of Europe. In passing through the Sound, at Elsinore, we were arrested by a British squadron, who brought us to, and sent a lieutenant on board to examine our crew. He ordered all the men to be mustered on deck, and the captain had no alternative but to comply. It was a most mortifying scene to an American. Every American seaman was obliged to show his protection, the same thing at sea as a passport on the land, to secure him from impressment by British cruisers. The officer examined every man carefully, to see whether his person corresponded with the description in his protection. He finally found one young man, who was a native of Charlestown, Massachusetts, within ten miles of where I was born; but his description was not correct, whether through the blunder of the man who wrote it, or because he had taken another man's protection, I do not know, but the officer said he had a good mind to take him, and if I had not been on board, as the bearer of a public commission in the service of the Government, I have no doubt that man would have been taken, and compelled to serve on board a British man of war, solely for the want of correspondence of the description with his person. I mention this to show that the value of a passport, according to the rules of those countries where such things are used, depends on the description of the person, and this is all left blank in the paper here presented us as a passport. There is not a particle of description by which even a single individual named could be identified. It is not worth a cent. I do not say it is a forgery, but I say its incompetency to answer the purpose of n passport is apparent on the face of it. Who knows, or how is this Court to ascertain, that the persons named in this paper are the same with those taken in the Amistad? No court, no tribunal, no officer, would accept such a document as a passport. And will this Court grant its decree in a case affecting both liberty and life on that paper ? It is impossible.

I now come to the case of the Antelope, as reported in 10 Wheaton, 66, and I ask particular attention to this case, not only because it brings a show of authority in favor of the delivery up of slaves, but because I feel bound to entreat the Court, whether they find a principle settled by that case or not, to settle the question now upon further and mature consideration. Chief Justice Marshall said, expressly, in delivering the opinion of the Court, that, as the Court was divided, " no principle is settled." If there was a principle settled, and that was in favor of delivering up persons held as slaves by foreign laws, I ask this Court to re—examine that principle and settle it anew. And if, upon re—examination, by what [should deem the greatest misfortune to this country, the Court should be divided in this case, as it was in that, I respectfully ask your Honors to give your separate opinions, with the reasons. I would not call in question the propriety of the determination of the Court in that day, severally, to withhold their reasons from the public; the state of the matter is now materially altered. It has become a point in which the morals, as well as the liberties of this country, are deeply interested. The public mind acquiesced before, in postponing the discussion, but now it is no longer a time for this course, the question must be met, and judicially decided.

THE CASE OF THE ANTELOPE REVIEWED.

Amistad Argument

The case of the Antelope was of so very extraordinary a character, and the decisions of the District, Circuit, and Supreme Courts of the United States, on the principles involved in it, were so variant from and conflicting with one another, that a review of its history will disclose, eminently, the progress of that moral, religious, and political revolution in the opinions of mankind which has been, from a period coeval with that of North American Independence, struggling against the combined powers and dominions of the earth and of darkness for the suppression of the African slave–trade.

In the month of December, 1819, at a time when piracy, from her sympathetic and favorite haunts of Chesapeake bay, and of Cuba, was habitually sallying forth against the commerce of the world, but chiefly under the many–colored banners of the newly emancipated colonies of Spain, transformed into a multitude of self–constituted sovereign and disunited States, capturing wherever they could be found the trading vessels of Portugal and of Spain, a privateer, named the Columbia, commanded by a citizen of the United States named Metcalf, came into the port of Baltimore under the flag of Venezuela—there clandestinely shipped a crew of thirty or forty men, not one of whom had ever owed allegiance to the Republic of Venezuela, and sailed in search of adventure, to pounce upon the defenseless upon any and every ocean for the spoils. She had scarcely got beyond the territorial jurisdiction of the United States when she changed her name of Columbia for that of Arraganta, hoisted the flag of Artigas, then ruler of the Oriental Republic of La Plata, and proceeded for the slave–coast of Africa—a mighty huntress, and her prey was man. There she fell in with sister pirates in abundance—first an American, from Bristol, Rhode Island, and borrowed twenty–five Negro captives from her; then sundry ostensible Portuguese vessels, from which she took nearly two hundred; and lastly, a Spaniard from Cuba, fitted out some months before by a slave trading house at the Havana, to catch a yet lawful human cargo from a region south of the equator; for the trade north of the equator had even then been declared unlawful by Spain. The name of this vessel was, at that time, the Antelope; and with her and her living merchandise the Arraganta steered for the coast of Brazil, for a market. There the Arraganta was shipwrecked; her master, Metcalf, either drowned, or made prisoner with the greater part of his crew; while the remainder, under the command of John Smith, a citizen of the United States, transhipping themselves and all their surviving African captives into the Antelope, changed her name to that of the General Ramirez, and stood for the southern coast of the United States, and a market.

Amistad Argument

In the month of June, 1820, this vessel, thus freighted, was found hovering on the coast of Florida, with the evident intention of surreptitiously introducing the Negroes and effecting the sale of them within the United States. She was there in flagrant violation of two classes of their laws—those intended to suppress the unlawful interference of our citizens in the civil war then raging between Spain and her South American Colonies contending for their independence, and those prohibiting their participation in the slave trade, and denouncing it as piracy.

She was reported to Captain John Jackson, then cruising on the same coast in the Revenue Cutter Dallas, as a vessel of piratical appearance. He, thereupon, boarded her; and finding her full of Negro slaves, and commanded by John Smith, holding forth at once a privateering commission from Artigas, and a protection as n citizen and seaman of the United States, he took possession of her, and brought her into the port of Savannah, in the judicial district of Georgia, for adjudication.

Upon this plain and simple statement of facts, can we choose but exclaim, if ever soul of an American citizen was polluted with the blackest and largest participation in the African slave–trade, when the laws of his country had pronounced it piracy, punishable with death, it was that of this same John Smith He had renounced and violated those rights, by taking a commission from Artigas to plunder the merchants and mariners of nations in friendship with his own; and yet he claimed the protection of that same country which he had abandoned and betrayed. Why was he not indicted upon the act of 15th May, 1820, so recently enacted before the commission of his last and most atrocious crime?

And can we choose but further exclaim—if ever hapless African, Kidnapped into slavery by one gang of ruffians, and then stolen by another, and by them attempted to be smuggled into our country as slaves, and by n fortunate casualty brought within our jurisdiction and the beneficent operation of our emancipating law*, was entitled to the blessing of freedom, and the right of being transported under our national protection to his native land, so was every individual African found by Captain Jackson on board of the Antelope, and brought within the jurisdiction of this Federal Union. Why were they not instantly liberated and sent home to Africa by the act of March 3d, 1819. Alas! far other. wise was, in the judicial district of Georgia, the disposal of this pirate, robber, and traitor to his country! Instead of being indicted for all or any one of his many violations of the laws of the United States, of nations, and of humanity, he was not only suffered to go at large, entirely unmolested, but was permitted to file his claim, before the District Court of the United States in Georgia, for the restitution to him of the Antelope and all her living cargo, as captured jure beli), by virtue of his commission from Artigas. This claim was, indeed, dismissed, with costs, by the judge of the District Court, William Davis. Smith appealed from that decision to the Circuit Court, the presiding judge of which, William Johnson, confirmed the decision of the District Court, and spoke with suitable severity, not of the wickedness, but of the absurdity of Smith's pretension. And here, and in freely commenting hereafter upon the opinions and decisions upon this case, of these two judges, William Davis and William Johnson, both long since deceased, truth and justice require the remark, with all the respect due to their memories as upright judges and honorable men, that they were both holders of slaves, adjudicating in a State where slavery is the law of the land. If this circumstance may account for the fact, that the ministers of national justice in Georgia slumbered over the manifold transgressions of John Smith, for, which he never was prosecuted, it will account no less for that division of opinion in the Supreme tribunal of the Union, which veiled from public examination and scrutiny the reasons of each judge for his own opinion, because, as the Chief Justice declared, NO PRINCIPLE WAS SETTLED. John Smith did not venture to appeal from the decisions of the District and Circuit Courts against his claim to the Supreme Court of the United States. His plunder slipped from his hands; but his treachery to his country for a commission from Artigas, his buccanier and slave– trade piracies, though not even undivulged crimes, yet remained unwhipped of justice.

On the 27th of July, 1820, Captain John Jackson, in behalf of himself, and of the officers and crew of the Revenue Cutter Dallas, filed in the District Court a libel against the Antelope, or General Ramirez, for forfeiture, under the act of Congress of 20th April, 1818, prohibiting American citizens from engaging in the African slave trade.

At the same Court, Charles Mulvey, vice–consul of Spain, and Francis Sorell, vice–consul of Portugal, at Savannah, filed each a libel for restitution, the former of 150, the latter of 130 African Negroes, composing the cargo of the Antelope. To these two libels Richard Habersham, district attorney of the United States, interposed in their name a claim to the freedom of all the Negroes, on the ground that some American citizen was interested or engaged in their transportation from Africa.

The Spanish vice–consul claimed the vessel and all the Negroes in behalf of the original fitters out of the Antelope, for the slave trading voyage, at the Havana.

Amistad Argument

And Captain Jackson claimed salvage for all the Negroes who might be adjudged to the Spanish and Portuguese vice-consuls; and twenty-five dollars a head for all those who might be declared free, according to the act of Congress.

The judge of the District Court, after rejecting the claim of John Smith, on the ground of the illegality of the fitting out of the Columbia, or Arraganta, at Baltimore, and thereby settling the principle, that no capture made by that vessel could be legal, seems to have forgotten, or overlooked, the violation by the same John Smith of the laws of the United States for the suppression of the slave-trade; at least, so far as concerned all the Negroes on board the Antelope, excepting only a small remnant of twenty-five, which had been taken from the American slave-trader, the Exchange, from Bristol, Rhode Island. John Smith had made no attempt to smuggle these into the United States separate from the rest. His attempt had been to smuggle them all in. Why, then, should those taken from the American vessel alone be declared free, and those taken from the Spaniards and Portuguese doomed to perpetual slavery?

The judge hunted up sundry old decisions in the Supreme Court of the United States, and, finally, the case of the Josafa et Segunda, 5 Wheaton, 338, for a principle "that, upon a piratical or illegal capture, the property of the original owners cannot be forfeited for the misconduct of the captors in violating the municipal laws of the country where the vessel seized by them is carried." The application of which principle to the rights of the respective parties in the case of the Antelope was, that the property of the Spanish owners of the Antelope could not be forfeited by the misconduct of John Smith in capturing it, in violation of the laws of the United States, by virtue of a commission from Artigas. Thus far the principle was correctly applied; but to that other misconduct of John Smith, the attempt to smuggle these Negroes into the United States, by which they became forfeited, and made free by the law, whoever might have been their owner; to that misconduct, the precedent of the Josafa et Segunda had no application whatever, and it was altogether overlooked in the decision of the district judge, although he decreed freedom to the chance chosen survivors of the twenty-five Negroes of the very same cargo, taken from the American vessel, though forfeited and liberated by the very same attempt of John Smith to smuggle them into the United States for sale. It was perfectly immaterial to the question of forfeiture and liberation to whom all or any of the Negroes had originally belonged. It was the attempt to smuggle them which induced their forfeiture by the rigor, and their consequent liberation by the beneficence, of the law.

Amistad Argument

But having once introduced this entirely extraneous question, to whom the Negroes on board the Antelope, when captured by Captain Jackson, had originally belonged the District Judge proceeded, upon such evidence as he deemed sufficient, to decide, that those captured in her by the Arraganta, were the property of Spaniards, and without one title of evidence, to infer, that all the Negroes taken from vessels under Portuguese colors, had been the property of Portuguese subjects, unknown; and upon these conclusions and assumptions, to adjudge all the Negroes, save the scanty surviving remnant of twenty– five taken from the Exchange of Rhode Island, to the Spanish and Portuguese Vice Consuls.

At this distance of time, who can read such an adjudication of an American judge, without amazement.

The claim of C. Mulvey [Spanish Vice Consul] was therefore sustained to the Antelope, and to as many of the Negroes, as should appear to be remaining of those found on board of her at the time of her capture by the Arraganta.

The libel of F. Sorrell, the Portuguese Vice Consul, was sustained against so many of the slaves as should appear to remain of those taken by the Arraganta from Portuguese vessels.

And it was further ordered with assent of parties, (that is, of these two parties the Spanish and Portuguese Vice Consuls, and well they might assent!) that the chim of John Jackson to salvage, should be sustained as regarded the Negroes claimed by and adjudged to them—and as regarded those adjudged to the United States, to an allowance of twenty five dollars for each according the Act of Congress of 3d March, 1819.

This decree was pronounced on the 21st of February 1821— and the clerk of the court was directed on or before the 26th day of the same month to report to the court the number of Spanish and Portuguese Negroes in the hands of the marshal, distinguishing the Negroes respectively belonging to each. He was also required to designate the very small number adjudged to the United States, that is, to the blessed enjoyment of themselves and their own liberty; and associating with himself two resident merchants, was at the same time to report the quantum or proportion of salvage to be allowed to Captain Jackson for the Negroes thus reputably and substantially sold by the judicial authority of the United States to the Spanish and Portuguese Vice Consuls.

Amistad Argument

This unblushing bargain and sale of human captives, entitled at least by the intention of the United States laws to their freedom' was the first incident which brought to a pause the legal standard of morality of a Connecticut District Judge of the United States in the case of the Amistad captives. An estimate in dollars and cents of the value at New Haven, of from two to three hundred living men and women, for the purpose of allowing salvage upon them as merchandise, was too much for the nerves of a Yankee judge. The authority of the case of the Antelope was in this particular no precedent for him. The very proposal shocked his moral sense, and he instantly decided that men and women were not articles for a price current in the markets overt of Connecticut.

In the markets of Savannah, nothing was more simple. The clerk of the District Court, with his two associated resident merchants, in obedience to the order of the judge appraised the Negroes taken from the Spanish and Portuguese vessels at three hundred dollars per head, making the aggregate of sixty–one thousand five hundred dollars [for 205 souls]; and they were of opinion that there should be an allowance of one fourth of said sum to Captain Jackson, his officers and crew, for salvage on the said Negroes.

Seventy–five dollars per head! Fifteen thousand three hundred and seventy five dollars for two hundred and five men and women! What a revolution in the relative value of slaves and of freemen, since the age of Homer! In the estimate of that Prince of Grecian Poets.

Jove fix'd it certain that whatever day

Makes man a slave, takes half his worth away—

and in the political statistics of the author of the Declaration of Independence the degradation of the character of man, by the infliction upon him of slavery is far greater than is asserted by the blind old rhapsodist of Smyrna. But here we have an inverted proportion of relative value, and Captain Jackson, by the decree of a Judicial Court of the United States receives twenty–five dollars a head for redeeming one parcel of Africans from slavery to freedom, while at the same time he was to receive seventy–five dollars a head for reducing by the same act two other parcels of the same company from freedom to slavery!

Amistad Argument

Nor was the manner in which the clerk of the District Court executed the order to report the relative numbers of the three classes of the captured Africans, the least extraordinary part of these proceedings.

He reported that two hundred and fifty–eight Negroes had been delivered by Captain John Jackson, Commander of the Revenue Cutter Dallas, on the 25th of July, 1820, to the marshal of Georgia, from on board the General Ramirez [the Antelope.] That of that number forty–four had died in the space of seven months —one was missing and one discharged by order of court, and that the marshal returned two hundred and twelve Negroes which remained to be apportioned.

What kind become of the missing one neither the clerk nor the judge seems to have thought it worth his while to inquire—why should they ? it was but one man—and that man a Negro ! no further trace of him appears upon the record.

Neither was it thought necessary to record the reason of the favor bestowed by the court upon one other man in ordering his discharge. The very nature of the order is its own justification.

But mark the mortality of the Negroes! out of 258, four deaths in the space of seven months! and that, not while crammed between the decks of a slaver in the middle passage, but on the soil of the American Union, in the mild and healthy climate of Georgia—in the custody of an officer commissioned by the President of the United States, and under the protection of their judicial magistracy. In the case of the Amistad, the mortality ceased, as soon as the captives were admitted to the privilege of breathing in the atmosphere of freedom.

But if the death of one man in six, in the space of seven months, is deeply distressing to the sympathies of our nature, what shall we say to a mortality of eighteen out of twenty five, which the clerk reported as the proportion of deaths among the Negroes taken from the American vessel, the Exchange, and who were by the final decree of the judge to be liberated? The clerk in his report denominates them American Negroes, and he reduces their number to SEVEN. Seven African captives out of two hundred and fifty–eight, was the number to whom the benignity of the laws of the American Union enacted for the suppression of the African slave trade, and expounded by the District Court of the United States in Georgia, would have extended the inestimable blessings of freedom and

91

Amistad Argument

restoration to their country!

The clerk had been required to report the number of Spanish, Portuguese, and American Negroes— distinguishing those respectively belonging to each of the se classes. He could obtain no evidence worth a straw upon which to found his report, the Negroes were all huddled together in one crowd– John Smith, the pirate, was the only witness who could tell him which were the Negroes taken out of the American vessel, and he told him that sixteen out of the twenty–five had died, before the capture of the Antelope by Capt. Jackson. The clerk reported accordingly, and added two to the number of deaths, as the average loss since the 25th of July; that is, since they had been in the custody of the marshal.

It further appears from his report that the whole number captured by the Arraganta had been 331, of which 213 were Portuguese, 93 Spanish, and 25 American. That of the whole number 119 had died, but in what proportions from the general classes he could not ascertain. John Smith testified that sixteen of the 25 American Negroes had died before the Antelope was taken by Captain Jackson, and the clerk guessed that two more had died since, because that was the average loss of 9 to 44 out of 258. But neither John Smith nor any one else could point out the individual survivors of each separate class, and the clerk therefore reported that there had been captured by the Arraganta 213 Portuguese Negroes, of which the average loss was 71;—93 Spanish Negroes of which the average loss was 30, and 25 American Negroes, of whom the deaths attested by John Smith were 16, and the subsequent average loss 2, leaving as before stated 212 to be apportioned—that is, 142 to the Portuguese Vice Consul, 63 to the Spanish Vice Consul, and 7 to the United States, to be sent home to Africa; freemen by the mandate of our laws.

That the whole 212 were entitled to the benefit of the same laws, I cannot possibly doubt—but such was not the decision of the District Judge. Exceptions were taken to the report of the clerk, by the District Attorney of the United States, Richard W. Habersham, and by Spanish Vice Consul Mulvey. The District Attorney still claiming the freedom of all the Negroes, and objecting to the allowance of 75 dollars a head to Captain Jackson for salvage, though not to the allowance of 25 dollars a head for their liberation. The Spanish Vice Consul insisting that the number of slaves allowed to the Spanish claimants was too few and not supported by any testimony in the case—and that the allowance to Captain Jackson for salvage was too high, and ought to be regulated by the act of

Amistad Argument

Congress in relation to the compensation given in case the said slaves had been decreed to be delivered to the United States.

The Judge confirmed the report of the Clerk in all its parts; and the District Attorney, in behalf of the United States, and the Spanish Vice Consul, in behalf of the Spanish claimants, appealed to the Circuit Court, then next to be held at Milledgeville on the 8th day of May, 1821.

In these decisions of the District Court, is it possible to avert one's eyes from the glaring light of an over–ruling propensity to narrow down, if not wholly to nullify, the laws of the United States for the suppression of the African slave trade? To sustain the claim of the Spanish Vice Consul, the irrelevant question to whom the Antelope had originally belonged, was introduced; and upon that was engrafted the deeply controverted question, whether the African slave trade was or was not contrary to the law of nations. To redeem from forfeiture the Antelope and the Negroes captured in her by the Arraganta, the judge resorted to an argument of counsel in the recently reported case of she Josefa Segundas, (Wheaton, 338,) where it was said, that as piracy can neither divest nor convey property, a pirate cannot, by a subsequent violation of the laws of his own country, forfeit the property of which he has acquired possession by preceding piracy. This seems equivalent to a principle that a second act of piracy protects the pirate from punishment for the first. However conformable this maxim may be to the legal standard of morality, the Supreme Court did not so decide in the case of the Josefa Segunda. They decided, that the capture of a Spanish vessel and Negroes by privateer, with a commission from Arismendi, under the Republic of Venezuela, was not piracy; and that the Josefa Segunda, a Spanish vessel, and her cargo of Negroes, captured by authority of such a commission, were forfeited by a subsequent attempt of the captors to smuggle them into the United States, though taken from the Spanish owners only by the Venezuelan commission from Arismendi. Now the Columbia had entered Baltimore, and there enlisted her crew under those identical colors of Venezuela, and, DO doubt, with a commission from the same Arismendi. When metamorphosed into the Arraganta, she took the Antelope and her Negroes, by a commission from Artigas, quite as efficient to legitimate a prize as that of Arismendi; and John Smith, when captured with the Antelope and her Negroes, by Captain Jackson, produced this commission from Artigas as his warrant for his possession of the vessel and the slaves. As between the Arraganta and the Antelope, therefore, the capture of the latter by a commission from Artigas was not piratical but belligerent, it did divest the Spanish owners of the property and vest it in the captors, at least sufficiently to make it forfeitable

93

by their subsequent attempt to smuggle it into the United States; and the decision of the Supreme Court, in the case of the Josefa Segunda, instead of sustaining that of the District Judge, in the case of the Antelope, is an authority point blank against it.

For the allotment of 142 of the Negroes to the Portuguese Vice Consul, there was not even the apology of a Portuguese claimant, other than the Vice Consul himself to the property. There was not a shadow of evidence that they were the property of Portuguese subjects, and none were ever found to claim them. He took the testimony of the capturing crew, that some of them were taken from vessels under Portuguese colors; and as he had no evidence that Portugal had then prohibited the slave trade, he took it for granted that the Negroes were all slaves, and, as such, he decreed that they should be delivered to the Vice Consul.

With regard to the question, whether Slavery was or was not contrary to the laws of nations, his decision was such as might be expected from a judge, himself a holder of slaves, in a land where slavery has the sanction of law. The question, as I have endeavored to show, did not belong to the case. "But it is contended," (says the District judge) " on the authority of some recent decisions in the British Admiralty Court, that Africans are to be considered free, until it is shown that they are slaves, and that the burden of proof is with those who set up a claim to them. The doctrine may be correct in England, since there Negroes have al. ways been held to be free, except in cases where they have voluntarily entered into engagements binding them to service. And yet, inconsistent and contradictory as it may be, slavery has been recognized in all the British American colonies.

" But it does not appear to me that I can admit the proposition in the form and manner in which it is here presented. The period is not very remote when all the Governments of Europe, and the several States of the United States when they were British colonies, and many of them after they became independent, recognized slavery. But a few years have elapsed since the Government of the United States permitted her citizens to engage in the African trade. Under such a state of things, it appears to me that this Court is bound to consider the unfortunate Africans, when found in the possession of the subjects or citizens of any Government which has heretofore permitted this traffic as slaves, until the contrary be shown. That this trade, however inhuman it may be, and however obnoxious it is to every benevolent feeling, must now be considered legal, notwithstanding its injustice, until it is shown to have been prohibited by that Government whose subjects claim the right of– engaging in it.

"When it shall have been ascertained that the different Governments of the civilized world have consented to abolish the trade or after it shall have been ascertained that any particular State or Government has determined to abolish it, this Court would consider the claims set up in favor of Africans found in the situation of those before the Court, in a different point of view. In the one case they would, I think, uniformly be considered free, until the contrary was shown; in the other case, they would be so considered when they were found in the possession of the subjects or citizens of that Government which had determined to abolish the trade.

" If it could be made to appear to this Court that, at the time these Africans were taken from the possession of the Spanish and Portuguese claimants Spain and Portugal had agreed to prohibit their subjects from engaging in the trade, this Court, I think, would be bound to restore to these people their liberty.

"It is true this Court will not enforce the municipal laws of another country, by punishing the subjects of that country for the infraction of them; but this Court could feel bound to respect the rights of Africans no less than it could respect the rights of any other class of persons. Spain, however' had not, at the time I am speaking of, abolished the trade to Africa, although she had placed it under certain restrictions. Can it be permitted to this Court to examine the commercial regulations or the conventional engagement of Spain?"

It is unnecessary further to repeat verbatim et literatim this argument of the District judge to sustain his decree. Every word and letter of it teems with anxiety to sustain the institution of Slavery, and to prostrate instead of enforcing the laws of the United States for the suppression of the slave trade. What he calls certain restrictions placed on the trade by Spain, was the total prohibition of it north of the equator, even then stipulated by Spain in a treaty with Great Britain, and enacted accordingly by her law. But what of that? The judge admits that the trade is inhuman, that it is obnoxious to every benevolent feeling, but he is bound to consider it legal, notwithstanding its injustice, because many years before it had been practiced by Great Britain' and not many years before by the United States themselves." Is this reasoning for a Court of JUSTICE? When all the civilized nations of the earth shall have abolished the African slave trade, the judge thinks that captured Africans would be considered free, unless proved to be slaves: and if Spain and Portugal should abolish the slave trade, he thinks the burden of proof that Negroes captured in their vessels were slaves, would rest upon their captors. In that case, the Court would respect the rights of Africans as much as those of any other class of persons; but, until then, how could the Court be permitted to examine into treaty stipulations of Spain, or into any restriction imposed by Spain upon the traffic of her subjects in slaves ?

Such was the reasoning of a slave–holding judge upon slavery and the slave trade, and by such reasoning did he' out of two hundred and twelve Africans, forfeit to the United States, to receive from them the blessing of freedom, and restoration to their native country reduce the number who should enjoy that privilege to seven individuals, consigning all the rest to perpetual, hopeless Spanish and Portuguese slavery!—Seven freemen to two hundred and five slaves!

The appeal from these decrees to the Circuit Court of the United States came up before Judge William Johnson, in May, 1821. His opinions differed toto coelo from those of the District judge. He increased the number of the Africans to be liberated, as survivors of the twenty–five taken from the American vessels, from seven to sixteen: he rejected the incredible testimony of the pirate, John Smith, that while the mortality of the whole cargo of Negroes had averaged not more than one in three, the number of deaths among those taken from the American vessel had amounted to two–thirds of the whole. He reversed the decree of the District judge, which had allotted one hundred and forty–two Negroes to the Portuguese Vice Consul; and reserved his claim for further proof, which never was produced. He reduced the allowance of salvage to Captain Jackson, and the crew of the revenue cutter, to fifty dollars a head for the Negroes to be delivered to the Spanish Vice Consul, and expressed a strong doubt whether it was a case for salvage at all. He intimated, very significantly, an opinion, that if a claim had been interposed by an agent of Venezuela, or of the Oriental Republic, the capture of the Antelope, by Captain Jackson, must have been pronounced illegal—a mere marine trespass—punishable in damages rather than rewardable for salvage; and yet he allowed him a salvage of fifty dollars a head for the Negroes surrendered to the Spanish Vice Consul. He concurred, however in the most exceptionable of all the opinions of the District judge; namely, that because John Smith had no forfeitable interest in the Antelope and in the Negroes, originally belonging to Spanish owners, but then in his possession, and which he was when captured, in the act of smuggling into the United States; therefore they were not forfeited at all, and must be delivered up to the Spanish Vice Consul. The judge of the Circuit Court, sitting alone, after stating the circumstances of the capture by Captain Jackson, and the claims of the respective parties, promptly and without hesitation pronounces, that John Smith was taken in the act of violating the laws of the United States for the suppression of the slave trade; and that, " if the case rested here there would be no difficulty in adjudging the vessel forfeited, for taking these Africans on board at sea, with intent to dispose of them as slaves. But this, although perhaps literally within the provisions of the statute, is obviously not within the intent and meaning." Why perhaps, literally within the provisions of the statute? No reader of the English language can read the provisions of the statute and entertain a doubt that they extend literally to the case—why not within its intent and meaning? Never was an obiter dictum of a judge more peremptory or more gratuitous! There is not a word, not a letter in the statute to authorize the intention of shielding from forfeiture a slave trading smuggler, because the captain was not her owner. The forfeiture attaches to the action, the violation of the laws against the slave trade, and to the instrument used for that violation, without inquiring to whom that instrument belongs. The mischief to be remedied by the law, was the introduction of African slaves into the United States.—The vessel is the instrument with which the violation of the law was effected, and by which the forfeiture was incurred. Neither justice nor policy could require an exemption from the forfeiture, because the captain in possession of the vessel and employing her in violation of the law, was not her lawful owner. The judge says, there are reiterated decisions of the American courts, that a capture made under an illegal American outfit is not belligerent, but void, and producing no change of right; and from this it followers, that Smith had no interest on which the forfeiture inflicted by law for this offense could attach. The judge names no one of these reiterated decisions, and we have seen that the only one specifically cited by the District judge, in support of the same principle, was a clear authority against it. There were no doubt decisions that captures of friendly foreign vessels, by American privateers illegally fitted out in our ports) and bearing South American commissions, did not so divest the property, but that it might be restored by our courts, in controversy between the captors and the original owners—but that the laws of the United States, prescribing penalties of forfeiture for crimes, should be violated with impunity, because the slave smuggler had stolen the instrument with which he committed the crime! No! I trust the Antelope is, and will for ever remain, the solitary case in which such a principle can claim the sanction of the courts of the United States!

The wild and glaring inconsistency not only between the opinions and decrees of the District and Circuit Courts of the United States, in the case of the Antelope, but between the opinions and decrees of each of those Courts and itself discloses in crystal transparency an internal conflict of mind between the duty of suppressing the African

Amistad Argument

slave trade, and the desire to maintain and fortify the institution of slavery, little auspicious to the composure of justice or to the impartial exercise of the judicial faculty. Both the Judges profess a sentimental abhorrence of the trade. The Circuit Judge discusses at great length the question whether the slave trade is contrary to the Law of Nations. He admits that the British Court of Admiralty have of latter years asserted a doctrine of this nature; but after commenting sarcastically upon the motive of the British Judges and Government, and descanting upon mental dependence, and interference with the family concerns of others, in which no nation has a right to volunteer, he quotes a passage from the decision of the British Court in the case of the Amedee [Actor, 240,] and says, "I must until better advised assume an opposite language."

" I feel," says he, " no inclination to justify or even palliate the trade. I thank God I have lived to see its death−blow. But it was from religion or policy, not from national humanity, that the blow was received. On the contrary, British policy struggled against the effort to abolish it, and all the efforts of the Quakers, the Methodists and Mr. Wilberforce proved abortive until the horrors acted in St. Domingo opened the eyes of Government to consequences that it became political to guard against. From that time, philanthropy like the pent up vapor, began freely to diffuse itself, and extended its spread even to the British Court of Admiralty."

"That slavery, (says again the Judge of the Circuit Court,) is a national evil no one will deny except him [he] who would maintain that national wealth is the supreme national good. But what" ever it be, it was entailed upon us by our ancestors, and actually provided for in the constitution first received from the Lords Proprietors under which the southern colonies were planted. During the Royal government it was fostered as the means of improving the colonies, and affording a lucrative trade to the mother country, and however revolting to humanity, may be the reflection, the laws of any country on the subject of the slave trade are nothing more in the eyes of any other nation than a class of the trade laws of the nation that enacts them.',

Both the Judges acknowledge the inherent, inextinguishable wickedness of the trade, and both have an invincible repugnance to consider it contrary to the laws of nations. The Judge of the District Court admits that the doctrine that Africans taken at sea must be presumed to be free, until proved to be slaves, may be correct in England, but cannot entirely recognize it in the State of Georgia. The Judge of the Circuit Court, repudiates it altogether—says he must until better advised hold opposite language— assails with great

Amistad Argument

bitterness the decision of Sir William Grant in the case of the Amedee: thanks God that he has lived to see the death blow of the African slave trade; but allows no credit to Great Britain on the score of humanity for striking it. No! it was religion or policy. The horrors of the scenes in St. Domingo had alarmed the British Government for the safety of their West Indian colonies, and so the pent up vapor of philanthropy was let loose and extended even to the British Courts of Vice Admiralty. As for slavery, every one knows it an evil, but it was entailed upon us by our ancestors; it was provided for by the constitution granted by the Lords Proprietors; it was encouraged from motives of policy by the Royal Government, and what right has any one to question our practice of it now? It was once lawful— who shall say it shall not be lawful forever ?

Upon the tone of this judicial argumentation I shall not indulge myself in commenting; but in comparing the spirit of the reasoning of these two judges with that of Sir William Grant in the decision which they reject and oppose, how stands the account of moral principle ? The reasons of the British Judge glow with the flame of human liberty, those of the American Judges are wedged in thrilling regions of thick ribbed ice. Vituperation of the slave trade in words, with a broad shield of protection carefully extended over it in deeds. Slavery acknowledged an evil, and the inveteracy of its abuse urged as an unanswerable argument for its perpetuity: the best of actions imputed to the worst of motives, and a bluster of mental energy to shelter a national crime behind a barrier of national independence; these are the characteristics exhibited by American in collision with British Admiralty Courts. Or again, examine the respective opinions and decrees in their beating upon the trade itself: those of the British Court went directly to its suppress sign; those of the American Courts, to its encouragement, security and promotion. The British Court has at least the consistency of harmonizing practice and profession. The American Courts profess humanity and practice oppression.

The decrees of the American Circuit Court are if possible more extraordinary than its opinions. After deciding that the Negroes taken by the Arraganta in the Antelope, and from the Portuguese vessels shall be delivered to the Spanish and Portuguese Vice Consuls, because he must maintain that it is A question altogether inter altos, whether the Spanish and Portuguse nations had authorized the traffic in which their vessels were engaged, the Judge adds: " Not so as to the American vessel. I have a law to direct me as to that, and the slaves taken out of her must be liberated." The laws had literally directed that all the Negroes whom John Smith had attempted to smuggle into the United States for sale, should be liberated, but the Judge had pronounced that this was not its intent and

99

meaning. But now another difficulty occurs. No competent witness can tell which of the surviving Negroes were taken from the American vessels, which from the Portuguese vessels, and which from the Antelope. The individuals belonging to each of the three vessels cannot be identified. How shall he distribute his doom of freedom and of slavery among the prize goods and the pirated merchandise of John Smith? With a full consciousness of the gross and glaring injustice of the decree he says, THE LOT MOST DECIDE ! Where did he get his law for that? He says he has a law to direct him, and he flies in the face of that law to enslave hundreds and emancipate sixteen human beings on the cast of a die. Let me do no wrong to his words—hear them.

" I would that it were in my power to do perfect justice in their behalf. BUT THIS IS HOW IMPOSSIBLE. I can decree freedom to a certain number, but I may decree that to A, which is the legal right of B. It is impossible to identify the individuals who were taken from the American vessel, and yet it is not less certain that the benefit of this decree is their right end theirs alone. Poor would be the consolation to them to know that because we could not identify them we had given away their freedom to others.— Yet shall we refuse to act because not gifted with the power of divination? We can only do the best in our power. The lot must decide their fate, and the Almighty will direct the hand that acts in the selection. But I cannot consent to reduce this number from twenty–five to nine, [to seven,] for this depends upon testimony that was interested to deceive, since in those twenty–fire, Smith could have no hope to sustain his claims though he might succeed as to the residue. The reduction of the number must therefore be averaged upon a scale with the rest, and as they consisted of twenty–three men and two boys, the lot must select them accordingly from the men and boys.

" Some doubts have been stated as to the national character of the vessel and as to the Spanish and Portuguese interest in the slaves. On the vessel I entertain no doubt. She was captured as Spanish, and the evidence is sufficient to prove the Spanish interest in her—and the slaves taken on board of her, must necessarily follow her fate. But I am induced to think that the evidence preponderates to prove that there were but ninety–three, and, that number must also be reduced by the general scale of loss. Concerning the residue, the evidence appears so conclusive, that reluctant as I feel to keep the case open I cannot adjudge them to the Portuguese Consul, without further proof."

Amistad Argument

In examining the claim of Capt. Jackson to salvage, the judge becomes exceedingly doubtful whether it is a case for salvage at all, and enters a caveat against his own decree for allowing it. He thinks if a Venezuelan agent had interposed a claim to the property as prize of war, he should have been still more puzzled how to shape his decree than he was. He does not appear to be at all aware that if a Venezuelan agent could have claimed the property as prize of war there could have been no Spanish claimant to whom it could hare been restored. The decree of restoration to Spanish owners was therefore ipso facto equivalent to a decree for salvage, the quantum of which alone remained for consideration. His caveat against his allowance for salvage, was therefore a caveat against his whole decree, and thus far was an approach to the definition of justice—Jus suum cuique.

The decrees of the Circuit Court (for there were two) like the state of mind disclosed by these opinions of the judge, were a chaos of confusion. By the first, delivered on the 11th of May, 1803, the Decree of the District Court, so far as related to the vessel, the Antelope, was affirmed, and so far as related to the slaves imported in her was reversed and annulled. The District Court had decreed the restoration of the Antelope to the Spanish claimants, on the ground that she had not been forfeited to the United States, for the violation of the laws for the suppression of the slave trade. She had not been forfeited, though taken by Captain Jackson in the act of smuggling into the United States for sale near three hundred Africans, and though the law literally declares all Africans thus imported free, and the vessel in which they are imported forfeited to the United States. From this forfeiture the Decree of the District Court, exempted the Antelope, because before the commission of this smuggling piracy she had been taken by another act of piracy, from certain virtuous Spanish slave traders, whose property in her, and consequently in the slaves with which she was laden, was too sacred to be divested either by piratical capture or by the laws of the United States against the importation of slaves, or against the African slave trade. With this part of the Decree of the District Court, the judge of the Circuit Court concurs. The laws of the United States for the suppression of the execrable slave trade, and against the importation of African slaves are baffled, defeated, prostrated, nullified— three hundred wretched victims of that trade, are deprived of the benefit of that just and generous provision that the very act of importing them shall operate in their favor as an act of emancipation. They are re- consigned to hopeless and perpetual slavery, from mere reverence for the property of Spanish slave traders! Well might such a decision divide the opinions of the judges of the Supreme tribunal when it came up to them for adjudication. Well might Chief Justice Marshall

101

declare that upon this point no principle was settled, and well may every friend of human liberty, and every sincere wishes for the suppression of that detested traffic indignantly deny that the case of the Antelope can ever be cited as authority for any such principle of law.

But as the Circuit Court, reversed and annulled every part of the decree of the District Court for the disposal and distribution of the slaves, so the final decree of the Supreme Court passed the same sweeping sentence of reversal, upon all the dispositions of the Circuit Court, not excepting that reliance upon an Almighty hand to direct that designation by lot, which was to give to one man what was the right of another, and to emancipate a slave as an equivalent for enslaving a freeman.

The judge of the Circuit Court at first decreed the manner, in which the sixteen freemen should be drawn by lot from the whole surviving cargo of the Antelope, as taken by Captain Jackson. He allowed a certain average portion of the survivors of 93 to the whole number j to be delivered to the Spanish Vice Consul, together with the proceeds of the vessels, and with suitable deductions for the salvage, forthwith—and he reserved for further consideration, and further evidence, till the next term of the court, the final distribution of the residue of the slaves between the Spanish and Portuguese Vice Consuls.

On the 16th of July, 1821, the designation was accordingly made by lot of the sixteen persons drawn from 204, and delivered to the marshal of the United States to abide the order of the court—that is, for emancipation. It does not appear that the Spanish Vice Consul received those which had been provisionally assigned to him. On the 27th day of December, 1821, the judge of the Circuit Court held, together with Jeremiah Cuyler, the newly appointed judge of the District Court in the place of William Davis deceased, a special court, at which the case was argued, and further evidence filed—and on the next day, the court " Ordered and decreed, that the residue of the Negroes imported in the General Ramirez [Antelope] be divided between the Spanish and Portuguese claimants in the ratio of one hundred and sixty–six on be half of the Spanish claimants, and one hundred and thirty on behalf of the Portuguese claimants, and that they be delivered up to the agents of the individuals as soon as their respective powers of attorney shall be duly authenticated and filed with the clerk of this court; and they shall respectively comply with the Decorated Order of this court, in paying the expenses incurred on said Negroes in the ratio above stated, and in giving bond and security as therein directed for

Amistad Argument

transporting them beyond the limits of the United States to some permitted port, allowing however six months from the date of the bond instead of three months as in that decretal order aforesaid' and that the proceed sales of the vessel, after deducting the costs of court, exclusive of marshal's bills for maintenance, be paid over to the Spanish claimants."

On the 2d of January, 1822, the District Attorney of the United States, appealed in their behalf to the Supreme Court of the United States from so much of the said decree, of the said Circuit Court as decreed the said African Negroes to the Portuguese Vice Consul.

And thus, in February, 1822, the case of the Antelope, and her cargo, came up for adjudication of the Supreme Court of the United States, the result of which is reported in the 10th, 11th, and 12th volumes of Wheaton's Reports.

Three long years passed away before the first judgment of the court in the case was pronounced. Nearly two years before had elapsed from the capture of the Antelope by Captain Jackson. For little short of the space of five years, nearly three hundred captured Africans had been kept as prisoners of the United States, and to abide the decision of their tribunals for the enjoyment of their inalienable right to liberty. What had they been doing, during this long captivity? They had been maintained at the cost of the United States, we shall see hereafter to what tune. While the slow, solemn and majestic march of the law was progressing in the search " for the legal standard of morality" to fix the destiny of these human victims, time and chance had disposed of them more mercifully than the decrees of the District or of the Circuit Court. The marshal had bound most of them out to labor in the sweat of their brows, at the erection of fortifications, for the defense of the LIBERTIES of this, our beloved country. The judges who passed upon the fate of these their fellow men—the wives—the children—the property the neighbors—the country, of those judges were armed in panoply against foreign aggression by the daily labor of these stolen Africans, whose lives, and liberty American judges were committing by the legal standard of morality to the cast of a die. During those five years it may be well conjectured that the condition of those captives of the Antelope thus employed was less rigorous and afflicted than it was made by the lottery judgment of the court.

The judgment of the Supreme Court in 1825, reversed this lottery judgment of the Circuit Court. It reversed the whole allotment of one hundred and thirty to the Portuguese Vice Consul, and awarded to them the blessing of liberty intended for them by the law, and yet

103

so harshly denied them by the decrees of the courts below. It reduced the number to be delivered to the Spanish claimants from a ratio of 166 to 93 to the whole number, and vigorously exacted proof to the satisfaction of the Circuit Court of the identity of every individual to be delivered up, as having been of the number taken by the Arraganta in the Antelope. The allowances of salvage and of gratuity to Captain Jackson and the crew of the Revenue Cutter were confirmed. One step further and the case of the Antelope would have conferred unfading glory on the Supreme Court. One step more and the heartless sophistry would have beep silenced, and the cold blooded apathy to human suffering would have been stung into sensibility, which delivered up to Spanish slave traders, a vessel, forfeited by the just severity, and thirty–nine Africans emancipated by the benignly, of the laws of this Union for the suppression of the African slave trade.

That step was not taken; there lacked one voice in a divided court to reverse the whole of that decree of the Circuit Court of which so many parts were annulled. One obnoxious principle was left to have its sway in that particular case, because there wanted a casting vote to reverse it—but Chief Justice Marshall himself, in announcing the affimation of the sentence on this point of the Circuit Court, guarded against any and every future attempt to allege it as an authority by explicitly declaring that in this judgment of the court NO PRINCIPLE WAS SETTLED.

The opinion delivered by him on this first decision of the case in the Supreme Court, must be considered as that of the Chief Justice himself. It is in a tone entirely different from that in which the judges of the lower courts had indulged themselves. It contains no angry invective, no sneering sarcasm, no direct defiance, on the motives of the British government, and the solicitude of the British tribunals, for the suppression of the slave trade. It states with a sincere and painful effort of impartiality the reasons for and against the principle that the trade is contrary to the laws of nations. It admits and emphatically declares it contrary to the laws of nature. It cites and analyzes the general decisions upon the same point in the British Courts of Admiralty, and examines them with freedom, but without asperity. The Chief Justice says that as no principle was settled by the affirmance of the decree of the Circuit Court, the judges had concluded not to assign their respective reasons for their conflicting opinions; but was to him was assigned the duty of pronouncing the decree of the court, his argumemt was necessarily on the side of that division which sustained the decree of the Circuit Court, and consequently there is no coumteracting opinion upon the records to balance it. But it almost balances itself. The argument with much hesitation concludes that the African slave trade is not contrary to the Law of Nations —but it begins with admitting, also with hesitation, that it is contrary to the law of nature. He says—" That it is contrary to the law of nature will scarcely be denied. That every man has a natural right to the fruits of his own labor, is generally admitted; and that no other person can rightfully deprive him of those fruits, and appropriate them against his will seems to be the necessary result of this admission.

" Seems, Madam—Nay it is—I know not seems."

Surely never was this exclamation more suitable than on this occasion; but the cautious and wary manner of stating the moral principle, proclaimed in the Declaration of Independence, as self–evident truth, is because the argument is obliged to encounter it with matter of fact. To the moral principle the Chief Justice opposes general usage—fact against right. " From the earliest times war has existed, and war confers rights in which all have acquiesced. Among the most enlightened nations of antiquity, one of these was, that the victor might enslave the vanquished——

"Slavery, then, has its origin in force; but as the world has agreed that it is a legitimate result of force, the state of things which is thus produced by general consent cannot be pronounced unlawful.

" Throughout Christendom, this harsh rule has been exploded, and war is no longer considered as giving a right to enslave cap. tires. But this triumph of humanity has not been universal The parties to the modern law of nations do not propagate their principles by force; and Africa has not yet adopted them. Throughout the whole extent of that immense continent, so far as we know its history, it is still the law of nations that prisoners are slaves. Can those who hare themselves renounced this law, be permitted to participate in its effects, by purchasing the beings who are its victims ?

"Whatever might be the answer of a moralist to this question, a jurist must search for its legal solution in those principles of action which are sanctioned by the usages, the national acts, and the general assent, of that portion of the world of which he con. eiders himself a part, and to whose law the appeal is made. If we resort to this standard as the test of international law, the question as has already been observed, is decided in favor of the legality of the trade. Both Europe and America embarked in it; and for nearly two centuries, it –was carried on without opposition and without censure."

Amistad Argument

With all possible reverence for the memory of Chief Justice Marshall, and with all due respect for his argument in this case, I must here be permitted to say, that here begins its fallacy. He admits that throughout all Christendom, the victors in war have no right to enslave the vanquished. As between Christian nations therefore, slavery as a legitimate consequence of war is totally abolished. So totally abolished that slaves captured in war, cannot be held by the captors, as slaves; but must be emancipated, or exchanged as prisoners of war.

But Africa, says the Chief Justice, still enslaves her captives in war, and for nearly two centuries, Europe and America purchased African slaves without " opposition and without censure." This may prove that the African slave–trade was heretofore, not contrary to the international law of Europe and of Christendom. But how was it, when the Antelope was in judgment before Christian Admiralty Courts in 1820—01, and '25? How is it now?

For nearly forty years it has been prohibited by the laws of the United States, as a crime of enormous magnitude—and when the Antelope was tried by their judicial Courts, it was proclaimed piracy, punishable with death—

It was piracy by the laws of Great Britain.

By the 10th Article of the Treaty of Ghent, concluded on the 84th of December, 1814, between Great Britain and the United States, the traffic in slaves had been declared irreconcilable with the principles of humanity and justice, and both parties did there by stipulate and contract to use their best endeavors to promote Its entire abolition.

On the 8th of February, 1815, the Ambassadors at the Congress of Vienna, from Austria, France, Great Britain, Portugal, Prussia, Russia, and Sweden, had issued a Declaration, " in the face of Europe, that considering the universal abolition of the slave–trade as n measure worthy of their attention, conformable to the spirit of the times, and to the generous principles of their august Sovereigns, they are animated with the sincere desire of concurring in the most prompt and effectual execution of this measure, by all the means at their disposal, and of acting in the employment of those means with all the zeal and perseverance which is due to so noble a cause." And again,

Amistad Argument

" In communicating this Declaration to the knowledge of Europe, and of all civilized countries, the said plenipotentiaries hope to prevail on every other Government, and particularly on those which in abolishing the slave–trade have already manifested the same sentiments, to give them their support in a cause, the final triumph of which will be one of the noblest monuments of the age which embraced it, and which shall have brought it to a glorious termination."

On the 20th of May, 1814, Louis the 18th, on his first restoration, had stipulated by treaty with Great Britain, to unite all his efforts with hers, at this then approaching Congress of Vienna, to induce all the Powers of Christendom to decree the abolition of the slave–trade, so that the said trade should cease, universally, as it should cease definitely, under any circumstances, on the part of France, within five years.

Within one year from that time, the Emperor Napoleon, on the 29th of March, 1815, upon his return from Elba, within the hundred days of his authority, decreed the immediate and total abolition of the slave–trade on the part of France—which decree Louis the 18th, upon his second restoration, repeated and confirmed—and on the 20th of November, 1815, a Treaty, of which the following was one of the Articles, was concluded between Great Britain and France.

" The high contracting powers, sincerely desiring to give effect to the measures on which they deliberated at the Congress of Vienna, relative to the complete and universal abolition of the slave–trade, and having each in their respective dominions, prohibited without restriction, their colonies and subjects from taking any part whatever in this traffic, engage to renew conjointly their efforts, with the view of securing signal success to those principles, which they proclaimed in the Declaration of the 8th of February, 1815, and of concerning without loss of time, through their ministers at the Courts of London and of Paris, the most effectual measures for the active and definitive abolition of a commerce so odious and so strongly condemned by the laws of religion and of nature."

Spain had not been a party to the Declaration of the Allied Powers, at the Congress of Vienna, of 8th of February, 1815—but in a treaty with Great Britain, concluded on the 20th of August, 1814, his Catholic Majesty, concurring in the fullest manner in the sentiments of his Britannic Majesty with respect to the injustice and inhumanity of the traffic in slaves, stipulated that he would take into consideration with the deliberation which the state of his possessions in America demanded, the means of acting in conformity with those sentiments.

And on the 23d of September, 1817, by a treaty concluded between the same two powers, his Catholic Majesty engaged, that the slave–trade should be abolished throughout the entire dominions of Spain, on the 30th day of May, 1820; and that from and after that period, it shall not be lawful for any of the subjects of the crown of Spain, to purchase slaves, or to carry on the slave trade, on any parts of the coast of Africa, upon any pretext, or in any manner whatever; provided, however, that a term of five months from the said date of the 30th of May, 1820, should be allowed for completing the voyages of vessels cleared out lawfully, previously to the said 30th of May.

A decree of the King of Spain, of December, 1817, conformable to the above treaty–stipulation, prohibited all Spanish subjects from engaging in the African slave–trade, from and after the 30th of May, 1820.

The case of the Antelope first came before the District Court of the United States for adjudication, on the 27th of July, 1820. At that time the African slave–trade was forbidden to all Spanish subjects throughout the world, by a decree issued nearly three years before. But the Antelope had been fitted out at the Havana, upon her slave—trading expedition, and had even been captured by the Arraganta, before the 20th of May, 1820, and consequently before the legal prohibition had taken effect. The capture of her by the Arraganta had been made, not for breach of laws against the slave– trade, but as prize of war under a commission from the Oriental Republic. It was her captor who had incurred her forfeiture, and the liberation of the Africans taken in her by the violation of the laws of the United States against the slave–trade—not by purchasing or shipping the Negroes in Africa, but for importing them into the United States contrary to law.— To the question of that forfeiture, that of the original property of the vessel and cargo was altogether foreign. That was res inter alios, with which the Courts of the United States had nothing to do. The smuggler was a citizen of the United States. He had proprietary possession of the vessel and of the Negroes, which he was smuggling in to be sold as slaves. It was the identical offense against which the laws of Congress had provided, and the Negroes had by those laws, and by the violation of them committed by John Smith, acquired a right to freedom, infinitely more sacred, one would have thought, in an American Court of Justice, than the property in and to them, of the Spanish slave–traders who had kidnapped or bought them in Africa, and had not yet consummated their property by bringing them within the exclusive jurisdiction of Spain.

Amistad Argument

All the Courts of the United States did however think proper to go back to the proprietary right of the Spanish slave-trader; and two of them to sanctify that at the expense of the freedom of the captives, and of the vital spirit of the laws of the Union for the suppression of the African slave trade. This sacrifice was made, by the District and Circuit Courts of the United States, in Georgia. It was never sanctioned by the Supreme Court of the Union. On this single point, the judgment of the Circuit Court, was saved from reversal, by a divided Court; but on all the collateral points the decisions of both the lower Courts were reversed, and on the single point of the Circuit Court, affirmed: the Chief Justice in affirming it gave explicit and emphatic warning, that no principle was settled.

In all the three courts, the restoration of the Antelope, and of the Africans captured by the Arraganta on board of her to the Spanish claimants, was explicitly decreed on the fact that at the time of her expedition from the Havana, and of her capture by the Arraganta the prohibition of the slave trade by the King of Spain had not yet taken effect. All the courts agreed that if the case had occurred after the abolition of the trade by Spain, the judgment would have been cliff renu That is, it must and would have been the emancipation and the restoration to their native country as freemen, of every individual African captured by Captain Jackson in the Antelope.

With what color of reason then was the case of the Antelope made the corner stone of the Attorney General's report to the President of the United States, that the captives of the Amistad should be, by mere Executive warrant, delivered up in a mass, untold and unidentified, to the Spanish minister. Whatever there was or could be of authority in the case of the Antelope led directly to the opposite conclusion. The Supreme Court had toppled down headlong the decree of the Circuit Court for the distribution of the victims between the Spanish and Portuguese Vice Consuls by lot. They had scattered to the winds this gambling of human bones, this cross and pile distribution of justice between liberty and bondage. They had rescued from the grasp of the overseer all the prisoners taken from the vessels bearing Portuguese colors, they had exacted proof of the number and identification of the individuals, to be given up to the Vice Consul of Spain. They had allowed salvage for them to captain Jack. son, to be deducted from their estimated value; and from two hundred and ninety-six adjudicated by the courts below, to perpetual slavery, they had reduced the number to an estimate which could not exceed thirty-nine. The only principle to which half the court adhered, and thereby left the decree of the Circuit Court unreversed was, that the Spanish prohibition of the slave trade had not

109

quickened into life quite in time to save these thirty—nine unfortunates from the clutches of their oppressors.

Apply these principles to the case of the Amistad captives. They had been imported into the Havana in open and undisguised defiance of the Spanish prohibition of the slave trade enacted nearly twenty years before; but connived at by the Spanish authorities in Cuba for gold—for a doubloon a head. They had been shipped coast—wise, in continuance and for consummation of the slave—trading voyage from Africa. They had been clandestinely transferred to Ruiz and Montes, who were furnished with printed pretended passports, false and fraudulent upon their face, and these were the only title to property they could show. The captives of the Amistad were, when taken by Lieut. Gedney, not even in the condition of slaves; they were freemen, in possession not only of themselves, but of the vessel with which they were navigating the common property and jurisdiction of all nations, the Ocean: in possession of the cargo of the vessel, and of the Spaniards Ruiz and Montes themselves. Lieut. Gedney seized them as charged with the crimes of piracy and murder. The captives of the Antelope were taken by Captain Jackson in the condition of slaves. The courts of the United States were not called on to change their condition. The courts of the United must have enslaved the captives of the Amistad before they could restore them to their pretended masters.

The decision of the courts of the United States against the captives of the Antelope were all apologetic. They leaned almost entirely upon a decision of Sir William Scott in the case of the Louis, apparently if not really conflicting with that of Sir William Grant in the case of the Amedee. It is apparent that the Admiralty Courts of Great Britain have been divided on the question not less than those of the United States. Sir William Scott, who, during the war of the French Revolution, had been the main pillar of belligerent rights and arbitrary searches and visitations of neutral vessels, after the peace and the agitation of the slavery question among all the nations of Europe, took a very different lurch, and became the most fervent champion of the slave trade and of the unqualified exemption of all merchant vessels from visitation or search by the armed ships of every nation other than their own. In the case of the slave Grace, he decided that a West Indian female slave following her mistress to England, and emancipated by mere contact with English soil, became re—enslaved by returning to the West Indian Islands,—a decision the reverse of which has been repeatedly decided in one of the principal slave states of this Union. In the case of the Louis he laid it down in most unqualified terms, which Chief Justice Marshall in the case of the Antelope repeats with seeming approbation, that the right of

Amistad Argument

search is confined to a state of war. That it is a right strictly belligerent in its character, which can never be exercised by a nation at peace, except against professed pirates, who are the enemies of the human race: a position which, if true, would at once decide that both the capture of the Antelope by Captain Jackson, and of the Amistad by Lieut. Gedney, were unlawful and unjustifiable. I must pause before I assent to the doctrine to that extent.

In the same case of the Louis, Sir William Scott travels out of his record, to start a hypothetical objection to the universality of this exemption of foreign vessels from visitation and search. " It is pressed as a difficulty," says the Judge, " what is to be done, if a French ship laden with slaves is brought in ? I answer without hesitation, restore the possession which has been unlawfully divested: rescind the illegal act done by your own subject, and leave the foreigner to the justice of his own country."

Chief Justice Marshall, in the case of the Antelope, cites also this passage of the decision of Sir William Scott; but besides that it is a mere obiter dictum upon an imaginary case not before the court, it is assuredly not law within these United States. By the act of Congress of 2d of March, 1799, to regulate the collection of duties, [section 99. U. S. Laws 3, 226,] " the officers of the revenue cutters are authorized, required and directed to go on board all ships or vessels which shall arrive within the United States, or within four leagues of the coast thereof if bound for the United States, and to search and examine the same, and every part thereof," for the purposes of revenue.

By the act of 2d of March, 1807, to prohibit the importation of slaves into the United States, [section 7, U. S. Laws 2, 96,] it is provided that " if any ship or vessel shall be found, from and after the first day of January, 1808, in any river, port, bay, or harbor, or on the high seas, within the jurisdictional limits of the United States, or hovering on the coast thereof, having on board any Negro, mulato, or person of color, for the purpose of selling them as slaves, or with intent to land the same in any port or place within the jurisdiction of the United States, contrary to the prohibition of this act, every such ship or vessel, together with her tackle, apparel and furniture, and the goods or effects which shall be found on board the same, shall be forfeited to the use of the United States, and may be seized, prosecuted and condemned in any court of the United States having jurisdiction thereof. And it shall be lawful for the President of the United States, and he is hereby authorized, should he deem it expedient, to cause any of the armed vessels of the United States, to be manned and employed to cruise on any part of the coast of the United

States or territories thereof, where he may judge attempts will be made to violate the provisions of this act, and to instruct and direct the commanders of armed vessels of the United States, to seize, take, and bring into any port of the United States all such ships or vessels, and moreover to seize, take and bring into any port of the United States, all ships or vessels of the United States wheresoever found on the high seas, contravening the provisions of this act, to be proceeded against according to law,"

Here then are two very extensive limitations, by the laws of the United States, upon the doctrines of Sir William Scott, pronounced in the case of the Louis. These limitations embrace both the cases of the Antelope and of the Amistad. Yet in the case of the Antelope, Chief Justice Marshall cites the opinions of Sir William Scott in the case of the Louis, without any notice whatever of the statute laws of the United States contradictory to those opinions, and the Attorney General Grundy cites, in the case of the Amistad, the opinions of Chief Justice Marshall in that of the Antelope, as authority for a principle which in that very opinion the Chief justice declares not settled.

The truth is, that the opinions of Sir William Scott in the case of the Louis, have reference only to the slave trade, and the shipment of slaves on the coast of Africa: the case of the Antelope was for the violation of the laws of the United States against the importation of slaves into the United States for sale. In all these cases the right of visitation and search of foreign vessels is not a merely belligerent right; it is exercised at all times, in peace or war, and if a French ship laden with slaves were found hovering on the coast of the United States, or within at least four leagues of their shores, and brought in, neither would the possession be unlawfully divested, nor would the foreigner be left to the justice of his own country. There is no act of Parliament against the importation of slaves into England for sale: the opinions of Sir William Scott look to no such case, for no such crime could then be committed. They had no application therefore to the case of the Antelope, and were very erroneously cited as warranting the surrender of that vessel and her cargo of Africans to the Spanish claimants.

I have said that the decisions of all the courts of the United States in that case directing that surrender, are apologetic. They admit that the traffic in slaves is contrary to the law of nature; that it is inhuman, cruel, odious, detestable; but that it is not contrary to the law of nations, and therefore must be acknowledged, defended, protected and carried into execution for other nations by the Courts of the United States, although as abhorrent to our laws as to the laws of nature. For this distinction also, our courts are indebted to Sir

Amistad Argument

William Scott, whose ingenuity in that same case of the Louis, lays down the following position, cited also approvingly, by Chief Justice Marshall, in his opinion upon the case of the Antelope.

"A court," says the British Judge, " in the administration of law, cannot attribute criminality to an act where the law imputes none. It must look to the legal standard of morality; and upon a question of this nature, that standard must be found in the law of nations, as fixed and evidenced by general and ancient and admitted practice, by treaties, and by the general tenor of the laws and ordinances, and the formal transactions of civilized states: and looking to these authorities, he found a difficulty in maintaining that the transaction was legally criminal."

In the Declaration of Independence the Laws of Nature are announced and appealed to as identical with the laws of nature's God, and as the foundation of all obligatory human laws. But here Sir William Scott proclaims a legal standard of morality, differing from, opposed to, and transcending the standard of nature and of nature's God. This legal standard of morality must, he says, in the administration of law, be held, by a Court, to supersede the laws of God, and justify, before the tribunals of man, the most atrocious of crimes in the eyes of God. With such a principle it is not surprising that Sir William Scott should have found a difficulty in maintaining that the African slave trade was legally criminal, nor that one half the Supreme Court of the United States should have adopted his conclusions. It is consolatory to the friends of human virtue and of human freedom to know, that this error of the first concoction, in the moral principle of a British judge, has been, so far as relates to the African slave trade, laid prostrate by the moral sense of his own country, which has overcome the difficulty of finding the slave trade criminal, by the legal and national abolition of slavery itself.

The decree of the Supreme Court, in 1825, " proceeding to give such decree as the Circuit Court ought to have given, did direct and order that the restitution to be made to the Spanish claimant should be according to the ratio which 93 (instead of 166) bears to the whole number, comprehending as well those originally on board the Antelope as those which were put on board that vessel by the captain of the Arraganta. After making the apportionment according to this ratio, and deducting from the number the rateable loss which must fall on the slaves, to which the Spanish claimants were originally entitled, the residue of the said 93 were to be delivered to the Spanish claimant, on the terms mentioned in the decree of the Circuit Court: and all the remaining Africans were to be delivered to the United States, to be disposed of according to law."

A mandate issued to the Circuit Court for the district of Georgia for the execution of this decree. One would suppose that the Supreme Court had sufficiently manifested its disapprobation of the mode of settling the question of freedom and slavery, by lot; and yet was their decree, on this point, not 80 explicit, but that one of the two judges of the Circuit Court believed that the selection between the Africans to be delivered to the Spanish claimants as slaves, and those claimed by the Portuguese Vice Consul, but whom the Supreme Court had declared free, might still be made by lot. The other judge understood better the spirit of the Supreme tribunal; and hence arose a dilberence of opinion between the two judges of the Circuit Court, which sent the case back for a second judgment of the appellate court. The second judgment of the Supreme Court, in the case of the Antelope, was rendered at their February term, 1826, and is reported (11 Wheaton, 413) as follows:—" Certificate.—A mandate having issued to the Circuit Court for the District of Georgia, to carry into execution the decree of this Court, pronounced at the February term, 1825, to deliver certain Africans, in the said decree mentioned, to the Spanish Consul for Spanish claimants; and the judges of that court having been divided in opinion respecting the mode of designating the said slaves to be delivered, and separating them from others to be delivered to the United States, whether the same should be made by lot, or upon proof on the part of the Spanish claimant, it is ordered to be certified to the said Circuit Court of Georgia, that, in executing the said mandate, the Africans to be delivered must be designated by proof made to the satisfaction of the Court."

To understand this difference of opinion, with regard to the mode of designating the Africans to be delivered up to the Spanish claimant and to slavery, it is to be remembered, that the libel of the Spanish Vice Consul before the District Court had claimed 150 of the Africans captured by Captain Jackson, and the libel of the Portuguese Vice Consul 130. That the decree of the District Court, founded on the report of the clerk, had awarded 142 of the 212 surviving Africans to the Portuguese, and 63 to the Spanish Vice Consul; while the subsequent decree of the Circuit Court, after a delay of one term and the admission of further evidence, had allotted in the ratio of 166 to the Spanish, and 130 to the Portuguese claimants. That is, deducting from the Spanish number the 16 persons drawn by lot and liberated, this decree gave to the Spanish and Portuguese Vice Consuls the ratio of the full number claimed by each of them in his respective libel. The Supreme Court, reversing this decree of the Circuit Court, had directed that the ratio of the whole number, to be delivered up to the Spanish Vice Consul should be reduced from

166 to 93; and that number was still to be reduced by the rateable loss, which the clerk of the District Court had reported to be 30. And all the rest, by the decree of the Supreme Court, were to be liberated. If, then, the Africans to be delivered to the Spanish Vice Consul had been drawn from the whole number by lot, he would have received 63; but the Supreme Court having, upon this second appeal, decreed that the Spanish claimant must identify by proof of having been taken by the Arraganta, in the Antelope, every individual, to be delivered up to him, explicitly rejected, for the second time, the lot, as a mode of ascertaining freemen among slaves, and actually diminished the number of victims delivered up to the Spaniard, from 63 to 39. And this was the number finally delivered up by the decree of the Supreme Court of the United States of the captives of the Antelope to the Spanish Vice Consul. But this was not the last decision of the Supreme Court in the case.

It was remanded to the Circuit Court, with directions to make a final disposition of the controversy between the parties pursuant to the principles of the decrees of 1825 and 1826. And now came up the question, to use a vulgar but significant phrase, Who should pay the piper ?

"The Circuit Court, [says the Report, 12 Wheaton, 547,] in order to enable it to decree finally in the case, directed the register to take and report an account of the costs, and also of the expenses of keeping, maintaining, of the Africans, by the marshal, and which account (amounting to upwards of thirty–six thousand dollars) was accordingly reported. Exceptions were filed to the report by both the Portuguese and Spanish claimants. The Circuit Court also caused proofs to be taken, for the purpose of identifying. individually the Africans to be delivered to the Spanish claimants, as directed by the decree of 1816.

Thus circumstanced, the case came on for final hearing before the Circuit Court. The Court decreed that the Portuguese claimant should not be made liable for costs, or any proportion of the expenses and charges of the marshal, for maintaining, the Africans: and being of opinion that 39 of the Africans were sufficiently identified, by proof, as being the property of the Spanish claimants, directed the 39 Africans, so identified, to be delivered to the Spanish claimants, upon their paying a proportion of the costs and expenses reported by the registrar, in the ratio of the number of Africans delivered to the whole number. And the Circuit Court was further of opinion, that the residue of the Africans not directed to be delivered to the Spanish claimants should be delivered to the United States, to be disposed of according to law: but on the question, whether they shall

115

be delivered absolutely, or on condition of payment of the balance of the expenses which will remain unsatisfied, after charging the Africans adjudged to the Spanish claimants in their due ratio, the Judges of the Circuit Court being divided in opinion, ordered this difference of opinion to be "certified to this Court."

The United States District Attorney appealed from so much of this final order of the Circuit Court as related to the apportionment among the several parties of the costs and expenses in the preservation, maintenance, and custody of the said Africans, and of the costs and expenses of the various proceedings had in relation to the said Africans; and also from so much of said order as decreed 39 of the said Africans to the Spanish claimants.

So extraordinary, so anti–judicial is every thing upon the records in this case of the Antelope, that the Supreme Court actually did not know what was the question upon which the judges of the Circuit Court were opposed in opinion—they supposed it was, whether the Africans not directed to be delivered to the Spanish claimants should be delivered by the marshal to the United States, absolutely and unconditionally, to be disposed of according to law, that is, to be liberated and sent home; or whether it should be imposed on the United States, as a condition precedent to their delivery, that the United States should pay to the marshal his claim for expenses, at the rate of sixteen cents a day for each African, (for several years) in the ratio of the number to be delivered to the United States.

This, it will be perceived, was still the question of freedom or slavery to the poor Africans. If the decree had been, that the payment of these expenses, amounting to about 350 dollars a head, was a condition precedent to their delivery to the United States, in the event of nonpayment, the marshal had a lien upon the Africans, and they would have been his slaves.

The mode of proof admitted by the Circuit Court to identify the individuals to be doomed to slavery and delivery to the Spanish claimants cannot commend itself to the sense of justice, of humanity, or of freedom. Fifty of them, employed upon the fortifications, had been selected by the marshal, and recognized by a man named Grondona, who had been second officer on board the Antelope when the slaves were purchased and shipped in Africa. Grondona had since disappeared, and was said to be dead; but there were witnesses in Court who had been present at the examination when Grondona recognized

116

thirty-four of the Negroes and they him, by speaking together, and by signs, though the witnesses knew no. thing of the language in which they spoke. Other witnesses testified to his having recognized five more. The Africans had no notice that their fate, as freemen or slaves, was to depend on this recognition. They had no one to defend them, and protest for them, against the manner of disposing of their free dom. The examination was in open court, but the only evidence furnished was testimony to individuals whom Grondona had recognized and who had recognized him. Hearsay evidence of one whose language the witnesses did not understand!

Yet the Supreme Court thought this evidence sufficient, under the very peculiar circumstances of this case, reasonably to satisfy the mind of the identity of thirty-nine of the Africans, as belonging to the Spanish claimants, and affirmed the decree of the Circuit Court for their delivery up to the Spanish Vice Consul.

Under the very peculiar circumstances of the case, in order to enslave 39 human beings, otherwise entitled to freedom, evidence was deemed sufficient, which, upon an ordinary question of property, of five dollars value, between man and man, would have been rejected as inadmissible.

The very peculiar circumstances of the case are quite as strongly masked, in the opinion of the judge of the Circuit Court, in December, 1826, as they had been in his preceding opinion, delivered in 1821. In apologizing for the enormous amount of the marshal's bill, allowed by the court, which he is aware must expose the court, and the administration of justice in the country, to certain imputations, he says, "What could the court do? The United States regard the subjects of this suit as men and not things. They could not be sold, and the money lodged fin the registry. They were then prisoners, and necessarily to be kept and treated as such." Had he judge allowed his reason to advance one step further, he would have seen, that precisely because they were men and not things, precisely because they could not be sold, precisely because they must be kept and treated, if at all, as prisoners they could not be restored entire as merchandize, nor therefore, come within the purview of the 9th article of our treaty with Spain.

" The next question," says the judge of the Circuit Court, " is, by whom these costs are to be paid? That the maintenance of the Africans was n legal charge on the United States, in the first instance, is perfectly clear. By the act of February 28, 1799, in forcing them into the hands of the marshal, the United States became bound for their subsistence."

117

Amistad Argument

The judge of the Circuit Court further affirms, that the Supreme Court, by its decree of 1825, and explanatory decree of 1826, established seven principles; the first of which, in his enumeration, is—" That the lay of nations recognized both slavery and the slave–trade."

But Chief Justice Marshall, in delivering the opinion and pronouncing the decree of the Supreme Court in 1825, declared that, on the question of the restitution to the Spanish claimant, which depended entirely upon the recognition of the slave–trade by the LAW of nations, " the Court is divided on it, and, consequently, NO PRINCIPLE IS SETTLED. '

The judge of the Circuit Court was, therefore, in manifest error when he said that the Supreme Court had, by the decrees of 1825 and 1826, established the principle, that the law of nations recognized both slavery and the slave–trade. And this mistake discloses the source of that great perplexity, which troubles him, to find a consistency between the principle which he erroneously supposes them to have established, and their decree for carrying it into execution. It is not our business to inquire into the reasons of that Court. " We must give effect to it according to what we understand to be its meaning. And, upon collating and combining their decree of 1825 with the explanatory decree of 1826, the two will be found to amount to this—that the rights of the Spaniards shall be recognized; but, in reducing that right to possession, they shall be held to have established a claim originally to ninety–three, which number shall be reduced by the average of deaths; and to the number so ascertained, they shall be held to produce proof of individual identity. But all the cargo, with the exception of those to be thus identified, shall be delivered over to the United States. This will be doing what that Court certainly intended to do: it will make a final disposition of a most troublesome charge. It is our duty (says he) to find out the meaning of the decree of the Supreme Court, and to obey it. And here it is evident, that although their reasoning, and the principles recognized, would seem to go fully up to the maintenance of the Spanish right, yet the decree, in its details, sustains those rights under very important limits and modifications."

And such is the history of the case of the Antelope in the judicial tribunals of the United States. That vessel, commanded by a citizen of the United States, was taken in the very act of smuggling 258 Africans into the United States for sale as slaves, and by the plain, unquestionable letter of the 4th section of an act of Congress of 20th April, 1818, was forfeited; while, by an act in addition to the acts prohibiting the slave–trade, of 3d March,

Amistad Argument

1819, every African thus imported in the Antelope was made free, —subject only to safe keeping, support, and removal beyond the limits of the United States, by direction of their President.

After seven years of litigation in the Courts of the United States, and, of course, of captivity to nearly all of these Africans who survived the operation; after decrees of the District Court, reversed by the Circuit Court, and three successive annual reversals by the Supreme Court of the decrees of the Circuit Court; what was the result of this most troublesome charge ?

The vessel was restored to certain Spanish slave–traders in the island of Cuba. Of the Africans, about fifty had perished by the benignity of their treatment in this land of liberty, during its suspended animation as to them; sixteen, drawn by lot from the whole number, (by the merciful dispensation of the Circuit Court, under the arbitrary enlargement of the tender mercies of the District Judge, which had limited the number to seven,)—sixteen had drawn the prize of liberty, to which the whole number were entitled by the letter of the law; and of the remainder, THIRTY–NINE upon evidence inadmissible upon the most trifling question of property in any court of justice, were, under the very peculiar circumstances of the case, surrendered! delivered up to the Spanish vice–consul—AS SLAVES! To the rest was at last extended the benefit of the laws which had foreordained their emancipation. They were delivered over to safe keeping, support, and transportation, as freemen, beyond the limits of the United States, by the Chief Magistrate of the Union.

And now, by what possible process of reasoning can any decision of the Supreme Court of the United States in the case of the Antelope, be adduced as authorizing the President of the United States to seize and deliver up to the order of the Spanish minister the captives of the Amistad? Even the judge of the District Court in Georgia, who would have enslaved all the unfortunates of the Antelope but seven, distinctly admitted, that, if they had been bought in Africa after the prohibition of the trade by Spain, he would have liberated them all.

In delivering the opinion of the Supreme Court, on their first decree in the case of the Antelope, Chief Justice Marshall, after reviewing the decisions in the British Courts of Admiralty, says, " The principle common to these cases is, that the legality of the capture of a vessel engaged in the slave–trade depends on the law of the country to which the vessel belongs. If that law gives its sanction to the trade, restitution will be decreed: if that law prohibits it, the vessel and cargo will be condemned as good prize."

It was by the application of this principle, to the fact, that, at the time when the Antelope was taken by the Arraganta, the slave–trade, in which the Antelope was engaged, had not yet been made unlawful by Spain, that the Supreme Court affirmed so much of the decree of the Circuit Court as directed restitution to the Spanish claimant of the Africans found on board the Antelope when captured by the Arraganta.

But by the same identical principle, applied to the case of the Amistad, if, when captured by Lieutenant Gedney, she and her cargo had been in possession of the Spaniards, and the Africans in the condition of slaves, the vessel would have been condemned, and the slaves liberated, by the laws of the United States; because she was engaged in the slave–trade in violation of the laws of Spain. She was in possession of the Africans, self–emancipated, and not in the condition of slaves. That, surely, could not legalize the trade in which she had been engaged. By the principle asserted in the opinion of the Supreme Court, declared by Chief Justice Marshall, it would have saved the vessel, at once, from condemnation and from restitution, and would have relieved the Court from the necessity of restoring to the Africans their freedom. Thus the opinion of the Supreme Court, as declared by the Chief Justice, in the case of the Antelope, was a fact, an authority in point, against the surrender of the Amistad, and in favor of the liberation of the Africans taken in her, even if they had been, when taken, in the condition of slaves. How monstrous, then, is the claim upon the Courts of the United States to re–inslave them, as thralls to the Spaniards, Ruiz and Montes! or to transport them beyond the seas, at the demand of the Minister of Spain!

I said, when I began this plea, that my final reliance for success in this case was on this Court as a court of JUSTICE; and in the confidence this fact inspired that, in the administration of justice, in a case of no less importance than the liberty and the life of a large number of persons, this Court would not decide but on a due consideration of all the rights, both natural and social, of every one of these individuals. I have endeavored to show that they are entitled to their liberty from this Court. I have avoided, purposely avoided, and this Court will do justice to the motive for which I have avoided, a recurrence to those first principles of liberty which might well have been invoked in the argument of this cause. I have shown that Ruiz and Montes, the only parties in interest here, for whose sole benefit this suit is carried on by the Government, were acting at the time in a way that is forbidden by the laws of Great Britain, of Spain, and of the United States, and that the mere signature of the Governor General of Cuba ought not to prevail over the ample evidence in the case that these Negroes were free and had a right to assert their liberty. I have shown that the papers in question are absolutely null and insufficient as passports for persons, and still more invalid to convey or prove a title to property.

The review of the case of the Antelope, and my argument in behalf of the captives of the Amistad, is closed.

May it please your Honors: On the 7th of February, 1804, now more than thirty-seven years past, my name was entered, and yet stands recorded, on both the rolls, as one of the Attorneys and Counsellors of this Court. Five years later, in February and March, 1809, I appeared for the last time before this Court, in defence of the cause of justice' and of important rights, in which many of my fellow-citizens had property to a large amount at stake. Very shortly afterwards, I was called to the discharge of other duties—first in distant lands, and in later years, within our own country, but in different departments of her Government.

Little did I imagine that I should ever again be required to claim the right of appearing in the capacity of an officer of this Court; yet such has been the dictate of my destiny—and I appear again to plead the cause of justice, and now of liberty and life, in behalf of many of my fellow men, before that same Court, which in a former age I had addressed in support of rights of property I stand again, I trust for the last time, before the same Court— 'hic caestus, artemque repono." I stand before the same Court, but not before the same judges—nor aided by the same associates —nor resisted by the same opponents. As I cast my eyes along those seats of honor and of public trust, now occupied by you, they seek in vain for one of those honored and honorable persons whose indulgence listened then to my voice. Marshall—Cushing—Chase—Washington—Johnson—Livingston—Todd—Where are they ? Where is that eloquent statesman and learned lawyer who was my associate counsel in the management of that cause, Robert Goodloe Harper? Where is that brilliant luminary, so long the pride of Maryland and of the American Bar, then my opposing counsel, Luther Martin? Where is the excellent clerk of that day, whose name has been inscribed on the shores of Africa, as a monument of his abhorrence of the African slave-trade, Elias B. Caldwell, Where is the marshal—where are the criers of the Court I Alas! where is one of the very judges of the Court, arbiters of life and death, before whom I commenced this anxious argument, even now prematurely closed? Where are they all I Gone ! Gone ! All gone!— Gone from the services which, in their day and generation, they faithfully rendered to their country. From the excellent characters which they sustained in life, so far as I have had the means of knowing, I humbly hope, and fondly trust, that they have gone to receive the rewards of blessedness on high. In taking, then, my final leave of this Bar, and of this Honorable Court, I can only ejaculate a fervent petition to Heaven, that every member of it may go to his final account with as little of earthly frailty to answer for as those illustrious dead, and that you may, every one, after the close of a long and virtuous career in this world, be received at the portals of the next with the approving sentence—" Well done, good and faithful servant; enter thou into the joy of thy Lord."

THE STATE OF THE
UNION ADDRESSES

State of the Union Addresses

John Quincy Adams

- December 6, 1825
- December 5, 1826
- December 4, 1827
- December 2, 1828

State of the Union Address John Quincy Adams

December 6, 1825

Fellow Citizens of the Senate and of the House of Representatives:

In taking a general survey of the concerns of our beloved country, with reference to subjects interesting to the common welfare, the first sentiment which impresses itself upon the mind is of gratitude to the Omnipotent Disposer of All Good for the continuance of the signal blessings of His providence, and especially for that health which to an unusual extent has prevailed within our borders, and for that abundance which in the vicissitudes of the seasons has been scattered with profusion over our land. Nor ought we less to ascribe to Him the glory that we are permitted to enjoy the bounties of His hand in peace and tranquillity — in peace with all the other nations of the earth, in tranquillity among our selves. There has, indeed, rarely been a period in the history of civilized man in which the general condition of the Christian nations has been marked so extensively by

1

peace and prosperity.

Europe, with a few partial and unhappy exceptions, has enjoyed 10 years of peace, during which all her Governments, what ever the theory of their constitutions may have been, are successively taught to feel that the end of their institution is the happiness of the people, and that the exercise of power among men can be justified only by the blessings it confers upon those over whom it is extended.

During the same period our intercourse with all those nations has been pacific and friendly; it so continues. Since the close of your last session no material variation has occurred in our relations with any one of them. In the commercial and navigation system of Great Britain important changes of municipal regulation have recently been sanctioned by acts of Parliament, the effect of which upon the interests of other nations, and particularly upon ours, has not yet been fully developed. In the recent renewal of the diplomatic missions on both sides between the two Governments assurances have been given and received of the continuance and increase of the mutual confidence and cordiality by which the adjustment of many points of difference had already been effected, and which affords the surest pledge for the ultimate satisfactory adjustment of those which still remain open or may hereafter arise.

The policy of the United States in their commercial intercourse with other nations has always been of the most liberal character. In the mutual exchange of their respective productions they have abstained altogether from prohibitions; they have interdicted themselves the power of laying taxes upon exports, and when ever they have favored their own shipping by special preferences or exclusive privileges in their own ports it has been only with a view to countervail similar favors and exclusions granted by the nations with whom we have been engaged in traffic to their own people or shipping, and to the disadvantage of ours. Immediately after the close of the last war a proposal was fairly made by the act of Congress of 1815–03–03, to all the maritime nations to lay aside the system of retaliating restrictions and exclusions, and to place the shipping of both parties to the common trade on a footing of equality in respect to the duties of tonnage and impost. This offer was partially and successively accepted by Great Britain, Sweden, the Netherlands, the Hanseatic cities, Prussia, Sardinia, the Duke of Oldenburg, and Russia. It was also adopted, under certain modifications, in our late commercial convention with France, and by the act of Congress of 1824–01–08, it has received a new confirmation with all the nations who had acceded to it, and has been offered again to all those who are or may here after be willing to abide in reciprocity by it. But all these regulations, whether established by treaty or by municipal enactments, are still subject to one important restriction.

The removal of discriminating duties of tonnage and of impost is limited to articles of the growth, produce, or manufacture of the country to which the vessel belongs or to such articles as are most usually first shipped from her ports. It will deserve the serious consideration of Congress whether even this remnant of restriction may not be safely abandoned, and whether the general tender of equal competition made in the act of 1824-01-08, may not be extended to include all articles of merchandise not prohibited, of what country so ever they may be the produce or manufacture. Propositions of this effect have already been made to us by more than one European Government, and it is probable that if once established by legislation or compact with any distinguished maritime state it would recommend itself by the experience of its advantages to the general accession of all.

The convention of commerce and navigation between the United States and France, concluded on 1822-06-24, was, in the understanding and intent of both parties, as appears upon its face, only a temporary arrangement of the points of difference between them of the most immediate and pressing urgency. It was limited in the first instance to two years from 1822-10-01, but with a proviso that it should further continue in force 'til the conclusion of a general and definitive treaty of commerce, unless terminated by a notice, 6 months in advance, of either of the parties to the other. Its operation so far as it extended has been mutually advantageous, and it still continues in force by common consent. But it left unadjusted several objects of great interest to the citizens and subjects of both countries, and particularly a mass of claims to considerable amount of citizens of the United States upon the Government of France of indemnity for property taken or destroyed under circumstances of the most aggravated and outrageous character. In the long period during which continual and earnest appeals have been made to the equity and magnanimity of France in behalf of these claims their justice has not been, as it could not be, denied.

It was hoped that the accession of a new Sovereign to the throne would have afforded a favorable opportunity for presenting them to the consideration of his Government. They have been presented and urged hither to without effect. The repeated and earnest representations of our minister at the Court of France remain as yet even without an

3

answer. Were the demands of nations upon the justice of each other susceptible of adjudication by the sentence of an impartial tribunal, those to which I now refer would long since have been settled and adequate indemnity would have been obtained.

There are large amounts of similar claims upon the Netherlands, Naples, and Denmark. For those upon Spain prior to 1819 indemnity was, after many years of patient forbearance, obtained; and those upon Sweden have been lately compromised by a private settlement, in which the claimants themselves have acquiesced. The Governments of Denmark and of Naples have been recently reminded of those yet existing against them, nor will any of them be forgotten while a hope may be indulged of obtaining justice by the means within the constitutional power of the Executive, and without resorting to those means of self-redress which, as well as the time, circumstances, and occasion which may require them, are within the exclusive competency of the Legislature.

It is with great satisfaction that I am enabled to bear witness to the liberal spirit with which the Republic of Colombia has made satisfaction for well-established claims of a similar character, and among the documents now communicated to Congress will be distinguished a treaty of commerce and navigation with that Republic, the ratifications of which have been exchanged since the last recess of the Legislature. The negotiation of similar treaties with all of the independent South American States has been contemplated and may yet be accomplished. The basis of them all, as proposed by the United States, has been laid in two principles — the one of entire and unqualified reciprocity, the other the mutual obligation of the parties to place each other permanently upon the footing of the most favored nation. These principles are, indeed, indispensable to the effectual emancipation of the American hemisphere from the thralldom of colonizing monopolies and exclusions, an event rapidly realizing in the progress of human affairs, and which the resistance still opposed in certain parts of Europe to the acknowledgment of the Southern American Republics as independent States will, it is believed, contribute more effectually to accomplish. The time has been, and that not remote, when some of those States might, in their anxious desire to obtain a nominal recognition, have accepted of a nominal independence, clogged with burdensome conditions, and exclusive commercial privileges granted to the nation from which they have separated to the disadvantage of all others. They are all now aware that such concessions to any European nation would be incompatible with that independence which they have declared and maintained.

Among the measures which have been suggested to them by the new relations with one another, resulting from the recent changes in their condition, is that of assembling at the Isthmus of Panama a congress, at which each of them should be represented, to deliberate upon objects important to the welfare of all. The Republics of Colombia, of Mexico, and of Central America have already deputed plenipotentiaries to such a meeting, and they have invited the United States to be also represented there by their ministers. The invitation has been accepted, and ministers on the part of the United States will be commissioned to attend at those deliberations, and to take part in them so far as may be compatible with that neutrality from which it is neither our intention nor the desire of the other American States that we should depart.

The commissioners under the 7th article of the treaty of Ghent have so nearly completed their arduous labors that, by the report recently received from the agent on the part of the United States, there is reason to expect that the commission will be closed at their next session, appointed for May 22 of the ensuing year.

The other commission, appointed to ascertain the indemnities due for slaves carried away from the United States after the close of the late war, have met with some difficulty, which has delayed their progress in the inquiry. A reference has been made to the British Government on the subject, which, it may be hoped, will tend to hasten the decision of the commissioners, or serve as a substitute for it.

Among the powers specifically granted to Congress by the Constitution are those of establishing uniform laws on the subject of bankruptcies throughout the United States and of providing for organizing, arming, and disciplining the militia and for governing such part of them as may be employed in the services of the United States. The magnitude and complexity of the interests affected by legislation upon these subjects may account for the fact that, long and often as both of them have occupied the attention and animated the debates of Congress, no systems have yet been devised for fulfilling to the satisfaction of the community the duties prescribed by these grants of power.

To conciliate the claim of the individual citizen to the enjoyment of personal liberty, with the effective obligation of private contracts, is the difficult problem to be solved by a law of bankruptcy. These are objects of the deepest interest to society, affecting all that is precious in the existence of multitudes of persons, many of them in the classes essentially dependent and helpless, of the age requiring nurture, and of the sex entitled to protection

5

from the free agency of the parent and the husband. The organization of the militia is yet more indispensable to the liberties of the country. It is only by an effective militia that we can at once enjoy the repose of peace and bid defiance to foreign aggression; it is by the militia that we are constituted an armed nation, standing in perpetual panoply of defense in the presence of all the other nations of the earth. To this end it would be necessary, if possible, so to shape its organization as to give it a more united and active energy. There are laws establishing an uniform militia throughout the United States and for arming and equipping its whole body. But it is a body of dislocated members, without the vigor of unity and having little of uniformity but the name. To infuse into this most important institution the power of which it is susceptible and to make it available for the defense of the Union at the shortest notice and at the smallest expense possible of time, of life, and of treasure are among the benefits to be expected from the persevering deliberations of Congress.

Among the unequivocal indications of our national prosperity is the flourishing state of our finances. The revenues of the present year, from all their principal sources, will exceed the anticipations of the last. The balance in the Treasury on the first of January last was a little short of $2,000,000, exclusive of $2,500,000, being the moiety of the loan of $5,000,000 authorized by the act of 1824-05-26. The receipts into the Treasury from the first of January to the 30th of September, exclusive of the other moiety of the same loan, are estimated at $16,500,000, and it is expected that those of the current quarter will exceed $5,000,000, forming an aggregate of receipts of nearly $22,000,000, independent of the loan. The expenditures of the year will not exceed that sum more than $2,000,000. By those expenditures nearly $8,000,000 of the principal of the public debt that have been discharged.

More than $1,500,000 has been devoted to the debt of gratitude to the warriors of the Revolution; a nearly equal sum to the construction of fortifications and the acquisition of ordnance and other permanent preparations of national defense; $500,000 to the gradual increase of the Navy; an equal sum for purchases of territory from the Indians and payment of annuities to them; and upward of $1,000,000 for objects of internal improvement authorized by special acts of the last Congress. If we add to these $4,000,000 for payment of interest upon the public debt, there remains a sum of $7,000,000, which have defrayed the whole expense of the administration of Government in its legislative, executive, and judiciary departments, including the support of the military and naval establishments and all the occasional contingencies of a government

6

coextensive with the Union.

The amount of duties secured on merchandise imported since the commencement of the year is about $25,500,000, and that which will accrue during the current quarter is estimated at $5,500,000; from these $31,000,000, deducting the draw–backs, estimated at less than $7,000,000, a sum exceeding $24,000,000 will constitute the revenue of the year, and will exceed the whole expenditures of the year. The entire amount of the public debt remaining due on the first of January next will be short of $81,000,000.

By an act of Congress of the 3d of March last a loan of $12,000,000 was authorized at 4.5%, or an exchange of stock to that amount of 4.5% for a stock of 6%, to create a fund for extinguishing an equal amount of the public debt, bearing an interest of 6%, redeemable in 1826. An account of the measures taken to give effect to this act will be laid before you by the Secretary of the Treasury. As the object which it had in view has been but partially accomplished, it will be for the consideration of Congress whether the power with which it clothed the Executive should not be renewed at an early day of the present session, and under what modifications.

The act of Congress of the 3d of March last, directing the Secretary of the Treasury to subscribe, in the name and for the use of the United States, for 1,500 shares of the capital stock of the Chesapeake and Delaware Canal Company, has been executed by the actual subscription for the amount specified; and such other measures have been adopted by that officer, under the act, as the fulfillment of its intentions requires. The latest accounts received of this important undertaking authorize the belief that it is in successful progress.

The payments into the Treasury from the proceeds of the sales of the public lands during the present year were estimated at $1,000,000. The actual receipts of the first two quarters have fallen very little short of that sum; it is not expected that the second half of the year will be equally productive, but the income of the year from that source may now be safely estimated at $1,500,000. The act of Congress of 1824–05–18, to provide for the extinguishment of the debt due to the United States by the purchasers of public lands, was limited in its operation of relief to the purchaser to the 10th of April last. Its effect at the end of the quarter during which it expired was to reduce that debt from $10,000,000 to $7,000,000 By the operation of similar prior laws of relief, from and since that of 1821–03–02, the debt had been reduced from upward of $22,000,000 to $10,000,000.

7

It is exceedingly desirable that it should be extinguished altogether; and to facilitate that consummation I recommend to Congress the revival for one year more of the act of 1824–05–18, with such provisional modification as may be necessary to guard the public interests against fraudulent practices in the resale of the relinquished land.

The purchasers of public lands are among the most useful of our fellow citizens, and since the system of sales for cash alone has been introduced great indulgence has been justly extended to those who had previously purchased upon credit. The debt which had been contracted under the credit sales had become unwieldy, and its extinction was alike advantageous to the purchaser and to the public. Under the system of sales, matured as it has been by experience, and adapted to the exigencies of the times, the lands will continue as they have become, an abundant source of revenue; and when the pledge of them to the public creditor shall have been redeemed by the entire discharge of the national debt, the swelling tide of wealth with which they replenish the common Treasury may be made to reflow in unfailing streams of improvement from the Atlantic to the Pacific Ocean.

The condition of the various branches of the public service resorting from the Department of War, and their administration during the current year, will be exhibited in the report of the Secretary of War and the accompanying documents herewith communicated. The organization and discipline of the Army are effective and satisfactory. To counteract the prevalence of desertion among the troops it has been suggested to withhold from the men a small portion of their monthly pay until the period of their discharge; and some expedient appears to be necessary to preserve and maintain among the officers so much of the art of horsemanship as could scarcely fail to be found wanting on the possible sudden eruption of a war, which should take us unprovided with a single corps of cavalry.

The Military Academy at West Point, under the restrictions of a severe but paternal superintendence, recommends itself more and more to the patronage of the nation, and the numbers of meritorious officers which it forms and introduces to the public service furnishes the means of multiplying the undertakings of the public improvements to which their acquirements at that institution are peculiarly adapted. The school of artillery practice established at Fortress Monroe Hampton, VA is well suited to the same purpose, and may need the aid of further legislative provision to the same end. The reports of the various officers at the head of the administrative branches of the military service, connected with the quartering, clothing, subsistence, health, and pay of the Army, exhibit the assiduous vigilance of those officers in the performance of their respective duties, and the faithful accountability which has pervaded every part of the system.

Our relations with the numerous tribes of aboriginal natives of this country, scattered over its extensive surface and so dependent even for their existence upon our power, have been during the present year highly interesting. An act of Congress of 1824–05–25, made an appropriation to defray the expenses of making treaties of trade and friendship with the Indian tribes beyond the Mississippi. An act of 1825–03–03, authorized treaties to be made with the Indians for their consent to the making of a road from the frontier of Missouri to that of New Mexico, and another act of the same date provided for defraying the expenses of holding treaties with the Sioux, Chippeways, Menomenees, Sauks, Foxes, etc., for the purpose of establishing boundaries and promoting peace between said tribes.

The first and last objects of these acts have been accomplished, and the second is yet in a process of execution. The treaties which since the last session of Congress have been concluded with the several tribes will be laid before the Senate for their consideration conformably to the Constitution. They comprise large and valuable acquisitions of territory, and they secure an adjustment of boundaries and give pledges of permanent peace between several tribes which had been long waging bloody wars against each other.

On the 12th of February last a treaty was signed at the Indian Springs between commissioners appointed on the part of the United States and certain chiefs and individuals of the Creek Nation of Indians, which was received at the seat of Government only a very few days before the close of the last session of Congress and of the late Administration. The advice and consent of the Senate was given to it on the 3d of March, too late for it to receive the ratification of the then President of the United States; it was ratified on the 7th of March, under the unsuspecting impression that it had been negotiated in good faith and in the confidence inspired by the recommendation of the Senate. The subsequent transactions in relation to this treaty will form the subject of a separate communication.

The appropriations made by Congress for public works, as well in the construction of fortifications as for purposes of internal improvement, so far as they have been expended, have been faithfuly applied. Their progress has been delayed by the want of suitable officers for superintending them. An increase of both the corps of engineers, military and

9

topographical, was recommended by my predecessor at the last session of Congress. The reasons upon which that recommendation was founded subsist in all their force and have acquired additional urgency since that time. The Military Academy at West Point will furnish from the cadets there officers well qualified for carrying this measure into effect.

The Board of Engineers for Internal Improvement, appointed for carrying into execution the act of Congress of 1824-04-30, "to procure the necessary surveys, plans, and estimates on the subject of roads and canals", have been actively engaged in that service from the close of the last session of Congress. They have completed the surveys necessary for ascertaining the practicability of a canal from the Chesapeake Bay to the Ohio River, and are preparing a full report on that subject, which, when completed, will be laid before you. The same observation is to be made with regard to the two other objects of national importance upon which the Board have been occupied, namely, the accomplishment of a national road from this city to New Orleans, and the practicability of uniting the waters of Lake Memphramagog with Connecticut River and the improvement of the navigation of that river. The surveys have been made and are nearly completed. The report may be expected at an early period during the present session of Congress.

The acts of Congress of the last session relative to the surveying, marking, or laying out roads in the Territories of Florida, Arkansas, and Michigan, from Missouri to Mexico, and for the continuation of the Cumberland road, are, some of them, fully executed, and others in the process of execution. Those for completing or commencing fortifications have been delayed only so far as the Corps of Engineers has been inadequate to furnish officers for the necessary superintendence of the works. Under the act confirming the statutes of Virginia and Maryland incorporating the Chesapeake and Ohio Canal Company, three commissioners on the part of the United States have been appointed for opening books and receiving subscriptions, in concert with a like number of commissioners appointed on the part of each of those States. A meeting of the commissioners has been post-poned, to await the definitive report of the board of engineers.

The light-houses and monuments for the safety of our commerce and mariners, the works for the security of Plymouth Beach and for the preservation of the islands in Boston Harbor, have received the attention required by the laws relating to those objects respectively. The continuation of the Cumberland road, the most important of them all,

10

after surmounting no inconsiderable difficulty in fixing upon the direction of the road, has commenced under the most promising of auspices, with the improvements of recent invention in the mode of construction, and with advantage of a great reduction in the comparative cost of the work.

The operation of the laws relating to the Revolutionary pensioners may deserve the renewed consideration of Congress. The act of 1818–03–18, while it made provision for many meritorious and indigent citizens who had served in the War of Independence, opened a door to numerous abuses and impositions. To remedy this the act of 1820–05–01, exacted proofs of absolute indigence, which many really in want were unable and all susceptible of that delicacy which is allied to many virtues must be deeply reluctant to give. The result has been that some among the least deserving have been retained, and some in whom the requisites both of worth and want were combined have been stricken from the list. As the numbers of these venerable relics of an age gone by diminish; as the decays of body, mind, and estate of those that survive must in the common course of nature increase, should not a more liberal portion of indulgence be dealt out to them? May not the want in most instances be inferred from the demand when the service can be proved, and may not the last days of human infirmity be spared the mortification of purchasing a pittance of relief only by the exposure of its own necessities? I submit to Congress the expediency of providing for individual cases of this description by special enactment, or of revising the act of 1820–05–01, with a view to mitigate the rigor of its exclusions in favor of persons to whom charity now bestowed can scarcely discharge the debt of justice.

The portion of the naval force of the Union in actual service has been chiefly employed on three stations — the Mediterranean, the coasts of South America bordering on the Pacific Ocean, and the West Indies. An occasional cruiser has been sent to range along the African shores most polluted by the traffic of slaves; one armed vessel has been stationed on the coast of our eastern boundary, to cruise along the fishing grounds in Hudsons Bay and on the coast of Labrador, and the first service of a new frigate has been performed in restoring to his native soil and domestic enjoyments the veteran hero whose youthful blood and treasure had freely flowed in the cause of our country's independence, and whose whole life has been a series of services and sacrifices to the improvement of his fellow men.

State of the Union Addresses

The visit of General Lafayette, alike honorable to himself and to our country, closed, as it had commenced, with the most affecting testimonials of devoted attachment on his part, and of unbounded gratitude of this people to him in return. It will form here–after a pleasing incident in the annals of our Union, giving to real history the intense interest of romance and signally marking the unpurchasable tribute of a great nation's social affections to the disinterested champion of the liberties of human–kind.

The constant maintenance of a small squadron in the Mediterranean is a necessary substitute for the humiliating alternative of paying tribute for the security of our commerce in that sea, and for a precarious peace, at the mercy of every caprice of four Barbary States, by whom it was liable to be violated. An additional motive for keeping a respectable force stationed there at this time is found in the maritime war raging between the Greeks and the Turks, and in which the neutral navigation of this Union is always in danger of outrage and depredation. A few instances have occurred of such depredations upon our merchant vessels by privateers or pirates wearing the Grecian flag, but without real authority from the Greek or any other Government. The heroic struggles of the Greeks themselves, in which our warmest sympathies as free men and Christians have been engaged, have continued to be maintained with vicissitudes of success adverse and favorable.

Similar motives have rendered expedient the keeping of a like force on the coasts of Peru and Chile on the Pacific. The irregular and convulsive character of the war upon the shores has been extended to the conflicts upon the ocean. An active warfare has been kept up for years with alternate success, though generally to the advantage of the American patriots. But their naval forces have not always been under the control of their own Governments. Blockades, unjustifiable upon any acknowledged principles of international law, have been proclaimed by officers in command, and though disavowed by the supreme authorities, the protection of our own commerce against them has been made cause of complaint and erroneous imputations against some of the most gallant officers of our Navy. Complaints equally groundless have been made by the commanders of the Spanish royal forces in those seas; but the most effective protection to our commerce has been the flag and the firmness of our own commanding officers.

The cessation of the war by the complete triumph of the patriot cause has removed, it is hoped, all cause of dissension with one party and all vestige of force of the other. But an unsettled coast of many degrees of latitude forming a part of our own territory and a flourishing commerce and fishery extending to the islands of the Pacific and to China still require that the protecting power of the Union should be displayed under its flag as well upon the ocean as upon the land.

The objects of the West India Squadron have been to carry into execution the laws for the suppression of the African slave trade; for the protection of our commerce against vessels of piratical character, though bearing commissions from either of the belligerent parties; for its protection against open and unequivocal pirates. These objects during the present year have been accomplished more effectually than at any former period. The African slave trade has long been excluded from the use of our flag, and if some few citizens of our country have continued to set the laws of the Union as well as those of nature and humanity at defiance by persevering in that abominable traffic, it has been only by sheltering themselves under the banners of other nations less earnest for the total extinction of the trade of ours.

The active, persevering, and unremitted energy of Captain Warrington and of the officers and men under his command on that trying and perilous service have been crowned with signal success, and are entitled to the approbation of their country. But experience has shown that not even a temporary suspension or relaxation from assiduity can be indulged on that station without reproducing piracy and murder in all their horrors; nor is it probably that for years to come our immensely valuable commerce in those seas can navigate in security without the steady continuance of an armed force devoted to its protection.

It were, indeed, a vain and dangerous illusion to believe that in the present or probable condition of human society a commerce so extensive and so rich as ours could exist and be pursued in safety without the continual support of a military marine — the only arm by which the power of this Confederacy can be estimated or felt by foreign nations, and the only standing military force which can never be dangerous to our own liberties at home. A permanent naval peace establishment, therefore, adapted to our present condition, and adaptable to that gigantic growth with which the nation is advancing in its career, is among the subjects which have already occupied the foresight of the last Congress, and which will deserve your serious deliberations. Our Navy, commenced at an early period of our present political organization upon a scale commensurate with the incipient energies, the scanty resources, and the comparative indigence of our infancy, was even then found adequate to cope with all the powers of Barbary, save the first, and

13

with one of the principle maritime powers of Europe.

At a period of further advancement, but with little accession of strength, it not only sustained with honor the most unequal of conflicts, but covered itself and our country with unfading glory. But it is only since the close of the late war that by the numbers and force of the ships of which it was composed it could deserve the name of a navy. Yet it retains nearly the same organization as when it consisted only of 5 frigates. The rules and regulations by which it is governed earnestly call for revision, and the want of a naval school of instruction, corresponding with the Military Academy at West Point, for the formation of scientific and accomplished officers, is felt with daily increasing aggravation.

The act of Congress of 1824–05–26, authorizing an examination and survey of the harbor of Charleston, in South Carolina, of St. Marys, in Georgia, and of the coast of Florida, and for other purposes, has been executed so far as the appropriation would admit. Those of the 3d of March last, authorizing the establishment of a navy yard and depot on the coast of Florida, in the Gulf of Mexico, and authorizing the building of ten sloops of war, and for other purposes, are in the course of execution, for the particulars of which and other objects connected with this Department I refer to the report of the Secretary of the Navy, herewith communicated.

A report from the PostMaster General is also submitted, exhibiting the present flourishing condition of that Department. For the first time for many years the receipts for the year ending on the first of July last exceeded the expenditures during the same period to the amount of more than $45,000. Other facts equally creditable to the administration of this Department are that in two years from 1823–07–01, an improvement of more than $185,000 in its pecuniary affairs has been realized; that in the same interval the increase of the transportation of the mail has exceeded 1,500,000 miles annually, and that 1,040 new post offices have been established. It hence appears that under judicious management the income from this establishment may be relied on as fully adequate to defray its expenses, and that by the discontinuance of post roads altogether unproductive, others of more useful character may be opened, 'til the circulation of the mail shall keep pace with the spread of our population, and the comforts of friendly correspondence, the exchanges of internal traffic, and the lights of the periodical press shall be distributed to the remotest corners of the Union, at a charge scarcely perceptible to any individual, and without the cost of a dollar to the public Treasury.

State of the Union Addresses

Upon this first occasion of addressing the Legislature of the Union, with which I have been honored, in presenting to their view the execution so far as it has been effected of the measures sanctioned by them for promoting the internal improvement of our country, I can not close the communication without recommending to their calm and persevering consideration the general principle in a more enlarged extent. The great object of the institution of civil government is the improvement of the condition of those who are parties to the social compact, and no government, in what ever form constituted, can accomplish the lawful ends of its institution but in proportion as it improves the condition of those over whom it is established. Roads and canals, by multiplying and facilitating the communications and intercourse between distant regions and multitudes of men, are among the most important means of improvement. But moral, political, intellectual improvement are duties assigned by the Author of Our Existence to social no less than to individual man.

For the fulfillment of those duties governments are invested with power, and to the attainment of the end — the progressive improvement of the condition of the governed — the exercise of delegated powers is a duty as sacred and indispensable as the usurpation of powers not granted is criminal and odious.

Among the first, perhaps the very first, instrument for the improvement of the condition of men is knowledge, and to the acquisition of much of the knowledge adapted to the wants, the comforts, and enjoyments of human life public institutions and seminaries of learning are essential. So convinced of this was the first of my predecessors in this office, now first in the memory, as, living, he was first in the hearts, of our country- men, that once and again in his addresses to the Congresses with whom he cooperated in the public service he earnestly recommended the establishment of seminaries of learning, to prepare for all the emergencies of peace and war — a national university and a military academy. With respect to the latter, had he lived to the present day, in turning his eyes to the institution at West Point he would have enjoyed the gratification of his most earnest wishes; but in surveying the city which has been honored with his name he would have seen the spot of earth which he had destined and bequeathed to the use and benefit of his country as the site for a university still bare and barren.

In assuming her station among the civilized nations of the earth it would seem that our country had contracted the engagement to contribute her share of mind, of labor, and of expense to the improvement of those parts of knowledge which lie beyond the reach of individual acquisition, and particularly to geographical and astronomical science. Looking back to the history only of the half century since the declaration of our independence, and observing the generous emulation with which the Governments of France, Great Britain, and Russia have devoted the genius, the intelligence, the treasures of their respective nations to the common improvement of the species in these branches of science, is it not incumbent upon us to inquire whether we are not bound by obligations of a high and honorable character to contribute our portion of energy and exertion to the common stock? The voyages of discovery prosecuted in the course of that time at the expense of those nations have not only redounded to their glory, but to the improvement of human knowledge.

We have been partakers of that improvement and owe for it a sacred debt, not only of gratitude, but of equal or proportional exertion in the same common cause. Of the cost of these undertakings, if the mere expenditures of outfit, equipment, and completion of the expeditions were to be considered the only charges, it would be unworthy of a great and generous nation to take a second thought. One hundred expeditions of circumnavigation like those of Cook and La Prouse would not burden the exchequer of the nation fitting them out so much as the ways and means of defraying a single campaign in war. but if we take into account the lives of those benefactors of man–kind of which their services in the cause of their species were the purchase, how shall the cost of those heroic enterprises be estimated, and what compensation can be made to them or to their countries for them? Is it not by bearing them in affectionate remembrance? Is it not still more by imitating their example — by enabling country–men of our own to pursue the same career and to hazard their lives in the same cause?

In inviting the attention of Congress to the subject of internal improvements upon a view thus enlarged it is not my desire to recommend the equipment of an expedition for circumnavigating the globe for purposes of scientific research and inquiry. We have objects of useful investigation nearer home, and to which our cares may be more beneficially applied. The interior of our own territories has yet been very imperfectly explored. our coasts along many degrees of latitude upon the shores of the Pacific Ocean, though much frequented by our spirited commercial navigators, have been barely visited by our public ships. The River of the West, first fully discovered and navigated by a country–man of our own, still bears the name of the ship in which he ascended its waters, and claims the protection of our armed national flag at its mouth. With the establishment of a military post there or at some other point of that coast, recommended by my predecessor and already matured in the deliberations of the last Congress, I would suggest the expediency of connecting the equipment of a public ship for the exploration of the whole north–west coast of this continent.

The establishment of an uniform standard of weights and measures was one of the specific objects contemplated in the formation of our Constitution, and to fix that standard was on of the powers delegated by express terms in that instrument to Congress. The Governments of Great Britain and France have scarcely ceased to be occupied with inquiries and speculations on the same subject since the existence of our Constitution, and with them it has expanded into profound, laborious, and expensive researches into the figure of the earth and the comparative length of the pendulum vibrating seconds in various latitudes from the equator to the pole. These researches have resulted in the composition and publication of several works highly interesting to the cause of science. The experiments are yet in the process of performance. Some of them have recently been made on our own shores, within the walls of one of our own colleges, and partly by one of our own fellow citizens. It would be honorable to our country if the sequel of the same experiments should be countenanced by the patronage of our Government, as they have hitherto been by those of France and Britain.

Connected with the establishment of an university, or separate from it, might be undertaken the erection of an astronomical observatory, with provision for the support of an astronomer, to be in constant attendance of observation upon the phenomena of the heavens, and for the periodical publication of his observances. it is with no feeling of pride as an American that the remark may be made that on the comparatively small territorial surface of Europe there are existing upward of 130 of these light–houses of the skies, while throughout the whole American hemisphere there is not one. If we reflect a moment upon the discoveries which in the last four centuries have been made in the physical constitution of the universe by the means of these buildings and of observers stationed in them, shall we doubt of their usefulness to every nation? And while scarcely a year passes over our heads without bringing some new astronomical discovery to light, which we must fain receive at second hand from Europe, are we not cutting ourselves off from the means of returning light for light while we have neither observatory nor observer upon our half of the globe and the earth revolves in perpetual darkness to our unsearching eyes?

State of the Union Addresses

When, on 1791-10-25, the first President of the United States announced to Congress the result of the first enumeration of the inhabitants of this Union, he informed them that the returns gave the pleasing assurance that the population of the United States bordered on 4,000,000 persons. At the distance of 30 years from that time the last enumeration, 5 years since completed, presented a population bordering on 10,000,000. Perhaps of all the evidence of a prosperous and happy condition of human society the rapidity of the increase of population is the most unequivocal. But the demonstration of our prosperity rests not alone upon this indication.

Our commerce, our wealth, and the extent of our territories have increased in corresponding proportions, and the number of independent communities associated in our Federal Union has since that time nearly doubled. The legislative representation of the States and people in the two Houses of Congress has grown with the growth of their constituent bodies. The House, which then consisted of 65 members, now numbers upward of 200. The Senate, which consisted of 26 members, has now 48. But the executive and, still more, the judiciary departments are yet in a great measure confined to their primitive organization, and are now not adequate to the urgent wants of a still growing community.

The naval armaments, which at an early period forced themselves upon the necessities of the Union, soon led to the establishment of a Department of the Navy. But the Departments of Foreign Affairs and of the Interior, which early after the formation of the Government had been united in one, continue so united to this time, to the unquestionable detriment of the public service. The multiplication of our relations with the nations and Governments of the Old World has kept pace with that of our population and commerce, while within the last 10 years a new family of nations in our own hemisphere has arisen among the inhabitants of the earth, with whom our intercourse, commercial and political, would of itself furnish occupation to an active and industrious department.

The constitution of the judiciary, experimental and imperfect as it was even in the infancy of our existing Government, is yet more inadequate to the administration of national justice at our present maturity. Nine years have elapsed since a predecessor in this office, now not the last, the citizen who, perhaps, of all others throughout the Union contributed most to the formation and establishment of our Constitution, in his valedictory address to Congress, immediately preceding his retirement from public life, urgently recommended the revision of the judiciary and the establishment of an additional executive department.

The exigencies of the public service and its unavoidable deficiencies, as now in exercise, have added yearly cumulative weight to the considerations presented by him as persuasive to the measure, and in recommending it to your deliberations I am happy to have the influence of this high authority in aid of the undoubting convictions of my own experience.

The laws relating to the administration of the Patent Office are deserving of much consideration and perhaps susceptible of some improvement. The grant of power to regulate the action of Congress upon this subject has specified both the end to be obtained and the means by which it is to be effected, "to promote the progress of science and useful arts by securing for limited times to authors and inventors the exclusive right to their respective writings and discoveries". If an honest pride might be indulged in the reflection that on the records of that office are already found inventions the usefulness of which has scarcely been transcended in the annals of human ingenuity, would not its exultation be allayed by the inquiry whether the laws have effectively insured to the inventors the reward destined to them by the Constitution — even a limited term of exclusive right to their discoveries?

On 1799–12–24, it was resolved by Congress that a marble monument should be erected by the United States in the Capitol at the city of Washington; that the family of General Washington should be requested to permit his body to be deposited under it, and that the monument be so designed as to commemorate the great events of his military and political life. In reminding Congress of this resolution and that the monument contemplated by it remains yet without execution, I shall indulge only the remarks that the works at the Capitol are approaching to completion; that the consent of the family, desired by the resolution, was requested and obtained; that a monument has been recently erected in this city over the remains of another distinguished patriot of the Revolution, and that a spot has been reserved within the walls where you are deliberating for the benefit of this and future ages, in which the mortal remains may be deposited of him whose spirit hovers over you and listens with delight to every act of the representatives of his nation which can tend to exalt and adorn his and their country.

The Constitution under which you are assembled is a charter of limited powers. After full and solemn deliberation upon all or any of the objects which, urged by an irresistible sense of my own duty, I have recommended to your attention should you come to the conclusion that, however desirable in themselves, the enactment of laws for effecting

19

them would transcend the powers committed to you by that venerable instrument which we are all bound to support, let no consideration induce you to assume the exercise of powers not granted to you by the people.

But if the power to exercise exclusive legislation in all cases what so ever over the District of Columbia; if the power to lay and collect taxes, duties, imposts, and excises, to pay the debts and provide for the common defense and general welfare of the United States; if the power to regulate commerce with foreign nations and among the several States and with the Indian tribes, to fix the standard of weights and measures, to establish post offices and post roads, to declare war, to raise and support armies, to provide and maintain a navy, to dispose of and make all needful rules and regulations respecting the territory or other property belonging to the United States, and to make all laws which shall be necessary and proper for carrying these powers into execution — if these powers and others enumerated in the Constitution may be effectually brought into action by laws promoting the improvement of agriculture, commerce, and manufactures, the cultivation and encouragement of the mechanic and of the elegant arts, the advancement of literature, and the progress of the sciences, ornamental and profound, to refrain from exercising them for the benefit of the people themselves would be to hide in the earth the talent committed to our charge — would be treachery to the most sacred of trusts.

The spirit of improvement is abroad upon the earth. It stimulates the hearts and sharpens the faculties not of our fellow citizens alone, but of the nations of Europe and of their rulers. While dwelling with pleasing satisfaction upon the superior excellence of our political institutions, let us not be unmindful that liberty is power; that the nation blessed with the largest portion of liberty must in proportion to its numbers be the most powerful nation upon earth, and that the tenure of power by man is, in the moral purposes of his Creator, upon condition that it shall be exercised to ends of beneficence, to improve the condition of himself and his fellow men.

While foreign nations less blessed with that freedom which is power than ourselves are advancing with gigantic strides in the career of public improvement, were we to slumber in indolence or fold up our arms and proclaim to the world that we are palsied by the will of our constituents, would it not be to cast away the bounties of Providence and doom ourselves to perpetual inferiority? In the course of the year now drawing to its close we have beheld, under the auspices and at the expense of one State of this Union, a new university unfolding its portals to the sons of science and holding up the torch of human improvement to eyes that seek the light. We have seen under the persevering and enlightened enterprise of another State the waters of our Western lakes mingle with those of the ocean. If undertakings like these have been accomplished in the compass of a few years by the authority of single members of our Confederation, can we, the representative authorities of the whole Union, fall behind our fellow servants in the exercise of the trust committed to us for the benefit of our common sovereign by the accomplishment of works important to the whole and to which neither the authority nor the resources of any one State can be adequate?

Finally, fellow citizens, I shall await with cheering hope and faithful cooperation the result of your deliberations, assured that, without encroaching upon the powers reserved to the authorities of the respective States or to the people, you will, with a due sense of your obligations to your country and of the high responsibilities weighing upon yourselves, give efficacy to the means committed to you for the common good. And may He who searches the hearts of the children of men prosper your exertions to secure the blessings of peace and promote the highest welfare of your country. JOHN QUNICY ADAMS

State of the Union Address John Quincy Adams

December 5, 1826

Fellow Citizens of the Senate and of the House of Representatives:

The assemblage of the representatives of our Union in both Houses of the Congress at this time occurs under circumstances calling for the renewed homage of our grateful acknowledgments to the Giver of All Good. With the exceptions incidental to the most felicitous condition of human existence, we continue to be highly favored in all the elements which contribute to individual comfort and to national prosperity. In the survey of our extensive country we have generally to observe abodes of health and regions of plenty. In our civil and political relations we have peace without and tranquillity within our borders. We are, as a people, increasing with unabated rapidity in population, wealth, and national resources, and whatever differences of opinion exist among us with regard to the mode and the means by which we shall turn the beneficence of Heaven to the improvement of our own condition, there is yet a spirit animating us all which will not suffer the bounties of Providence to be showered upon us in vain, but will receive them with grateful hearts, and apply them with unwearied hands to the advancement of the general good.

Of the subjects recommended to Congress at their last session, some were then definitively acted upon. Others, left unfinished, but partly matured, will recur to your attention without needing a renewal of notice from me. The purpose of this communication will be to present to your view the general aspect of our public affairs at this moment and the measures which have been taken to carry into effect the intentions of the Legislature as signified by the laws then and heretofore enacted.

In our intercourse with the other nations of the earth we have still the happiness of enjoying peace and a general good understanding, qualified, however, in several important instances by collisions of interest and by unsatisfied claims of justice, to the settlement of which the constitutional interposition of the legislative authority may become ultimately indispensable.

By the decease of the Emperor Alexander of Russia, which occurred contemporaneously with the commencement of the last session of Congress, the United States have been deprived of a long tried, steady, and faithful friend. Born to the inheritance of absolute power and trained in the school of adversity, from which no power on earth, however absolute, is exempt, that monarch from his youth had been taught to feel the force and value of public opinion and to be sensible that the interests of his own Government would best be promoted by a frank and friendly intercourse with this Republic, as those of his people would be advanced by a liberal intercourse with our country. A candid and confidential interchange of sentiments between him and the Government of the US upon the affairs of Southern America took place at a period not long preceding his demise, and contributed to fix that course of policy which left to the other Governments of Europe no alternative but that of sooner or later recognizing the independence of our southern neighbors, of which the example had by the United States already been set.

The ordinary diplomatic communications between his successor, the Emperor Nicholas, and the United States have suffered some interruption by the illness, departure, and subsequent decease of his minister residing here, who enjoyed, as he merited, the entire confidence of his new sovereign, as he had eminently responded to that of his predecessor. But we have had the most satisfactory assurances that the sentiments of the reigning Emperor toward the United States are altogether conformable to those which had so long and constantly animated his imperial brother, and we have reason to hope that they will serve to cement that harmony and good understanding between the two nations which, founded in congenial interests, can not but result in the advancement of the welfare and prosperity of both.

Our relations of commerce and navigation with France are, by the operation of the convention of 1822–06–24, with that nation, in a state of gradual and progressive improvement. Convinced by all our experience, no less than by the principles of fair and liberal reciprocity which the United States have constantly tendered to all the nations of the earth as the rule of commercial intercourse which they would universally prefer, that fair and equal competition is most conducive to the interests of both parties, the United States in the negotiation of that convention earnestly contended for a mutual renunciation of discriminating duties and charges in the ports of the two countries. Unable to obtain the immediate recognition of this principle in its full extent, after reducing the duties of discrimination so far as was found attainable it was agreed that at the expiration of two years from 1822–10–01, when the convention was to go into effect, unless a notice of 6 months on either side should be given to the other that the convention itself must terminate, those duties should be reduced 1/4, and that this reducation should be yearly repeated, until all discrimination should cease, while the convention itself should continue in force. By the effect of this stipulation 3/4 of the discriminating duties which had been levied by each party upon the vessels of the other in its ports have already been removed; and on the first of next October, should the convention be still in force, the remaining 1/4 will be discontinued. French vessels laden with French produce will be received in our ports on the same terms as our own, and ours in return will enjoy the same advantages in the ports of France.

By these approximations to an equality of duties and of charges not only has the commerce between the two countries prospered, but friendly dispositions have been on both sides encouraged and promoted. They will continue to be cherished and cultivated on the part of the United States. It would have been gratifying to have had it in my power to add that the claims upon the justice of the French Government, involving the property and the comfortable subsistence of many of our fellow citizens, and which have been so long and so earnestly urged, were in a more promising train of adjustment than at your last meeting; but their condition remains unaltered.

With the Government of the Netherlands the mutual abandonment of discriminating duties had been regulated by legislative acts on both sides. The act of Congress of 1818–04–20, abolished all discriminating duties of impost and tonnage upon the vessels and produce of the Netherlands in the ports of the United States upon the assurance given by the Government of the Netherlands that all such duties operating against the shipping and commerce of the United States in that Kingdom had been abolished. These reciprocal regulations had continued in force several years when the discriminating principle was resumed by the Netherlands in a new and indirect form by a bounty of 10% in the shape of a return of duties to their national vessels, and in which those of the United States are not permitted to participate. By the act of Congress of 1824–01–07, all discriminating duties in the United States were again suspended, so far as related to the vessels and produce of the Netherlands, so long as the reciprocal exemption should be extended to the vessels and produce of the United States in the Netherlands. But the same act provides that in the event of a restoration of discriminating duties to operate against the shipping and commerce of the United States in any of the foreign countries referred to therein the suspension of discriminating duties in favor of the navigation of such foreign country should cease and all the provisions of the acts imposing discriminating foreign tonnage and impost duties in the United States should revive and be in full force with regard to that nation.

In the correspondence with the Government of the Netherlands upon this subject they have contended that the favor shown to their own shipping by this bounty upon their tonnage is not to be considered a discriminating duty; but it can not be denied that it produces all the same effects. Had the mutual abolition been stipulated by treaty, such a bounty upon the national vessels could scarcely have been granted consistent with good faith. Yet as the act of Congress of 1824–01–07 has not expressly authorized the Executive authority to determine what shall be considered as a revival of discriminating duties by a foreign government to the disadvantage of the United States, and as the retaliatory measure on our part, however just and necessary, may tend rather to that conflict of legislation which we deprecate than to that concert to which we invite all commercial nations, as most conducive to their interest and our own, I have thought it more consistent with the spirit of our institutions to refer to the subject again to the paramount authority of the Legislature to decide what measure the emergency may require than abruptly by proclamation to carry into effect the minatory provisions of the act of 1824.

During the last session of Congress treaties of amity, navigation, and commerce were negotiated and signed at this place with the Government of Denmark, in Europe, and with the Federation of Central America, in this hemisphere. These treaties then received the constitutional sanction of the Senate, by the advice and consent to their ratification. They were accordingly ratified on the part of the US, and during the recess of Congress have been also ratified by the other respective contracting parties. The ratifications have been exchanged, and they have been published by proclamations, copies of which are herewith communicated to Congress.

These treaties have established between the contracting parties the principles of equality and reciprocity in their broadest and most liberal extent, each party admitting the vessels of the other into its ports, laden with cargoes the produce or manufacture of any quarter of the globe, upon the payment of the same duties of tonnage and impost that are chargeable upon their own. They have further stipulated that the parties shall hereafter grant no favor of navigation or commerce to any other nation which shall not upon the same terms be granted to each other, and that neither party will impose upon articles of merchandise the produce or manufacture of the other any other or higher duties than upon the like articles being the produce or manufacture of any other country. To these principles there is in the convention with Denmark an exception with regard to the colonies of that Kingdom in the arctic seas, but none with regard to her colonies in the West Indies.

In the course of the last summer the term to which our last commercial treaty with Sweden was limited has expired. A continuation of it is in the contemplation of the Swedish Government, and is believed to be desirable on the part of the United States. It has been proposed by the King of Sweden that pending the negotiation of renewal the expired treaty should be mutually considered as still in force, a measure which will require the sanction of Congress to be carried into effect on our part, and which I therefore recommend to your consideration.

With Prussia, Spain, Portugal, and, in general, all the European powers between whom and the United States relations of friendly intercourse have existed their condition has not materially varied since the last session of Congress. I regret not to be able to say the same of our commercial intercourse with the colonial possessions of Great Britain in America. Negotiations of the highest importance to our common interests have been for several years in discussion between the two Governments, and on the part of the United States have been invariably pursued in the spirit of candor and conciliation. Interests of great magnitude and delicacy had been adjusted by the conventions of 1815 and 1818, while that of 1822, mediated by the late Emperor Alexander, had promised a satisfactory compromise of claims which the Government of the US, in justice to the rights of a numerous class of their citizens, was bound to sustain.

But with regard to the commercial intercourse between the United States and the British colonies in America, it has been hitherto found impracticable to bring the parties to an understanding satisfactory to both. The relative geographical position and the respective products of nature cultivated by human industry had constituted the elements of a commercial intercourse between the United States and British America, insular and continental, important to the inhabitants of both countries; but it had been interdicted by Great Britain upon a principle heretofore practiced upon by the colonizing nations of Europe, of holding the trade of their colonies each in exclusive monopoly to herself.

After the termination of the late war this interdiction had been revived, and the British Government declined including this portion of our intercourse with her possessions in the negotiation of the convention of 1815. The trade was then carried on exclusively in British vessels 'til the act of Congress, concerning navigation, of 1818 and the supplemental act of 1820 met the interdict by a corresponding measure on the part of the United States. These measures, not of retaliation, but of necessary self defense, were soon succeeded by an act of Parliament opening certain colonial ports to the vessels of the United States coming directly from them, and to the importation from them of certain articles of our produce burdened with heavy duties, and excluding some of the most valuable articles of our exports. The United States opened their ports to British vessels from the colonies upon terms as exactly corresponding with those of the act of Parliament as in the relative position of the parties could be made, and a negotiation was commenced by mutual consent, with the hope on our part that a reciprocal spirit of accommodation and a common sentiment of the importance of the trade to the interests of the inhabitants of the two countries between whom it must be carried on would ultimately bring the parties to a compromise with which both might be satisfied. With this view the Government of the United States had determined to sacrifice something of that entire reciprocity which in all commercial arrangements with foreign powers they are entitled to demand, and to acquiesce in some inequalities disadvantageous to ourselves rather than to forego the benefit of a final and permanent adjustment of this interest to the satisfaction of Great Britain herself. The negotiation, repeatedly suspended by accidental circumstances, was, however, by mutual agreement and express assent, considered as pending and to be speedily resumed.

In the mean time another act of Parliament, so doubtful and ambiguous in its import as to have been misunderstood by the officers in the colonies who were to carry it into execution, opens again certain colonial ports upon new conditions and terms, with a threat to close them against any nation which may not accept those terms as prescribed by the British Government. This act, passed 1825–07, not communicated to the Government of the US, not understood by the British officers of the customs in the colonies where it was to be enforced, was never the less submitted to the consideration of Congress at their last session. With the knowledge that a negotiation upon the subject had long been in progress and pledges given of its resumption at an early day, it was deemed expedient to await the result of that negotiation rather than to subscribe implicitly to terms the import of which was not clear and which the British authorities themselves in this hemisphere were not prepared to explain.

Immediately after the close of the last session of Congress one of our most distinguished citizens was dispatched as envoy extraordinary and minister plenipotentiary to Great Britain, furnished with instructions which we could not doubt would lead to a conclusion of this long controverted interest upon terms acceptable to Great Britain. Upon his arrival, and before he had delivered his letters of credence, he was bet by an order of the British council excluding from and after the first of December now current the vessels of the United States from all the colonial British ports excepting those immediately bordering on our territories. In answer to his expostulations upon a measure thus unexpected he is informed that according to the ancient maxims of policy of European nations having colonies their trade is an exclusive possession of the mother country; that all participation in it by other nations is a boon or favor not forming a subject of negotiation, but to be regulated by the legislative acts of the power owning the colony; that the British Government therefore declines negotiating concerning it, and that as the US did not forthwith accept purely and simply the terms offered by the act of Parliament of 1825–07, Great Britain would not now admit the vessels of the United States even upon the terms on which she has opened them to the navigation of other nations.

We have been accustomed to consider the trade which we have enjoyed with the British colonies rather as an interchange of mutual benefits than as a mere favor received; that under every circumstance we have given an ample equivalent. We have seen every other nation holding colonies negotiate with other nations and grant them freely admission to the colonies by treaty, and so far are the other colonizing nations of Europe now from refusing to negotiate for trade with their colonies that we ourselves have secured access to the colonies of more than one of them by treaty. The refusal, however, of Great Britain to negotiate leaves to the United States no other alternative than that of regulating or interdicting altogether the trade on their part, according as either measure may effect the interests of our own country, and with that exclusive object I would recommend the whole subject to your calm and candid deliberations.

It is hoped that our unavailing exertions to accomplish a cordial good understanding on this interest will not have an unpropitious effect upon the other great topics of discussion between the two Governments. Our north-eastern and north-western boundaries are still unadjusted. The commissioners under the 7th article of the treaty of Ghent have nearly come to the close of their labors; nor can we renounce the expectation, enfeebled as it is, that they may agree upon their report to the satisfaction or acquiescence of both parties. The commission for liquidating the claims for indemnity for slaves carried away after the close of the war has been sitting, with doubtful prospects of success. Propositions of compromise have, however, passed between the two Governments, the result of which we flatter ourselves may yet prove unsatisfactory. Our own dispositions and purposes toward Great Britain are all friendly and conciliatory; nor can we abandon but with strong reluctance the belief that they will ultimately meet a return, not of favors, which we neither as nor desire, but of equal reciprocity and good will.

With the American Governments of this hemisphere we continue to maintain an intercourse altogether friendly, and between their nations and ours that commercial interchange of which mutual benefit is the source of mutual comfort and harmony the result is in a continual state of improvement. The war between Spain and them since the total expulsion of the Spanish military force from their continental territories has been little more than nominal, and their internal tranquillity, though occasionally menaced by the agitations which civil wars never fail to leave behind them, has not been affected by any serious calamity.

The congress of ministers from several of those nations which assembled at Panama, after a short session there, adjourned to meet again at a more favorable season in the neighborhood of Mexico. The decease of one of our ministers on his way to the Isthmus, and the impediments of the season, which delayed the departure of the other, deprived

United States of the advantage of being represented at the first meeting of the congress. There is, however, no reason to believe that any transactions of the congress were of a nature to affect injuriously the interests of the United States or to require the interposition of our ministers had they been present. Their absence has, indeed, deprived United States of the opportunity of possessing precise and authentic information of the treaties which were concluded at Panama; and the whole result has confirmed me in the conviction of the expediency to the United States of being represented at the congress. The surviving member of the mission, appointed during your last session, has accordingly proceeded to his destination, and a successor to his distinguished and lamented associate will be nominated to the Senate. A treaty of amity, navigation, and commerce has in the course of the last summer been concluded by our minister plenipotentiary at Mexico with the united states of that Confederacy, which will also be laid before the Senate for their advice with regard to its ratification.

In adverting to the present condition of our fiscal concerns and to the prospects of our revenue the first remark that calls our attention is that they are less exuberantly prosperous than they were at the corresponding period of the last year. The severe shock so extensively sustained by the commercial and manufacturing interests in Great Britain has not been without a perceptible recoil upon ourselves. A reduced importation from abroad is necessarily succeeded by a reduced return to the Treasury at home. The net revenue of the present year will not equal that of the last, and the receipts of that which is to come will fall short of those in the current year. The diminution, however, is in part attributable to the flourishing condition of some of our domestic manufactures, and so far is compensated by an equivalent more profitable to the nation.

It is also highly gratifying to perceive that the deficiency in the revenue, while it scarcely exceeds the anticipations of the last year's estimate from the Treasury, has not interrupted the application of more than $11M during the present year to the discharge of the principal and interest of the debt, nor the reduction of upward of $7,000,000 of the capital of the debt itself. The balance in the Treasury on the first of January last was $5,201,650.43; the receipts from that time to the 30th of September last were $19,585,932.50; the receipts of the current quarter, estimated at $6,000,000, yield, with the sums already received, a revenue of about $25,500,000 for the year; the expenditures for the first 3 quarters of the year have amounted to $18,714,226.66; the expenditures of the current quarter are expected, including the $2,000,000 of the principal of the debt to be paid, to balance the receipts; so that the expense of the year, amounting to upward of

$1,000,000 less than its income, will leave a proportionally increased balance in the Treasury on 1827-01-01, over that of the first of January last; instead of $5,200,000 there will be $6,400,000.

The amount of duties secured on merchandise imported from the commence of the year 'til September 30 is estimated at $21,250,000, and the amount that will probably accrue during the present quarter is estimated at $4,250,000, making for the whole year $25,500,000, from which the draw-backs being deducted will leave a clear revenue from the customs receivable in the year 1827 of about $20,400,000, which, with the sums to be received from the proceeds of public lands, the bank dividends, and other incidental receipts, will form an aggregate of about $23,000,000, a sum falling short of the whole expenses of the present year little more than the portion of those expenditures applied to the discharge of the public debt beyond the annual appropriation of $10,000,000 by the act of 1817-03-03. At the passage of that act the public debt amounted to $123,500,000. On the first of January next it will be short of $74,000,000. In the lapse of these 10 years $50,000,000 of public debt, with the annual charge of upward of $3,000,000 of interest upon them, have been extinguished. At the passage of tat act, of the annual appropriation of $10,000,000, $7,000,000 were absorbed in the payment of interest, and not more than $3,000,000 went to reduce the capital of the debt. Of the same $10,000,000, at this time scarcely $4,000,000 are applicable to the interest and upward of $6,000,000 are effective in melting down the capital.

Yet our experience has proved that a revenue consisting so largely of imposts and tonnage ebbs and flows to an extraordinary extent, with all the fluctuations incident to the general commerce of the world. It is within our recollection that even in the compass of the same last 10 years the receipts of the Treasury were not adequate to the expenditures of the year, and that in two successive years it was found necessary to resort to loans to meet the engagements of the nation. The returning tides of the succeeding years replenished the public coffers until they have again begun to feel the vicissitude of a decline. To produce these alternations of fullness and exhaustion the relative operation of abundant or unfruitful seasons, the regulations of foreign governments, political revolutions, the prosperous or decaying condition of manufactures, commercial speculations, and many other causes, not always to be traced, variously combine.

We have found the alternate swells and diminutions embracing periods of from two to three years. The last period of depression to United States was from 1819 to 1822. The corresponding revival was from 1823 to the commencement of the present year. Still, we have no cause to apprehend a depression comparable to that of the former period, or even to anticipate a deficiency which will intrench upon the ability to apply the annual $10M to the reduction of the debt. It is well for us, however, to be admonished of the necessity of abiding by the maxims of the most vigilant economy, and of resorting to all honorable and useful expedients for pursuing with steady and inflexible perseverance the total discharge of the debt.

Besides the $7,000,000 of the loans of 1813 which will have been discharged in the course of the present year, there are $9,000,000 which by the terms of the contracts would have been and are now redeemable. $13,000,000 more of the loan of 1814 will become redeemable from and after the expiration of the present month, and $9,000,000 other from and after the close of the ensuing year. They constitute a mass of $31,000,000, all bearing an interest of 6%, more than $20,000,000 of which will be immediately redeemable, and the rest within little more than a year. Leaving of this amount $15,000,000 to continue at the interest of 6%, but to be paid off as far as shall be found practicable in the years 1827 and 1828, there is scarcely a doubt that the remaining $16,000,000 might within a few months be discharged by a loan at not exceeding 5%, redeemable in the years 1829 and 1830. By this operation a sum of nearly $500,000 may be saved to the nation, and the discharge of the whole $31,000,000 within the 4 years may be greatly facilitated if not wholly accomplished.

By an act of Congress of 1835–03–03, a loan for the purpose now referred to, or a subscription to stock, was authorized, at an interest not exceeding 4.5%. But at that time so large a portion of the floating capital of the country was absorbed in commercial speculations and so little was left for investment in the stocks that the measure was but partially successful. At the last session of Congress the condition of the funds was still unpropitious to the measure; but the change so soon afterwards occurred that, had the authority existed to redeem the $9M now redeemable by an exchange of stocks or a loan at 5%, it is morally certain that it might have been effected, and with it a yearly saving of $90,000.

With regard to the collection of the revenue of imposts, certain occurrences have within the last year been disclosed in one or two of our principal ports, which engaged the attention of Congress at their last session and may hereafter require further consideration. Until within a very few years the execution of the laws for raising the revenue, like that of all our other laws, has been insured more by the moral sense of the community than by the rigors of a jealous precaution or by penal sanction. Confiding in the exemplary punctuality and unsullied integrity of our importing merchants, a gradual relaxation from the provisions of the collection laws, a close adherence to which have caused inconvenience and expense to them, had long become habitual, and indulgences had been extended universally because they had never been abused. It may be worthy of your serious consideration whether some further legislative provision may not be necessary to come in aid of this state of unguarded security.

From the reports herewith communicated of the Secretaries of War and of the Navy, with the subsidiary documents annexed to them, will be discovered the present condition and administration of our military establishment on the land and on the sea. The organization of the Army having undergone no change since its reduction to the present peace establishment in 1821, it remains only to observe that it is yet found adequate to all the purposes for which a permanent armed force in time of peace can be needed or useful. It may be proper to add that, from a difference of opinion between the late President of the United States and the Senate with regard to the construction of the act of Congress of 1821–03–02, to reduce and fix the military peace establishment of the US, it remains hitherto so far without execution that no colonel has been appointed to command one of the regiments of artillery. A supplementary or explanatory act of the Legislature appears to be the only expedient practicable for removing the difficulty of this appointment.

In a period of profound peace the conduct of the mere military establishment forms but a very inconsiderable portion of the duties devolving upon the administration of the Department of War. It will be seen by the returns from the subordinate departments of the Army that every branch of the service is marked with order, regularity, and discipline; that from the commanding general through all the gradations of superintendence the officers feel themselves to have been citizens before they were soldiers, and that the glory of a republican army must consist in the spirit of freedom, by which it is animated, and of patriotism, by which it is impelled. It may be confidently stated that the moral character of the Army is in a state of continual improvement, and that all the arrangements for the disposal of its parts have a constant reference to that end.

But to the War Department are attributed other duties, having, indeed, relation to a future possible condition of war, but being purely defensive, and in their tendency contributing rather to the security and permanency of peace — the erection of the fortifications provided for by Congress, and adapted to secure our shores from hostile invasion; the distribution of the fund of public gratitude and justice to the pensioners of the Revolutionary war; the maintenance of our relations of peace and protection with the Indian tribes, and the internal improvements and surveys for the location of roads and canals, which during the last 3 sessions of Congress have engaged so much of their attention, and may engross so large a share of their future benefactions to our country.

By the act of 1824-04-30, suggested and approved by my predecessor, the sum of $30K was appropriated for the purpose of causing to be made the necessary surveys, plans, and estimates of the routes of such roads and canals as the President of the United States might deem of national importance in a commercial or military point of view, or necessary for the transportation of the public mail. The surveys, plans, and estimates for each, when completed, will be laid before Congress.

In execution of this act a board of engineers was immediately instituted, and have been since most assiduously and constantly occupied in carrying it into effect. The first object to which their labors were directed, by order of the late President, was the examination of the country between the tide waters of the Potomac, the Ohio, and Lake Erie, to ascertain the practicability of a communication between them, to designate the most suitable route for the same, and to form plans and estimates in detail of the expense of execution.

On 1825-02-03, they made their first report, which was immediately communicated to Congress, and in which they declared that having maturely considered the circumstances observed by them personally, and carefully studied the results of such of the preliminary surveys as were then completed, they were decidedly of opinion that the communication was practicable.

At the last session of Congress, before the board of engineers were enabled to make up their second report containing a general plan and preparatory estimate for the work, the Committee of the House of Representatives upon Roads and Canals closed the session with a report expressing the hope that the plan and estimate of the board of engineers might at this time be prepared, and that the subject be referred to the early and favorable consideration of Congress at their present session. That expected report of the board of engineers is prepared, and will forthwith be laid before you.

State of the Union Addresses

Under the resolution of Congress authorizing the Secretary of War to have prepared a complete system of cavalry tactics, and a system of exercise and instruction of field artillery, for the use of the militia of the US, to be reported to Congress at the present session, a board of distinguished officers of the Army and of the militia has been convened, whose report will be submitted to you with that of the Secretary of War. The occasion was thought favorable for consulting the same board, aided by the results of a correspondence with the governors of the several States and Territories and other citizens of intelligence and experience, upon the acknowledged defective condition of our militia system, and of the improvements of which it is susceptible. The report of the board upon this subject is also submitted for your consideration.

In the estimates of appropriations for the ensuing year upward of $5M will be submitted for the expenditures to be paid from the Department of War. Less than 2/5 of this will be applicable to the maintenance and support of the Army. $1,500,000, in the form of pensions, goes as a scarcely adequate tribute to the services and sacrifices of a former age, and a more than equal sum invested in fortifications, or for the preparations of internal improvement, provides for the quiet, the comfort, and happier existence of the ages to come. The appropriations to indemnify those unfortunate remnants of another race unable alike to share in the enjoyments and to exist in the presence of civilization, though swelling in recent years to a magnitude burdensome to the Treasury, are generally not without their equivalents in profitable value, or serve to discharge the Union from engagements more burdensome than debt.

In like manner the estimate of appropriations for the Navy Department will present an aggregate sum of upward of $3,000,000M. About half of these, however, covers the current expenditures of the Navy in actual service, and half constitutes a fund of national property, the pledge of our future glory and defense. It was scarcely one short year after the close of the late war, and when the burden of its expenses and charges was weighing heaviest upon the country, that Congress, by the act of 1816-04-29, appropriated $1,000,000 annually for 8 years to the *gradual increase of the Navy*. At a subsequent period this annual appropriation was reduced to $0,500,000 for 6 years, of which the present year is the last. A yet more recent appropriation the last two years, for building 10 sloops of war, has nearly restored the original appropriation of 1816 of $1,000,000 for every year.

34

State of the Union Addresses

The result is before United States all. We have 12 line–of–battle ships, 20 frigates, and sloops of war in proportion, which, with a few months preparation, may present a line of floating fortifications along the whole range of our coast ready to meet any invader who might attempt to set foot upon our shores. Combining with a system of fortifications upon the shores themselves, commenced about the same time under the auspices of my immediate predecessor, and hitherto systematically pursued, it has placed in our possession the most effective sinews of war and has left us at once an example and a lesson from which our own duties may be inferred.

The gradual increase of the Navy was the principle of which the act of 1816–04–29, was the first development. It was the introduction of a system to act upon the character and history of our country for an indefinite series of ages. It was a declaration of that Congress to their constituents and to posterity that it was the destiny and the duty of these confederated States to become in regular process of time and by no petty advances a great naval power. That which they proposed to accomplish in 8 years is rather to be considered as the measure of their means that the limitation of their design. They looked forward for a term of years sufficient for the accomplishment of a definite portion of their purpose, and they left to their successors to fill up the canvas of which they had traced the large and prophetic outline. The ships of the line and frigates which they had in contemplation will be shortly completed. The time which they had allotted for the accomplishment of the work has more than elapsed. It remains for your consideration how their successors may contribute their portion of toil and of treasure for the benefit of the succeeding age in the gradual increase of our Navy.

There is perhaps no part of the exercise of the constitutional powers of the Federal Government which has given more general satisfaction to the people of the Union than this. The system has not been thus vigorously introduced and hitherto sustained to be now departed from or abandoned. In continuing to provide for the gradual increase of the Navy it may not be necessary or expedient to add for the present any more to the number of our ships; but should you deem it advisable to continue the yearly appropriation of $0.5M to the same objects, it may be profitably expended in a providing a supply of timber to be seasoned and other materials for future use in the construction of docks or in laying the foundations of a school for naval education, as to the wisdom of Congress either of those measures may appear to claim the preference.

Of the small portions of this Navy engaged in actual service during the peace, squadrons have continued to be maintained in the Pacific Ocean, in the West India seas, and in the Mediterranean, to which has been added a small armament to cruise on the eastern coast of South America. In all they have afforded protection to our commerce, have contributed to make our country advantageously known to foreign nations, have honorably employed multitudes of our sea men in the service of their country, and have inured numbers of youths of the rising generation to lives of manly hardihood and of nautical experience and skill.

The piracies with which the West India seas were for several years infested have been totally suppressed, but in the Mediterranean they have increased in a manner afflictive to other nations, and but for the continued presence of our squadron would probably have been distressing to our own.

The war which has unfortunately broken out between the Republic of Buenos Ayres and the Brazilian Government has given rise to very great irregularities among the naval officers of the latter, by whom principles in relation to blockades and to neutral navigation have been brought forward to which we can not subscribe and which our own commanders have found it necessary to resist. From the friendly disposition toward the United States constantly manifested by the Emperor of Brazil, and the very useful and friendly commercial intercourse between the United States and his dominions, we have reason to believe that the just reparation demanded for the injuries sustained by several of our citizens from some of his officers will not be withheld. Abstracts from the recent dispatches of the commanders of our several squadrons are communicated with the report of the Secretary of the Navy to Congress.

A report from the PostMaster General is likewise communicated, presenting in a highly satisfactory manner the result of a vigorous, efficient, and economical administration of that Department. The revenue of the office, even of the year including the latter half of 1824 and the first half of 1825, had exceeded its expenditures by a sum of more than $45,000. That of the succeeding year has been still more productive. The increase of the receipts in the year preceding the first of July last over that of the year before exceeds $136,000, and the excess of the receipts over the expenditures of the year has swollen from $45,000 to yearly $80,000.

During the same period contracts for additional transportation of the mail in stages for about 260,000 miles have been made, and for 70,000 miles annually on horse back. 714 new post offices have been established within the year, and the increase of revenue within the last 3 years, as well as the augmentation of the transportation by mail, is more than equal to the whole amount of receipts and of mail conveyance at the commencement of the present century, when the seat of the General Government was removed to this place. When we reflect that the objects effected by the transportation of the mail are among the choicest comforts and enjoyments of social life, it is pleasing to observe that the dissemination of them to every corner of our country has out– stripped in their increase even the rapid march of our population.

By the treaties with France and Spain, respectively ceding Louisiana and the Floridas to the United States, provision was made for the security of land titles derived from the Governments of those nations. Some progress has been made under the authority of various acts of Congress in the ascertainment and establishment of those titles, but claims to a very large extent remain unadjusted. The public faith no less than the just rights of individuals and the interest of the community itself appears to require further provision for the speedy settlement of those claims, which I therefore recommend to the care and attention of the Legislature.

In conformity with the provisions of the act of 1825–05–20, to provide for erecting a penitentiary in the District of Columbia, and for other purposes, 3 commissioners were appointed to select a site for the erection of a penitentiary for the District, and also a site in the county of Alexandria for a county jail, both of which objects have been effected. The building of the penitentiary has been commenced, and is in such a degree of forwardness as to promise that it will be completed before the meeting of the next Congress. This consideration points to the expediency of maturing at the present session a system for the regulation and government of the penitentiary, and of defining a system for the regulation and government of the penitentiary, and of defining the class of offenses which shall be punishable by confinement in this edifice.

In closing this communication I trust that it will not be deemed inappropriate to the occasion and purposes upon which we are here assembled to indulge a momentary retrospect, combining in a single glance the period of our origin as a national confederation with that of our present existence, at the precise interval of half a century from each other. Since your last meeting at this place the 50th anniversary of the day when our independence was declared has been celebrated throughout our land, and on that day, while every heart was bounding with joy and every voice was tuned to gratulation, amid the blessings of freedom and independence which the sires of a former age had handed down to their children, two of the principal actors in that solemn scene — the hand that penned the ever memorable Declaration and the voice that sustained it in debate — were by one summons, at the distance of 700 miles from each other, called before the Judge of All to account for their deeds done upon earth. They departed cheered by the benedictions of their country, to whom they left the inheritance of their fame and the memory of their bright example.

If we turn our thoughts to the condition of their country, in the contrast of the first and last day of that half century, how resplendent and sublime is the transition from gloom to glory! Then, glancing through the same lapse of time, in the condition of the individuals we see the first day marked with the fullness and vigor of youth, in the pledge of their lives, their fortunes, and their sacred honor to the cause of freedom and of man—kind; and on the last, extended on the bed of death, with but sense and sensibility left to breathe a last aspiration to Heaven of blessing upon their country, may we not humbly hope that to them too it was a pledge of transition from gloom to glory, and that while their mortal vestments were sinking into the clod of the valley their emancipated spirits were ascending to the bosom of their God! JOHN QUNICY ADAMS

State of the Union Address John Quincy Adams

December 4, 1827

Fellow Citizens of the Senate and of the House of Representatives:

A revolution of the seasons has nearly been completed since the representatives of the people and States of this Union were last assembled at this place to deliberate and to act upon the common important interests of their constituents. In that interval the never slumbering eye of a wise and beneficent Providence has continued its guardian care over the welfare of our beloved country; the blessing of health has continued generally to prevail throughout the land; the blessing of peace with our brethren of the human race has been enjoyed without interruption; internal quiet has left our fellow citizens in the full enjoyment of all their rights and in the free exercise of all their faculties, to pursue the impulse of their nature and the obligation of their duty in the improvement of their own condition; the productions of the soil, the exchanges of commerce, the vivifying labors of human industry, have combined to mingle in our cup a portion of enjoyment as large and liberal as the indulgence of Heaven has perhaps ever granted to the imperfect state of man upon earth; and as the purest of human felicity consists in its participation with others, it is no small addition to the sum of our national happiness at this time that peace and prosperity prevail to a degree seldom experienced over the whole habitable globe, presenting, though as yet with painful exceptions, a foretaste of that blessed period of promise when the lion shall lie down with the lamb and wars shall be no more.

To preserve, to improve, and to perpetuate the sources and to direct in their most effective channels the streams which contribute to the public weal is the purpose for which Government was instituted. Objects of deep importance to the welfare of the Union are constantly recurring to demand the attention of the Federal Legislature, and they call with accumulated interest at the first meeting of the two Houses after their periodical renovation. To present to their consideration from time to time subjects in which the interests of the nation are most deeply involved, and for the regulation of which the legislative will is alone competent, is a duty prescribed by the Constitution, to the performance of which the first meeting of the new Congress is a period eminently appropriate, and which it is now my purpose to discharge.

Our relations of friendship with the other nations of the earth, political and commercial, have been preserved unimpaired, and the opportunities to improve them have been cultivated with anxious and unremitting attention. A negotiation upon subjects of high and delicate interest with the Government of Great Britain has terminated in the adjustment of some of the questions at issue upon satisfactory terms and the postponement of others for future discussion and agreement.

The purposes of the convention concluded at St. Petersburg on 1822-07-12, under the mediation of the late Emperor Alexander, have been carried into effect by a subsequent convention, concluded at London on 1826-11-13, the ratifications of which were exchanged at that place on 1827-02-06. A copy of the proclamations issued on 1827-03-19, publishing this convention, is herewith communicated to Congress. The sum of $1,204,960, therein stipulated to be paid to the claimants of indemnity under the first article of the treaty of Ghent, has been duly received, and the commission instituted, comformably to the act of Congress of 1827-03-02, for the distribution of the indemnity of the persons entitled to receive it are now in session and approaching the consummation of their labors. This final disposal of one of the most painful topics of collision between the United States and Great Britain not only affords an occasion of gratulation to ourselves, but has had the happiest effect in promoting a friendly disposition and in softening asperities upon other objects of discussion; nor ought it to pass without the tribute of a frank and cordial acknowledgment of the magnanimity with which an honorable nation, by the reparation of their own wrongs, achieves a triumph more glorious than any field of blood can ever bestow.

The conventions of 1815–07–03, and of 1818–10–20, will expire by their own limitation on 1828–10–20. These have regulated the direct commercial intercourse between the United States and Great Britain upon terms of the most perfect reciprocity; and they effected a temporary compromise of the respective rights and claims to territory westward of the Rocky Mountains. These arrangements have been continued for an indefinite period of time after the expiration of the above mentioned conventions, leaving each party the liberty of terminating them by giving twelve months' notice to the other.

The radical principle of all commercial intercourse between independent nations is the mutual interest of both parties. It is the vital spirit of trade itself; nor can it be reconciled to the nature of man or to the primary laws of human society that any traffic should long be willingly pursued of which all the advantages are on one side and all the burdens on the other. Treaties of commerce have been found by experience to be among the most effective instruments for promoting peace and harmony between nations whose interests, exclusively considered on either side, are brought into frequent collisions by competition. In framing such treaties it is the duty of each party not simply to urge with unyielding pertinacity that which suits its own interest, but to concede liberally to that which is adapted to the interest of the other.

To accomplish this, little more is generally required than a simple observance of the rule of reciprocity, and were it possible for the states– men of 1 nation by stratagem and management to obtain from the weakness or ignorance of another an over–reaching treaty, such a compact would prove an incentive to war rather than a bond of peace.

Our conventions with Great Britain are founded upon the principles of reciprocity. The commercial intercourse between the two countries is greater in magnitude and amount than between any two other nations on the globe. It is for all purposes of benefit or advantage to both as precious, and in all probability far more extensive, than if the parties were still constituent parts of one and the same nation. Treaties between such States, regulating the intercourse of peace between them and adjusting interests of such transcendent importance to both, which have been found in a long experience of years mutually advantageous, should not be lightly cancelled or discontinued. Two conventions for continuing in force those above mentioned have been concluded between the plenipotentiaries of the two Governments on 1827–08–06, and will be forthwith laid before the Senate for the exercise of their constitutional authority concerning them.

In the execution of the treaties of peace of 1782–11 and 1783–09, between the United States and Great Britain, and which terminated the war of our independence, a line of boundary was drawn as the demarcation of territory between the two countries, extending over nearly 20 degrees of latitude, and ranging over seas, lakes, and mountains, then very imperfectly explored and scarcely opened to the geographical knowledge of the age. In the progress of discovery and settlement by both parties since that time several questions of boundary between their respective territories have arisen, which have been found of exceedingly difficult adjustment.

At the close of the last war with Great Britain four of these questions pressed themselves upon the consideration of the negotiators of the treaty of Ghent, but without the means of concluding a definitive arrangement concerning them. They were referred to three separate commissions consisting, of two commissioners, one appointed by each party, to examine and decide upon their respective claims. In the event of a disagreement between the commissioners, one appointed by each party, to examine and decide upon their respective claims. In the event of a disagreement between the commissioners it was provided that they should make reports to their several Governments, and that the reports should finally be referred to the decision of a sovereign the common friend of both.

Of these commissions two have already terminated their sessions and investigations, one by entire and the other by partial agreement. The commissioners of the 5th article of the treaty of Ghent have finally disagreed, and made their conflicting reports to their own Governments. But from these reports a great difficulty has occurred in making up a question to be decided by the arbitrator. This purpose has, however, been effected by a 4th convention, concluded at London by the plenipotentiaries of the two Governments on 1827–09–29. It will be submitted, together with the others, to the consideration of the Senate.

While these questions have been pending incidents have occurred of conflicting pretensions and of dangerous character upon the territory itself in dispute between the two nations. By a common understanding between the Governments it was agreed that no exercise of exclusive jurisdiction by either party while the negotiation was pending should change the state of the question of right to be definitively settled. Such collision has, never the less, recently taken place by occurrences the precise character of which has not yet been ascertained. A communication from the governor of the State of Maine, with accompanying documents, and a correspondence between the Secretary of State and the minister of Great Britain on this subject are now communicated. Measures have been taken to ascertain the state of the facts more correctly by the employment of a special agent to visit the spot where the alleged outrages have occurred, the result of those inquiries, when received, will be transmitted to Congress.

While so many of the subjects of high interest to the friendly relations between the two countries have been so far adjusted, it is a matter of regret that their views respecting the commercial intercourse between the United States and the British colonial possessions have not equally approximated to a friendly agreement.

At the commencement of the last session of Congress they were informed of the sudden and unexpected exclusion by the British Government of access in vessels of the United States to all their colonial ports except those immediately bordering upon our own territories. In the amicable discussions which have succeeded the adoption of this measure which, as it affected harshly the interests of the United States, became subject of expostulation on our part, the principles upon which its justification has been placed have been of a diversified character. It has been at once ascribed to a mere recurrence to the old, long established principle of colonial monopoly and at the same time to a feeling of resentment because the offers of an act of Parliament opening the colonial ports upon certain conditions had not been grasped at with sufficient eagerness by an instantaneous conformity to them.

At a subsequent period it has been intimated that the new exclusion was in resentment because a prior act of Parliament, of 1822, opening certain colonial ports, under heavy and burdensome restrictions, to vessels of the United States, had not been reciprocated by an admission of British vessels from the colonies, and their cargoes, without any restriction or discrimination what ever. But be the motive for the interdiction what it may, the British Government have manifested no disposition, either by negotiation or by corresponding legislative enactments, to recede from it, and we have been given distinctly to understand that neither of the bills which were under the consideration of Congress at their last session would have been deemed sufficient in their concessions to have been rewarded by any relaxation from the British interdict. It is one of the inconveniences inseparably connected with the attempt to adjust by reciprocal legislation interests of this nature that neither party can know what would be satisfactory to the other, and that after enacting a statute for the avowed and sincere purpose of conciliation it will generally be found utterly inadequate to the expectation of the other party, and will terminate in mutual disappointment.

The session of Congress having terminated without any act upon the subject, a proclamation was issued on 1827-03-17, conformably to the provisions of the 6th section of the act of 1823-03-01 declaring the fact that the trade and intercourse authorized by the British act of Parliament of 1822-06-24, between the United States and the British enumerated colonial ports had been by the subsequent acts of Parliament of 1825-07-05, and the order of council of 1826-07-27 prohibited. The effect of this proclamation, by the terms of the act under which it was issued, has been that each and every provision of the act concerning navigation of 1818-04-18, and of the act supplementary thereto of 1820-05-15, revived and is in full force.

Such, then is the present condition of the trade that, useful as it is to both parties it can, with a single momentary exception, be carried on directly by the vessels of neither. That exception itself is found in a proclamation of the governor of the island of St. Christopher and of the Virgin Islands, inviting for 3 months from 1827-08-28 the importation of the articles of the produce of the United States which constitute their export portion of this trade in the vessels of all nations.

That period having already expired, the state of mutual interdiction has again taken place. The British Government have not only declined negotiation upon this subject, but by the principle they have assumed with reference to it have precluded even the means of negotiation. It becomes not the self respect of the United States either to solicit gratuitous favors or to accept as the grant of a favor that for which an ample equivalent is exacted. It remains to be determined by the respective Governments whether the trade shall be opened by acts of reciprocal legislation. It is, in the mean time, satisfactory to know that apart from the inconvenience resulting from a disturbance of the usual channels of trade no loss has been sustained by the commerce, the navigation, or the revenue of the United

43

States, and none of magnitude is to be apprehended from this existing state of mutual interdict.

With the other maritime and commercial nations of Europe our intercourse continues with little variation. Since the cessation by the convention of 1822–06–24, of all discriminating duties upon the vessels of the United States and of France in either country our trade with that nation has increased and is increasing. A disposition on the part of France has been manifested to renew that negotiation, and in acceding to the proposal we have expressed the wish that it might be extended to other subjects upon which a good understanding between the parties would be beneficial to the interests of both.

The origin of the political relations between the United States and France is coeval with the first years of our independence. The memory of it is interwoven with that of our arduous struggle for national existence. Weakened as it has occasionally been since that time, it can by us never be forgotten, and we should hail with exultation the moment which should indicate a recollection equally friendly in spirit on the part of France.

A fresh effort has recently been made by the minister of the United States residing at Paris to obtain a consideration of the just claims of citizens of the United States to the reparation of wrongs long since committed, many of them frankly acknowledged and all of them entitled upon every principle of justice to a candid examination. The proposal last made to the French Government has been to refer the subject which has formed an obstacle to this consideration to the determination of a sovereign the common friend of both. To this offer no definitive answer has yet been received, but the gallant and honorable spirit which has at all times been the pride and glory of France will not ultimately permit the demands of innocent sufferers to be extinguished in the mere consciousness of the power to reject them.

A new treaty of amity, navigation, and commerce has been concluded with the Kingdom of Sweden, which will be submitted to the Senate for their advice with regard to its ratification. At a more recent date a minister plenipotentiary from the Hanseatic Republics of Hamburg, Lubeck, and Bremen has been received, charged with a special mission for the negotiation of a treaty of amity and commerce between that ancient and renowned league and the United States. This negotiation has accordingly been commenced, and is now in progress, the result of which will, if successful, be also submitted to the Senate for their consideration.

44

Since the accession of the Emperor Nicholas to the imperial throne of all the Russias the friendly dispositions toward the United States so constantly manifested by his predecessor have continued unabated, and have been recently testified by the appointment of a minister plenipotentiary to reside at this place. From the interest taken by this Sovereign in behalf of the suffering Greeks and from the spirit with which others of the great European powers are cooperating with him the friends of freedom and of humanity may indulge the hope that they will obtain relief from that most unequal of conflicts which they have so long and so gallantly sustained; that they will enjoy the blessing of self government, which by their sufferings in the cause of liberty they have richly earned, and that their independence will be secured by those liberal institutions of which their country furnished the earliest examples in the history of man–kind, and which have consecrated to immortal remembrance the very soil for which they are now again profusely pouring forth their blood. The sympathies which the people and Government of the United States have so warmly indulged with their cause have been acknowledged by their Government in a letter of thanks, which I have received from their illustrious President, a translation of which is now communicated to Congress, the representatives of that nation to whom this tribute of gratitude was intended to be paid, and to whom it was justly due.

In the American hemisphere the cause of freedom and independence has continued to prevail, and if signalized by none of those splendid triumphs which had crowned with glory some of the preceding years it has only been from the banishment of all external force against which the struggle had been maintained. The shout of victory has been superseded by the expulsion of the enemy over whom it could have been achieved.

Our friendly wishes and cordial good will, which have constantly followed the southern nations of America in all the vicissitudes of their war of independence, are succeeded by a solicitude equally ardent and cordial that by the wisdom and purity of their institutions they may secure to themselves the choicest blessings of social order and the best rewards of virtuous liberty. Disclaiming alike all right and all intention of interfering in those concerns which it is the prerogative of their independence to regulate as to them shall seem fit, we hail with joy every indication of their prosperity, of their harmony, of their persevering and inflexible homage to those principles of freedom and of equal rights which are alone suited to the genius and temper of the American nations.

It has been, therefore, with some concern that we have observed indications of intestine divisions in some of the Republics of the south, and appearances of less union with one another than we believe to be the interest of all. Among the results of this state of things has been that the treaties concluded at Panama do not appear to have been ratified by the contracting parties, and that the meeting of the congress at Tacubaya has been indefinitely postponed. In accepting the invitations to be represented at this congress, while a manifestation was intended on the part of the United States of the most friendly disposition toward the southern Republics by whom it had been proposed, it was hoped that it would furnish an opportunity for bringing all the nations of this hemisphere to the common acknowledgment and adoption of the principles in the regulation of their internal relations which would have secured a lasting peace and harmony between them and have promoted the cause of mutual benevolence throughout the globe. But as obstacles appear to have arisen to the reassembling of the congress, one of the 2 ministers commissioned on the part of the United States has returned to the bosom of his country, while the minister charged with the ordinary mission to Mexico remains authorized to attend the conferences of the congress when ever they may be resumed.

A hope was for a short time entertained that a treaty of peace actually signed between the Government of Buenos Ayres and of Brazil would supersede all further occasion for those collisions between belligerent pretensions and neutral rights which are so commonly the result of maritime war, and which have unfortunately disturbed the harmony of the relations between the United States and the Brazilian Governments. At their last session Congress were informed that some of the naval officers of that Empire had advanced and practiced upon principles in relation to blockades and to neutral navigation which we could not sanction, and which our commanders found it necessary to resist. It appears that they have not been sustained by the Government of Brazil itself. Some of the vessels captured under the assumed authority of these erroneous principles have been restored, and we trust that our just expectations will be realized that adequate indemnity will be made to all the citizens of the United States who have suffered by the unwarranted captures which the Brazilian tribunals themselves have pronounced unlawful.

In the diplomatic discussions at Rio de Janeiro of these wrongs sustained by citizens of the United States and of others which seemed as if emanating immediately from that Government itself the charge' d'affaires of the United States, under an impression that his representations in behalf of the rights and interests of his country—men were totally

46

disregarded and useless, deemed it his duty, without waiting for instructions, to terminate his official functions, to demand his pass– ports, and return to the United States. This movement, dictated by an honest zeal for the honor and interests of his country — motives which operated exclusively on the mind of the officer who resorted to it — has not been disapproved by me.

The Brazilian Government, however, complained of it as a measure for which no adequate intentional cause had been given by them, and upon an explicit assurance through their charge' d'affaires residing here that a successor to the late representative of the United States near that Government, the appointment of whom they desired, should be received and treated with the respect due to his character, and that indemnity should be promptly made for all injuries inflicted on citizens of the United States or their property contrary to the laws of nations, a temporary commission as charge' d'affaires to that country has been issued, which it is hopes will entirely restore the ordinary diplomatic intercourse between the 2 Governments and the friendly relations between their respective nations.

Turning from the momentous concerns of our Union in its intercourse with foreign nations to those of the deepest interest in the administration of our internal affairs, we find the revenues of the present year corresponding as nearly as might be expected with the anticipations of the last, and presenting an aspect still more favorable in the promise of the next.

The balance in the Treasury on 1827–01–01 was $6,358,686.18. The receipts from that day to 1827–09–30, as near as the returns of them yet received can show, amount to $16,886,581.32. The receipts of the present quarter, estimated at $4,515,000, added to the above form an aggregate of $21,400,000 of receipts.

The expenditures of the year may perhaps amount to $22,300,000 presenting a small excess over the receipts. But of these $22,000,000, upward of $6,000,000 have been applied to the discharge of the principal of the public debt, the whole amount of which, approaching $74,000,000 on 1827–01–01, will on 1828–01–01 fall short of $67,500,000. The balance in the Treasury on 1828–01–01 it is expected will exceed $5,450,000, a sum exceeding that of 1825–01–01, though falling short of that exhibited on 1827–01–01.

State of the Union Addresses

It was foreseen that the revenue of the present year 1827 would not equal that of the last, which had itself been less than that of the next preceding year. But the hope has been realized which was entertained, that these deficiencies would in no wise interrupt the steady operation of the discharge of the public debt by the annual $10,000,000 devoted to that object by the act of 1817-03-03.

The amount of duties secured on merchandise imported from the commencement of the year until 1827-09-30 is $21,226,000, and the probably amount of that which will be secured during the remainder of the year is $5,774,000, forming a sum total of $27,000,000. With the allowances for draw-backs and contingent deficiencies which may occur, though not specifically foreseen, we may safely estimate the receipts of the ensuing year at $22,300,000 — a revenue for the next equal to the expenditure of the present year.

The deep solicitude felt by our citizens of all classes throughout the Union for the total discharge of the public debt will apologize for the earnestness with which I deem it my duty to urge this topic upon the consideration of Congress — of recommending to them again the observance of the strictest economy in the application of the public funds. The depression upon the receipts of the revenue which had commenced with the year 1826 continued with increased severity during the two first quarters of the present year.

The returning tide began to flow with the third quarter, and, so far as we can judge from experience, may be expected to continue through the course of the ensuing year. In the mean time an alleviation from the burden of the public debt will in the three years have been effected to the amount of nearly $16,000,000, and the charge of annual interest will have been reduced upward of $1,000,000. But among the maxims of political economy which the stewards of the public moneys should never suffer without urgent necessity to be transcended is that of keeping the expenditures of the year within the limits of its receipts.

The appropriations of the two last years, including the yearly $10,000,000 of the sinking fund, have each equaled the promised revenue of the ensuing year. While we foresee with confidence that the public coffers will be replenished from the receipts as fast as they will be drained by the expenditures, equal in amount to those of the current year, it should not be forgotten that they could ill suffer the exhaustion of larger disbursements.

State of the Union Addresses

The condition of the Army and of all the branches of the public service under the superintendence of the Secretary of War will be seen by the report from that officer and the documents with which it is accompanied.

During the last summer a detachment of the Army has been usefully and successfully called to perform their appropriate duties. At the moment when the commissioners appointed for carrying into execution certain provisions of the treaty of 1825-08-19, with various tribes of the NorthWestern Indians were about to arrive at the appointed place of meeting the unprovoked murder of several citizens and other acts of unequivocal hostility committed by a party of the Winnebago tribe, one of those associated in the treaty, followed by indications of a menacing character among other tribes of the same region, rendered necessary an immediate display of the defensive and protective force of the Union in that quarter.

It was accordingly exhibited by the immediate and concerted movements of the governors of the State of Illinois and of the Territory of Michigan, and competent levies of militia, under their authority, with a corps of 700 men of United States troops, under the command of General Atkinson, who, at the call of Governor Cass, immediately repaired to the scene of danger from their station at St. Louis. Their presence dispelled the alarms of our fellow citizens on those disorders, and overawed the hostile purposes of the Indians. The perpetrators of the murders were surrendered to the authority and operation of our laws, and every appearance of purposed hostility from those Indian tribes has subsided.

Although the present organization of the Army and the administration of its various branches of service are, upon the whole, satisfactory, they are yet susceptible of much improvement in particulars, some of which have been heretofore submitted to the consideration of Congress, and others are now first presented in the report of the Secretary of War.

The expediency of providing for additional numbers of officers in the two corps of engineers will in some degree depend upon the number and extent of the objects of national importance upon which Congress may think it proper that surveys should be made conformably to the act of 1824-04-30. Of the surveys which before the last session of Congress had been made under the authority of that act, reports were made — Of the Board of Internal Improvement, on the Chesapeake and Ohio Canal. On the continuation

49

of the national road from Cumberland to the tide waters within the District of Columbia. On the continuation of the national road from Canton to Zanesville. On the location of the national road from Zanesville to Columbus. On the continuation of the same to the seat of government in Missouri. On a post road from Baltimore to Philadelphia. Of a survey of Kennebec River (in part). On a national road from Washington to Buffalo. On the survey of Saugatuck Harbor and River. On a canal from Lake PontChartrain to the Mississippi River. On surveys at Edgartown, Newburyport, and Hyannis Harbor. On survey of La Plaisance Bay, in the Territory of Michigan. And reports are now prepared and will be submitted to Congress — On surveys of the peninsula of Florida, to ascertain the practicability of a canal to connect the waters of the Atlantic with the Gulf of Mexico across that peninsula; and also of the country between the bays of Mobile and of Pensacola, with the view of connecting them together by a canal. On surveys of a route for a canal to connect the waters of James and Great Kenhawa rivers. On the survey of the Swash, in Pamlico Sound, and that of Cape Fear, below the town of Wilmington, in North Carolina. On the survey of the Muscle Shoals, in the Tennessee River, and for a route for a contemplated communication between the Hiwassee and Coosa rivers, in the State of Alabama. Other reports of surveys upon objects pointed out by the several acts of Congress of the last and preceding sessions are in the progress of preparation, and most of them may be completed before the close of this session. All the officers of both corps of engineers, with several other persons duly qualified, have been constantly employed upon these services from the passage of the act of 1824–04–30, to this time.

Were no other advantage to accrue to the country from their labors than the fund of topographical knowledge which they have collected and communicated, that alone would have been a profit to the Union more than adequate to all the expenditures which have been devoted to the object; but the appropriations for the repair and continuation of the Cumberland road, for the construction of various other roads, for the removal of obstructions from the rivers and harbors, for the erection of light houses, beacons, piers, and buoys, and for the completion of canals undertaken by individual associations, but needing the assistance of means and resources more comprehensive than individual enterprise can command, may be considered rather as treasures laid up from the contributions of the present age for the benefit of posterity than as unrequited applications of the accruing revenues of the nation.

To such objects of permanent improvement to the condition of the country, of real addition to the wealth as well as to the comfort of the people by whose authority and resources they have been effected, from $3,000,000 to $4,000,000 of the annual income of the nation have, by laws enacted at the three most recent sessions of Congress, been applied, without intrenching upon the necessities of the Treasury, without adding a dollar to the taxes or debts of the community, without suspending even the steady and regular discharge of the debts contracted in former days, which within the same three years have been diminished by the amount of nearly $16,000,000.

The same observations are in a great degree applicable to the appropriations made for fortifications upon the coasts and harbors of the United States, for the maintenance of the Military Academy at West Point, and for the various objects under the superintendence of the Department of the Navy. The report from the Secretary of the Navy and those from the subordinate branches of both the military departments exhibit to Congress in minute detail the present condition of the public establishments dependent upon them, the execution of the acts of Congress relating to them, and the views of the officers engaged in the several branches of the service concerning the improvements which may tend to their perfection.

The fortification of the coasts and the gradual increase and improvement of the Navy are parts of a great system of national defense which has been upward of 10 years in progress, and which for a series of years to come will continue to claim the constant and persevering protection and superintendence of the legislative authority. Among the measures which have emanated from these principles the act of the last session of Congress for the gradual improvement of the Navy holds a conspicuous place. The collection of timber for the future construction of vessels of war, the preservation and reproduction of the species of timber peculiarly adapted to that purpose, the construction of dry docks for the use of the Navy, the erection of a marine railway for the repair of the public ships, and the improvement of the navy yards for the preservation of the public property deposited in them have all received from the Executive the attention required by that act, and will continue to receive it, steadily proceeding toward the execution of all its purposes.

The establishment of a naval academy, furnishing the means of theoretic instruction to the youths who devote their lives to the service of their country upon the ocean, still solicits the sanction of the Legislature. Practical seamanship and the art of navigation may be acquired on the cruises of the squadrons which from time to time are dispatched to distant seas, but a competent knowledge even of the art of ship building, the higher mathematics, and astronomy; the literature which can place our officers on a level of polished education with the officers of other maritime nations; the knowledge of the laws, municipal and national, which in their intercourse with foreign states and their governments are continually called into operation, and, above all, that acquaintance with the principles of honor and justice, with the higher obligations of morals and of general laws, human and divine, which constitutes the great distinction between the warrior–patriot and the licensed robber and pirate — these can be systematically taught and eminently acquired only in a permanent school, stationed upon the shore and provided with the teachers, the instruments, and the books conversant with and adapted to the communication of the principles of these respective sciences to the youthful and inquiring mind.

The report from the PostMaster General exhibits the condition of that Department as highly satisfactory for the present and still more promising for the future. Its receipts for the year ending 1827–07–01 amounted to $1,473,551, and exceeded its expenditures by upward of $100,000. It can not be an over sanguine estimate to predict that in less than 10 years, of which half have elapsed, the receipts will have been more than doubled.

In the mean time a reduced expenditure upon established routes has kept pace with increased facilities of public accommodation and additional services have been obtained at reduced rates of compensation. Within the last year the transportation of the mail in stages has been greatly augmented. The number of post offices has been increased to 7,000, and it may be anticipated that while the facilities of intercourse between fellow citizens in person or by correspondence will soon be carried to the door of every villager in the Union, a yearly surplus of revenue will accrue which may be applied as the wisdom of Congress under the exercise of their constitutional powers may devise for the further establishment and improvement of the public roads, or by adding still further to the facilities in the transportation of the mails. Of the indications of the prosperous condition of our country, none can be more pleasing than those presented by the multiplying relations of personal and intimate intercourse between the citizens of the Union dwelling at the remotest distances from each other.

Among the subjects which have heretofore occupied the earnest solicitude and attention of Congress is the management and disposal of that portion of the property of the nation which consists of the public lands. The acquisition of them, made at the expense of the whole Union, not only in treasury but in blood, marks a right of property in them equally extensive. By the report and statements from the General Land Office now communicated it appears that under the present Government of the United States a sum little short of $33,000,000 has been paid from the common Treasury for that portion of this property which has been purchased from France and Spain, and for the extinction of the aboriginal titles. The amount of lands acquired is near 260,000,000 acres, of which on 1826-01-01, about 139,000,000 acres had been surveyed, and little more than 19,000,000 acres had been sold. The amount paid into the Treasury by the purchasers of the public lands sold is not yet equal to the sums paid for the whole, but leaves a small balance to be refunded. The proceeds of the sales of the lands have long been pledged to the creditors of the nation, a pledge from which we have reason to hope that they will in a very few years be redeemed.

The system upon which this great national interest has been managed was the result of long, anxious, and persevering deliberation. Matured and modified by the progress of our population and the lessons of experience, it has been hitherto eminently successful. More than 9/10 of the lands still remain the common property of the Union, the appropriation and disposal of which are sacred trusts in the hands of Congress.

Of the lands sold, a considerable part were conveyed under extended credits, which in the vicissitudes and fluctuations in the value of lands and of their produce became oppressively burdensome to the purchasers. It can never be the interest or the policy of the nation to wring from its own citizens the reasonable profits of their industry and enterprise by holding them to the rigorous import of disastrous engagements. In 1821-03, a debt of $22,000,000, due by purchasers of the public lands, had accumulated, which they were unable to pay. An act of Congress of 1821-03-02, came to their relief, and has been succeeded by others, the latest being the act of 1826-05-04, the indulgent provisions of which expired on 1827-07-04. The effect of these laws has been to reduce the debt from the purchasers to a remaining balance of about $4,300,000 due, more than 3/5 of which are for lands within the State of Alabama. I recommend to Congress the revival and continuance for a further term of the beneficent accommodations to the public debtors of that statute, and submit to their consideration, in the same spirit of equity, the remission, under proper discriminations, of the forfeitures of partial payments on account of purchases of the public lands, so far as to allow of their application to other payments.

There are various other subjects of deep interest to the whole Union which have heretofore been recommended to the consideration of Congress, as well by my predecessors as, under the impression of the duties devolving upon me, by myself. Among these are the debt, rather of justice than gratitude, to the surviving warriors of the Revolutionary war; the extension of the judicial administration of the Federal Government to those extensive since the organization of the present judiciary establishment, now constitute at least 1/3 of its territory, power, and population; the formation of a more effective and uniform system for the government of the militia, and the amelioration in some form or modification of the diversified and often oppressive codes relating to insolvency. Amidst the multiplicity of topics of great national concernment which may recommend themselves to the calm and patriotic deliberations of the Legislature, it may suffice to say that on these and all other measures which may receive their sanction my hearty cooperation will be given, conformably to the duties enjoined upon me and under the sense of all the obligations prescribed by the Constitution. JOHN QUNICY ADAMS

State of the Union Address John Quincy Adams

December 2, 1828

Fellow Citizens of the Senate and of the House of Representatives:

If the enjoyment in profusion of the bounties of Providence forms a suitable subject of mutual gratulation and grateful acknowledgment, we are admonished at this return of the season when the representatives of the nation are assembled to deliberate upon their concerns to offer up the tribute of fervent and grateful hearts for the never failing mercies of Him who ruleth over all. He has again favored us with healthful seasons and abundant harvests; He has sustained us in peace with foreign countries and in tranquillity within our borders; He has preserved us in the quiet and undisturbed possession of civil and religious liberty; He has crowned the year with His goodness, imposing on us no other condition than of improving for our own happiness the blessings bestowed by His hands, and, in the fruition of all His favors, of devoting his faculties with which we have been endowed by Him to His glory and to our own temporal and eternal welfare.

In the relations of our Federal Union with our brethren of the human race the changes which have occurred since the close of your last session have generally tended to the preservation of peace and to the cultivation of harmony. Before your last separation a war had unhappily been kindled between the Empire of Russia, one of those with which our intercourse has been no other than a constant exchange of good offices, and that of the Ottoman Porte, a nation from which geographical distance, religious opinions and maxims of government on their part little suited to the formation of those bonds of mutual benevolence which result from the benefits of commerce had department us in a state, perhaps too much prolonged, of coldness and alienation.

The extensive, fertile, and populous dominions of the Sultan belong rather to the Asiatic than the European division of the human family. They enter but partially into the system of Europe, nor have their wars with Russia and Austria, the European States upon which they border, for more than a century past disturbed the pacific relations of those States with the other great powers of Europe. Neither France nor Prussia nor Great Britain has ever taken part in them, nor is it to be expected that they will at this time. The declaration of war by Russia has received the approbation or acquiescence of her allies, and we may indulge the hope that its progress and termination will be signalized by the moderation and forbearance no less than by the energy of the Emperor Nicholas, and that it will afford the opportunity for such collateral agency in behalf of the suffering Greeks as will secure to them ultimately the triumph of humanity and of freedom.

The state of our particular relations with France has scarcely varied in the course of the present year. The commercial intercourse between the two countries has continued to increase for the mutual benefit of both. The claims of indemnity to numbers of our fellow citizens for depredations upon their property, heretofore committed during the revolutionary governments, remain unadjusted, and still form the subject of earnest representation and remonstrance. Recent advices from the minister of the United States at Paris encourage the expectation that the appeal to the justice of the French Government will ere long receive a favorable consideration.

The last friendly expedient has been resorted to for the decision of the controversy with Great Britain relating to the north–eastern boundary of the United States. By an agreement with the British Government, carrying into effect the provisions of the 5th article of the treaty of Ghent, and the convention of 1827–09–29, His Majesty the King of the Netherlands has by common consent been selected as the umpire between the parties. The proposal to him to accept the designation for the performance of this friendly office will be made at an early day, and the United States, relying upon the justice of their cause, will cheerfully commit the arbitrament of it to a prince equally distinguished for the independence of his spirit, his indefatigable assiduity to the duties of his station, and his inflexible personal probity.

Our commercial relations with Great Britain will deserve the serious consideration of Congress and the exercise of a conciliatory and forbearing spirit in the policy of both Governments. The state of them has been materially changed by the act of Congress, passed at their last session, in alteration of several acts imposing duties on imports, and by acts of more recent date of the British Parliament. The effect of the interdiction of direct trade, commenced by Great Britain and reciprocated by the United States, has been, as was to be foreseen, only to substitute different channels for an exchange of commodities indispensable to the colonies and profitable to a numerous class of our fellow citizens. The exports, the revenue, the navigation of the United States have suffered no diminution by our exclusion from direct access to the British colonies. The colonies pay more dearly for the necessaries of life which their Government burdens with the charges of double voyages, freight, insurance, and commission, and the profits of our exports are somewhat impaired and more injuriously transferred from one portion of our citizens to another.

The resumption of this old and otherwise exploded system of colonial exclusion has not secured to the shipping interest of Great Britain the relief which, at the expense of the distant colonies and of the United States, it was expected to afford. Other measures have been resorted to more pointedly bearing upon the navigation of the United States, and more pointedly bearing upon the navigation of the United States, and which, unless modified by the construction given to the recent acts of Parliament, will be manifestly incompatible with the positive stipulations of the commercial convention existing between the two countries. That convention, however, may be terminated with 12 months' notice, at the option of either party.

A treaty of amity, navigation, and commerce between the United States and His Majesty the Emperor of Austria, King of Hungary and Bohemia, has been prepared for signature by the Secretary of State and by the Baron de Lederer, intrusted with full powers of the Austrian Government. Independently of the new and friendly relations which may be thus commenced with one of the most eminent and powerful nations of the earth, the occasion has been taken in it, as in other recent treaties concluded by the United States, to extend those principles of liberal intercourse and of fair reciprocity which intertwine with the exchanges of commerce the principles of justice and the feelings of mutual benevolence.

This system, first proclaimed to the world in the first commercial treaty ever concluded by the United States — that of 1778–02–06, with France — has been invariably the cherished policy of our Union. It is by treaties of commerce alone that it can be made ultimately to prevail as the established system of all civilized nations. With this principle our fathers extended the hand of friendship to every nation of the globe, and to this policy our country has ever since adhered. What ever of regulation in our laws has ever been adopted unfavorable to the interest of any foreign nation has been essentially defensive and counteracting to similar regulations of theirs operating against us.

Immediately after the close of the War of Independence commissioners were appointed by the Congress of the Confederation authorized to conclude treaties with every nation of Europe disposed to adopt them. Before the wars of the French Revolution such treaties had been consummated with the United Netherlands, Sweden, and Prussia. During those wars treaties with Great Britain and Spain had been effected, and those with Prussia and France renewed. In all these some concessions to the liberal principles of intercourse proposed by the United States had been obtained; but as in all the negotiations they came occasionally in collision with previous internal regulations or exclusive and excluding compacts of monopoly with which the other parties had been trammeled, the advances made in them toward the freedom of trade were partial and imperfect. Colonial establishments, chartered companies, and ship building influence pervaded and encumbered the legislation of all the great commercial states; and the United States, in offering free trade and equal privilege to all, were compelled to acquiesce in many exceptions with each of the parties to their treaties, accommodated to their existing laws and anterior agreements.

The colonial system by which this whole hemisphere was bound has fallen into ruins, totally abolished by revolutions converting colonies into independent nations throughout the two American continents, excepting a portion of territory chiefly at the northern extremity of our own, and confined to the remnants of dominion retained by Great Britain over the insular archipelago, geographically the appendages of our part of the globe. With all the rest we have free trade, even with the insular colonies of all the European nations, except Great Britain. Her Government also had manifested approaches to the adoption of a free and liberal intercourse between her colonies and other nations, though by a sudden and scarcely explained revulsion the spirit of exclusion has been revived for operation upon the United States alone.

The conclusion of our last treaty of peace with Great Britain was shortly afterwards followed by a commercial convention, placing the direct intercourse between the two countries upon a footing of more equal reciprocity than had ever before been admitted. The same principle has since been much further extended by treaties with France, Sweden, Denmark, the Hanseatic cities, Prussia, in Europe, and with the Republics of Colombia and of Central America, in this hemisphere. The mutual abolition of discriminating duties and charges upon the navigation and commercial intercourse between the parties is the general maxim which characterizes them all. There is reason to expect that it will at no distant period be adopted by other nations, both of Europe and America, and to hope that by its universal prevalence one of the fruitful sources of wars of commercial competition will be extinguished.

Among the nations upon whose Governments many of our fellow citizens have had long–pending claims of indemnity for depredations upon their property during a period when the rights of neutral commerce were disregarded was that of Denmark. They were soon after the events occurred the subject of a special mission from the United States, at the close of which the assurance was given by His Danish Majesty that at a period of more tranquillity and of less distress they would be considered, examined, and decided upon in a spirit of determined purpose for the dispensation of justice. I have much pleasure in informing Congress that the fulfillment of this honorable promise is now in progress; that a small portion of the claims has already been settled to the satisfaction of the claimants, and that we have reason to hope that the remainder will shortly be placed in a train of equitable adjustment. This result has always been confidently expected, from the character of personal integrity and of benevolence which the Sovereign of the Danish dominions has through every vicissitude of fortune maintained.

The general aspect of the affairs of our neighboring American nations of the south has been rather of approaching than of settled tranquillity. Internal disturbances have been more frequent among them than their common friends would have desired. Our intercourse with all has continued to be that of friendship and of mutual good will. Treaties of commerce and of boundaries with the United Mexican States have been negotiated, but, from various successive obstacles, not yet brought to a final conclusion.

The civil war which unfortunately still prevails in the Republics of Central America has been unpropitious to the cultivation of our commercial relations with them; and the dissensions and revolutionary changes in the Republics of Colombia and of Peru have been seen with cordial regret by us, who would gladly contribute to the happiness of both. It is with great satisfaction, however, that we have witnessed the recent conclusion of a peace between the Governments of Buenos Ayres and of Brazil, and it is equally gratifying to observe that indemnity has been obtained for some of the injuries which our fellow citizens had sustained in the latter of those countries. The rest are in a train of negotiation, which we hope may terminate to mutual satisfaction, and that it may be succeeded by a treaty of commerce and navigation, upon liberal principles, propitious to a great and growing commerce, already important to the interests of our country.

The condition and prospects of the revenue are more favorable than our most sanguine expectations had anticipated. The balance in the Treasury on 1828–01–01, exclusive of the moneys received under the convention of 1826–11–13, with Great Britain, was $5,861,972.83. The receipts into the Treasury from 1828–01–01 to 1828–09–30, so far as they have been ascertained to form the basis of an estimate, amount to $18,633,580.27, which, with the receipts of the present quarter, estimated at $5,461,283.40, form an aggregate of receipts during the year of $24,094,863.67. The expenditures of the year may probably amount to $25,637,111.63, and leave in the Treasury on 1829–01–01 the sum of $5,125,638.14.

The receipts of the present year have amounted to near $2,000,000 more than was anticipated at the commencement of the last session of Congress.

The amount of duties secured on importations from the first of January to the 30th of September was about $22,997,000, and that of the estimated accruing revenue is $5,000,000, forming an aggregate for the year of near $28,000,000. This is $1,000,000 more than the estimate last December for the accruing revenue of the present year, which, with allowances for draw–backs and contingent deficiencies, was expected to produce an actual revenue of $22,300,000. Had these only been realized the expenditures of the year would have been also proportionally reduced, for of these $24,000,000 received upward of $9,000,000 have been applied to the extinction of public debt, bearing an interest of 6% a year, and of course reducing the burden of interest annually payable in future by the amount of more than $500,000. The payments on account of interest during the current year exceed $3,000,000, presenting an aggregate of more than $12,000,000 applied during the year to the discharge of the public debt, the whole of which remaining due on 1829–01–01 will amount only to $58,362,135.78.

That the revenue of the ensuing year will not fall short of that received in the one now expiring there are indications which can scarcely prove deceptive. In our country an uniform experience of 40 years has shown that what ever the tariff of duties upon articles imported from abroad has been, the amount of importations has always borne an average value nearly approaching to that of the exports, though occasionally differing in the balance, some times being more and some times less. It is, indeed, a general law of prosperous commerce that the real value of exports should by a small, and only a small, balance exceed that of imports, that balance being a permanent addition to the wealth of the nation.

The extent of the prosperous commerce of the nation must be regulated by the amount of its exports, and an important addition to the value of these will draw after it a corresponding increase of importations. It has happened in the vicissitudes of the seasons that the harvests of all Europe have in the late summer and autumn fallen short of their usual average. A relaxation of the interdict upon the importation of grain and flour from abroad has ensued, a propitious market has been opened to the granaries of our country, and a new prospect of reward presented to the labors of the husband–man, which for several years has been denied. This accession to the profits of agriculture in the middle and western portions of our Union is accidental and temporary. It may continue only for a single year. It may be, as has been often experienced in the revolutions of time, but the first of several scanty harvests in succession. We may consider it certain that for the approaching year it has added an item of large amount to the value of our exports and that it will produce a corresponding increase of importations. It may therefore confidently be foreseen that the revenue of 1829 will equal and probably exceed that of 1828, and will afford the means of extinguishing $10,000,000 more of the principal of the public debt.

This new element of prosperity to that part of our agricultural industry which is occupied in producing the first article of human subsistence is of the most cheering character to the feelings of patriotism. Proceeding from a cause which humanity will view with concern, the sufferings of scarcity in distant lands, it yields a consolatory reflection that this scarcity is in no respect attributable to us; that it comes from the dispensation of Him who ordains all in wisdom and goodness, and who permits evil itself only as an instrument of good; that, far from contributing to this scarcity, our agency will be applied only to the alleviation of its severity, and that in pouring forth from the abundance of our own garners the supplies which will partially restore plenty to those who are in need we shall ourselves reduce our stores and add to the price of our own bread, so as in some degree to participate in the wants which it will be the good fortune of our country to relieve.

The great interests of an agricultural, commercial, and manufacturing nation are so linked in union together that no permanent cause of prosperity to one of them can operate without extending its influence to the others. All these interests are alike under the protecting power of the legislative authority, and the duties of the representative bodies are to conciliate them in harmony together.

So far as the object of taxation is to raise a revenue for discharging the debts and defraying the expenses of the community, its operation should be adapted as much as possible to suit the burden with equal hand upon all in proportion with their ability of bearing it without oppression. But the legislation of one nation is some times intentionally made to bear heavily upon the interests of another. That legislation, adapted, as it is meant to be, to the special interests of its own people, will often press most unequally upon the several component interests of its neighbors.

Thus the legislation of Great Britain, when, as has recently been avowed, adapted to the depression of a rival nation, will naturally abound with regulations to interdict upon the productions of the soil or industry of the other which come in competition with its own, and will present encouragement, perhaps even bounty, to the raw material of the other State which it can not produce itself, and which is essential for the use of its manufactures, competitors in the markets of the world with those of its commercial rival.

Such is the state of commercial legislation of Great Britain as it bears upon our interests. It excludes with interdicting duties all importation (except in time of approaching famine) of the great staple of production of our Middle and Western States; it proscribes with equal rigor the bulkier lumber and live stock of the same portion and also of the Northern and Eastern part of our Union. It refuses even the rice of the South unless aggravated with a charge of duty upon the Northern carrier who brings it to them. But the cotton, indispensable for their looms, they will receive almost duty free to weave it into a fabric for our own wear, to the destruction of our own manufactures, which they are enabled thus to under-sell.

Is the self-protecting energy of this nation so helpless that there exists in the political institutions of our country no power to counter-act the bias of this foreign legislation; that the growers of grain must submit to this exclusion from the foreign markets of their

61

produce; that the shippers must dismantle their ships, the trade of the North stagnate at the wharves, and the manufacturers starve at their looms, while the whole people shall pay tribute to foreign industry to be clad in a foreign garb; that the Congress of the Union are impotent to restore the balance in favor of native industry destroyed by the statutes of another realm?

More just and generous sentiments will, I trust, prevail. If the tariff adopted at the last session of Congress shall be found by experience to bear oppressively upon the interests of any one section of the Union, it ought to be, and I can not doubt will be, so modified as to alleviate its burden. To the voice of just complaint from any portion of their constituents the representatives of the States and of the people will never turn away their ears.

But so long as the duty of the foreign shall operate only as a bounty upon the domestic article; while the planter and the merchant and the shepherd and the husbandman shall be found thriving in their occupations under the duties imposed for the protection of domestic manufactures, they will not repine at the prosperity shared with themselves by their fellow citizens of other professions, nor denounce as violations of the Constitution the deliberate acts of Congress to shield from the wrongs of foreigns the native industry of the Union.

While the tariff of the last session of Congress was a subject of legislative deliberation it was foretold by some of its opposers that one of its necessary consequences would be to impair the revenue. It is yet too soon to pronounce with confidence that this prediction was erroneous. The obstruction of one avenue of trade not unfrequently opens an issue to another. The consequence of the tariff will be to increase the exportation and to diminish the importation of some specific articles; but by the general law of trade the increase of exportation of one article will be followed by an increased importation of others, the duties upon which will supply the deficiencies which the diminished importation would otherwise occasion. The effect of taxation upon revenue can seldom be foreseen with certainty. It must abide the test of experience.

As yet no symptoms of diminution are perceptible in the receipts of the Treasury. As yet little addition of cost has even been experienced upon the articles burdened with heavier duties by the last tariff. The domestic manufacturer supplies the same or a kindred article at a diminished price, and the consumer pays the same tribute to the labor of his own country–man which he must otherwise have paid to foreign industry and toil.

The tariff of the last session was in its details not acceptable to the great interests of any portion of the Union, not even to the interest which it was specially intended to subserve. Its object was to balance the burdens upon native industry imposed by the operation of foreign laws, but not to aggravate the burdens of one section of the Union by the relief afforded to another. To the great principle sanctioned by that act — one of those upon which the Constitution itself was formed — I hope and trust the authorities of the Union will adhere. But if any of the duties imposed by the act only relieve the manufacturer by aggravating the burden of the planter, let a careful revisal of its provisions, enlightened by the practical experience of its effects, be directed to retain those which impart protection to native industry and remove or supply the place of those which only alleviate one great national interest by the depression of another.

The United States of America and the people of every State of which they are composed are each of them sovereign powers. The legislative authority of the whole is exercised by Congress under authority granted them in the common Constitution. The legislative power of each State is exercised by assemblies deriving their authority from the constitution of the State. Each is sovereign within its own province. The distribution of power between them presupposes that these authorities will move in harmony with each other. The members of the State and General Governments are all under oath to support both, and allegiance is due to the one and to the other. The case of a conflict between these two powers has not been supposed, nor has any provision been made for it in our institutions; as a virtuous nation of ancient times existed more than five centuries without a law for the punishment of parricide.

More than once, however, in the progress of our history have the people and the legislatures of one or more States, in moments of excitement, been instigated to this conflict; and the means of effecting this impulse have been allegations that the acts of Congress to be resisted were unconstitutional. The people of no one State have ever delegated to their legislature the power of pronouncing an act of Congress unconstitutional, but they have delegated to them powers by the exercise of which the execution of the laws of Congress within the State may be resisted. If we suppose the case of such conflicting legislation sustained by the corresponding executive and judicial authorities, patriotism and philanthropy turn their eyes from the condition in which the parties would be placed, and from that of the people of both, which must be its victims.

The reports from the Secretary of War and the various subordinate offices of the resort of that Department present an exposition of the public administration of affairs connected with them through the course of the current year. The present state of the Army and the distribution of the force of which it is composed will be seen from the report of the Major General. Several alterations in the disposal of the troops have been found expedient in the course of the year, and the discipline of the Army, though not entirely free from exception, has been generally good.

The attention of Congress is particularly invited to that part of the report of the Secretary of War which concerns the existing system of our relations with the Indian tribes. At the establishment of the Federal Government under the present Constitution of the United States the principle was adopted of considering them as foreign and independent powers and also as proprietors of lands. They were, moreover, considered as savages, whom it was our policy and our duty to use our influence in converting to Christianity and in bringing within the pale of civilization.

As independent powers, we negotiated with them by treaties; as proprietors, we purchased of them all the lands which we could prevail upon them to sell; as brethren of the human race, rude and ignorant, we endeavored to bring them to the knowledge of religion and letters. The ultimate design was to incorporate in our own institutions that portion of them which could be converted to the state of civilization. In the practice of European States, before our Revolution, they had been considered as children to be governed; as tenants at discretion, to be dispossessed as occasion might require; as hunters to be indemnified by trifling concessions for removal from the grounds from which their game was extirpated. In changing the system it would seem as if a full contemplation of the consequences of the change had not been taken.

We have been far more successful in the acquisition of their lands than in imparting to them the principles or inspiring them with the spirit of civilization. But in appropriating to ourselves their hunting grounds we have brought upon ourselves the obligation of providing them with subsistence; and when we have had the rare good fortune of teaching them the arts of civilization and the doctrines of Christianity we have unexpectedly found them forming in the midst of ourselves communities claiming to be independent of ours and rivals of sovereignty within the territories of the members of our Union. This state of things requires that a remedy should be provided — a remedy which, while it shall do justice to those unfortunate children of nature, may secure to the members of our confederation their rights of sovereignty and of soil. As the outline of a project to that effect, the views presented in the report of the Secretary of War are recommended to the consideration of Congress.

The report from the Engineer Department presents a comprehensive view of the progress which has been made in the great systems promotive of the public interest, commenced and organized under authority of Congress, and the effects of which have already contributed to the security, as they will hereafter largely contribute to the honor and dignity, of the nation.

The first of these great systems is that of fortifications, commenced immediately after the close of our last war, under the salutary experience which the events of that war had impressed upon our country–men of its necessity. Introduced under the auspices of my immediate predecessor, it has been continued with the persevering and liberal encouragement of the Legislature, and, combined with corresponding exertions for the gradual increase and improvement of the Navy, prepares for our extensive country a condition of defense adapted to any critical emergency which the varying course of events may bring forth. Our advances in these concerted systems have for the last 10 years been steady and progressive, and in a few years more will be so completed as to leave no cause for apprehension that our sea coast will ever again offer a theater of hostile invasion.

The next of these cardinal measures of policy is the preliminary to great and lasting works of public improvement in the surveys of roads, examination for the course of canals, and labors for the removal of the obstructions of rivers and harbors, first commenced by the act of Congress of 1824–04–30.

The report exhibits in one table the funds appropriated at the last and preceding sessions of Congress for all these fortifications, surveys, and works of public improvement, the manner in which these funds have been applied, the amount expended upon the several works under construction, and the further sums which may be necessary to complete them; in a second, the works projected by the Board of Engineers which have not been commenced, and the estimate of their cost; in a third, the report of the annual Board of Visitors at the Military Academy at West Point.

For 13 fortifications erecting on various points of our Atlantic coast, from Rhode Island to Louisiana, the aggregate expenditure of the year has fallen little short of $1,000,000. For the preparation of 5 additional reports of reconnoissances and surveys since the last session of Congress, for the civil construction upon 37 different public works commenced, 8 others for which specific appropriations have been made by acts of Congress, and 20 other incipient surveys under the authority given by the act of 1824–04–30, about $1,000,000 more has been drawn from the Treasury.

To these $2,000,000 is to be added the appropriation of $250,000 to commence the erection of a break–water near the mouth of the Delaware River, the subscriptions to the Delaware and Chesapeake, the Louisville and Portland, the Dismal Swamp, and the Chesapeake and Ohio canals, the large donations of lands to the States of Ohio, Indiana, Illinois, and Alabama for objects of improvements within those States, and the sums appropriated for light–houses, buoys, and piers on the coast; and a full view will be taken of the munificence of the nation in the application of its resources to the improvement of its own condition.

Of these great national under–takings the Academy at West Point is among the most important in itself and the most comprehensive in its consequences. In that institution a part of the revenue of the nation is applied to defray the expense of educating a competent portion of her youth chiefly to the knowledge and the duties of military life. It is the living armory of the nation. While the other works of improvement enumerated in the reports now presented to the attention of Congress are destined to ameliorate the face of nature, to multiply the facilities of communication between the different parts of the Union, to assist the labors, increase the comforts, and enhance the enjoyments of individuals, the instruction acquired at West Point enlarges the dominion and expands the capacities of the mind. Its beneficial results are already experienced in the composition of the Army, and their influence is felt in the intellectual progress of society. The institution is susceptible still of great improvement from benefactions proposed by several successive Boards of Visitors, to whose earnest and repeated recommendations I cheerfully add my own.

With the usual annual reports from the Secretary of the Navy and the Board of Commissioners will be exhibited to the view of Congress the execution of the laws relating to that department of the public service. The repression of piracy in the West Indian and in the Grecian seas has been effectually maintained, with scarcely any exception. During the war between the Governments of Buenos Ayres and of Brazil frequent collisions between the belligerent acts of power and the rights of neutral commerce occurred. Licentious blockades, irregularly enlisted or impressed sea men, and the property of honest commerce seized with violence, and even plundered under legal pretenses, are disorders never separable from the conflicts of war upon the ocean.

With a portion of them the correspondence of our commanders on the eastern aspect of the South American coast and among the islands of Greece discover how far we have been involved. In these the honor of our country and the rights of our citizens have been asserted and vindicated. The appearance of new squadrons in the Mediterranean and the blockade of the Dardanelles indicate the danger of other obstacles to the freedom of commerce and the necessity of keeping our naval force in those seas. To the suggestions repeated in the report of the Secretary of the Navy, and tending to the permanent improvement of this institution, I invite the favorable consideration of Congress.

A resolution of the House of Representatives requesting that one of our small public vessels should be sent to the Pacific Ocean and South Sea to examine the coasts, islands, harbors, shoals, and reefs in those seas, and to ascertain their true situation and description, has been put in a train of execution. The vessel is nearly ready to depart. The successful accomplishment of the expedition may be greatly facilitated by suitable legislative provisions, and particularly by an appropriation to defray its necessary expense. The addition of a 2nd, and perhaps a 3rd, vessel, with a slight aggravation of the cost, would contribute much to the safety of the citizens embarked on this under-taking, the results of which may be of the deepest interest to our country.

With the report of the Secretary of the Navy will be submitted, in conformity to the act of Congress of 1827-03-03, for the gradual improvement of the Navy of the United States, statements of the expenditures under that act and of the measures for carrying the same into effect. Every section of that statute contains a distinct provision looking to the great object of the whole — the gradual improvement of the Navy. Under its salutary sanction stores of ship timber have been procured and are in process of seasoning and preservation for the future uses of the Navy. Arrangements have been made for the preservation of the live oak timber growing on the lands of the United States, and for its reproduction, to supply at future and distant days the waste of that most valuable material for ship building by the great consumption of it yearly for the commercial as well as for the military marine of our country.

The construction of the two dry docks at Charlestown and at Norfolk is making satisfactory progress toward a durable establishment. The examinations and inquiries to ascertain the practicability and expediency of a marine railway at Pensacola, though not yet accomplished, have been post-poned but to be more effectually made. The navy yards of the United States have been examined, and plans for their improvement and the preservation of the public property therein at Portsmouth, Charlestown, Philadelphia, Washington, and Gosport, and to which 2 others are to be added, have been prepared and received my sanction; and no other portion of my public duties has been performed with a more intimate conviction of its importance to the future welfare and security of the Union.

With the report from the PostMaster General is exhibited a comparative view of the gradual increase of that establishment, from 5 to 5 years, since 1792 'til this time in the number of post offices, which has grown from less than 200 to nearly 8,000; in the revenue yielded by them, which from $67,000 has swollen to upward of $1,500,000, and in the number of miles of post roads, which from 5,642 have multiplied to 114,536. While in the same period of time the population of the Union has about thrice doubled, the rate of increase of these offices is nearly 40, and of the revenue and of traveled miles from 20 to 25 for one. The increase of revenue within the last 5 years has been nearly equal to the whole revenue of the Department in 1812.

The expenditures of the Department during the year which ended on 1828-07-01 have exceeded the receipts by a sum of about $25,000. The excess has been occasioned by the increase of mail conveyances and facilities to the extent of near 800,000 miles. It has been supplied by collections from the post masters of the arrearages of preceding years. While the correct principle seems to be that the income levied by the Department should defray all its expenses, it has never been the policy of this Government to raise from this establishment any revenue to be applied to any other purposes. The suggestion of the PostMaster General that the insurance of the safe transmission of moneys by the mail might be assumed by the Department for a moderate and competent remuneration will deserve the consideration of Congress.

A report from the commissioner of the public buildings in this city exhibits the expenditures upon them in the course of the current year. It will be seen that the humane and benevolent intentions of Congress in providing, by the act of 1826-05-20, for the erection of a penitentiary in this District have been accomplished. The authority of further legislation is now required for the removal to this tenement of the offenders against the laws sentenced to atone by personal confinement for their crimes, and to provide a code for their employment and government while thus confined.

The commissioners appointed, conformably to the act of 1827–03–02, to provide for the adjustment of claims of persons entitled to indemnification under the first article of the treaty of Ghent, and for the distribution among such claimants of the sum paid by the Government of Great Britain under the convention of 1826–11–13, closed their labors on 1828–08–30 last by awarding to the claimants the sum of $1,197,422.18, leaving a balance of $7,537.82, which was distributed ratably amongst all the claimants to whom awards had been made, according to the directions of the act.

The exhibits appended to the report from the Commissioner of the General Land Office present the actual condition of that common property of the Union. The amount paid into the Treasury from the proceeds of lands during the year 1827 and for the first half of 1828 falls little short of $2,000,000. The propriety of further extending the time for the extinguishment of the debt due to the United States by the purchasers of the public lands, limited by the act of 1828–03–21 to 1829–07–04, will claim the consideration of Congress, to whose vigilance and careful attention the regulation, disposal, and preservation of this great national inheritance has by the people of the United States been intrusted.

Among the important subjects to which the attention of the present Congress has already been invited, and which may occupy their further and deliberate discussion, will be the provision to be made for taking the 5th census of enumeration of the inhabitants of the United States. The Constitution of the United States requires that this enumeration should be made within every term of 10 years, and the date from which the last enumeration commenced was the first Monday of August of the year 1820.

The laws under which the former enumerations were taken were enacted at the session of Congress immediately preceding the operation; but considerable inconveniences were experienced from the delay of legislation to so late a period. That law, like those of the preceding enumerations, directed that the census should be taken by the marshals of the several districts and Territories of the Union under instructions from the Secretary of State. The preparation and transmission to the marshals of those instructions required more time than was then allowed between the passage of the law and the day when the enumeration was to commence. The term of 6 months limited for the returns of the marshals was also found even then too short, and must be more so now, when an additional population of at least 3,000,000 must be presented upon the returns.

As they are to be made at the short session of Congress, it would, as well as from other considerations, be more convenient to commence the enumeration from an earlier period of the year than the first of August. The most favorable season would be the spring.

On a review of the former enumerations it will be found that the plan for taking every census has contained many improvements upon that of its predecessor. The last is still susceptible of much improvement. The 3rd Census was the first at which any account was taken of the manufactures of the country. It was repeated at the last enumeration, but the returns in both cases were necessarily very imperfect. They must always be so, resting, of course, only upon the communications voluntarily made by individuals interested in some of the manufacturing establishments. Yet they contained much valuable information, and may by some supplementary provision of the law be rendered more effective.

The columns of age, commencing from infancy, have hitherto been confined to a few periods, all under the number of 45 years. Important knowledge would be obtained by extending these columns, in intervals of 10 years, to the utmost boundaries of human life. The labor of taking them would be a trifling addition to that already prescribed, and the result would exhibit comparative tables of longevity highly interesting to the country. I deem it my duty further to observe that much of the imperfections in the returns of the last and perhaps of preceding enumerations proceeded from the inadequateness of the compensations allowed to the marshals and their assistants in taking them.

In closing this communication it only remains for me to assure the Legislature of my continued earnest wish for the adoption of measures recommended by me heretofore and yet to be acted on by them, and of the cordial concurrence on my part in every constitutional provision which may receive their sanction during the session tending to the general welfare. JOHN QUNICY ADAMS

OTHER BOOKS BY
FREDERICK ELLIS

(Buy Direct at 35% off – Contact frederick659@yahoo.com)

Author - Jack London

MARTIN EDEN

WAR OF THE CLASSES

JOHN BARLEYCORN

THE PEOPLE OF THE ABYSS

JACK LONDON ON THE ROAD

THE ASSASSINATION BUREAU, LTD.

THE IRON HEEL

Author – B. Traven

GENERAL FROM THE JUNGLE

THE DEATH SHIP

THE REBELLION OF THE HANGED

THE WHITE ROSE

THE BRIDGE IN THE JUNGLE

MARCH TO THE MONTERIA

THE TREASURE OF THE SIERRA MADRE

   Author - Carl Frederick

est PLAYING THE GAME THE NEW WAY

   Authors - Frederick Ellis & Carl Frederick

THE OAKLAND STATEMENT

   Author – Mao Tsetung

QUOTATIONS FROM CHAIRMAN MAO TSETUNG

   Author – Upton Sinclair

OUR LADY

THE FLIVVER KING: THE STORY OF FORD-AMERICA

ONE HUNDRED PERCENT: THE STORY OF A PATRIOT

WORLD'S END I

WORLD'S END II

THE SECRET LIFE OF JESUS

THE MONEYCHANGERS

MENTAL RADIO

THE MILLENNIUM

A PERSONAL JESUS

PROFITS OF RELIGION

THEY CALL ME CARPENTER: A TALE OF
THE SECOND COMING

     Author – Thomas Paine

COMMON SENSE, THE RIGHTS OF MAN
& THE AGE OF REASON

THE AMERICAN CRISIS

     Author – Karl Marx

DAS KAPITAL

THE COMMUNIST MANIFESTO &
WAGES, PRICE AND PROFIT

WAGE-LABOUR AND CAPITAL
& VALUE. PRICE AND PROFIT

     Author – Eugene Debs

WALLS AND BARS

     Author – Jean-Jacques Rousseau

THE SOCIAL CONTRACT

Author – John Reed

TEN DAYS THAT SHOOK THE WORLD

INSURGENT MEXICO

Author – Antonio Gramsci

**THE MODERN PRINCE AND
SELECTED WRITINGS**

Author – V. I. Lenin

THE STATE AND REVOLUTION

**FIGHT AGAINST STALINISM & IMPERIALISM:
THE HIGHEST STAGE OF CAPITALISM**

Author – David Ricardo

**PRINCIPLES OF POLITICAL ECONOMY
AND TAXATION**

Author – Thomas Jefferson

**BIOGRAPHY OF THOMAS JEFFERSON & THE
LIFE AND MORALS OF JESUS OF NAZARETH**

Author – Emma Goldman

ANARCHISM AND OTHER WRITINGS

Author – Rosa Luxemburg

REFORM OR REVOLUTION & THE MASS STRIKE

Author – John Stuart Mill

ON SOCIALISM & THE SUBJECTION OF WOMEN

Author – THE HOLY SPIRIT

THE GOOD NEWS: AS TOLD BY MATTHEW, MARK, LUKE AND JOHN

Author – John Quincy Adams

THE AMISTAD ARGUMENT & THE STATE OF THE UNION ADDRESSES